"I wish this book had been around back when I was a girl. And I sure wish it had been around when my daughter was a girl. There's real wisdom between these covers. Do yourself a favor. Buy one copy for yourself (or your mother), and another to save for when your daughter is mother to a daughter."

—*Linda Ellerbee*

"As the largest informal education organization for girls in the world, we concur with Dr. Deak's insightful treatise on raising confident and competent girls. Throughout our 90-year history, the girl/adult partnership has been a key principle of Girl Scouting, and we can say from experience that it works! I encourage parents, guardians, and anyone who works with girls to read this book."

—*Marsha Johnson Evans, National Executive Director,*
  Girl Scouts of the USA

"*Girls Will Be Girls* is a required encounter for anyone who envisions a better future for girls. With clarity, insight, humor, and common sense, JoAnn Deak shares practical and strategic pearls to help good-intentioned people who live and work with girls become more effective with girls. I'm a mother, a pastor, and someone who has committed her professional life to listening to girls. JoAnn Deak has written what has now become my handbook."

—*The Rev. Emma Jordan-Simpson, Associate Pastor, Concord Baptist Church*
  of Christ and Executive Director, Girls Incorporated of New York City

"*Girls Will Be Girls* is a must-read for families, teachers, and others who live and work with girls. It guides us through the sometimes uncertain and confusing path of girls' passage from childhood to adulthood, helping us comprehend the subtle nuances of what it means to be a girl today. We owe it to our future moms, executives, leaders, co-workers, and friends to read this book."

—*Anita Benavides Mennucci, Executive Director, GENaustin (Girls*
  Empowerment Network, formerly The Ophelia Project)

"*Girls Will Be Girls* is a must-read for every parent! It provides thoughtful advice that will enrich your relationship with your daughter and help you enjoy the complex challenge of raising a strong and resilient person—one who can discover for herself the power of the words 'I can.' "

—*Frances A. Rubacha, Board Chair, Outward Bound USA*

"I love it! *Girls Will Be Girls* is helpful, reassuring, and wise. It provides invaluable guidance to today's parents, whose daughters face tremendous new challenges at the same time they are blessed with unprecedented opportunities."

—*Leslie Whitaker, co-author of* The Good Girls Negotiating Guide

"Dr. Deak, in examining the biological, social, and emotional reasons why raising girls is so complex, not only gives us concrete suggestions on how to prevent some of the problems, but also explains in wonderfully lucid and human terms why these approaches are effective. If you have a daughter or work with girls, this book will help you help them to negotiate the 'seeming chaos of life' that girls face today."

—*Agnes C. Underwood, Head, National Cathedral School, Washington, DC*

"Yes, girls ARE different. And so is this book. JoAnn Deak explains these differences in the context of the real world, and then proceeds to give both parents and educators solid, common-sense advice about how to address those differences in ways that will both support the adult-child relationship and allow each girl to grow in her ability to self-advocate."

—*Patricia E. Crone, Head, Atlanta Girls' School*

"Dr. Deak has a way with words—a way that is open, funny, engaging, wise, and, above all, human. Her stories are articulate and endearing, her tips relevant and meaningful, and her knowledge inspirational. Read this book and you will immediately feel more competent as a parent, more confident about your daughter's development, and more connected—both to her and to the parenting process."

—*Ellen Markowitz, Founder and President, PowerPlay NYC*

"A great book—get it now! Practical and grounded in its head-to-toe understanding of girls, it's also inspirational and motivating. It will help

"JoAnn Deak thoughtfully informs us of the rough waters that girls (and to some extent boys) must navigate as they mature into adulthood. But she also highlights the many strengths upon which we can help them build their present and future lives. This is a must-read for parents, educators, and policy makers."

—Rosemary Salomone, Professor of Law, St. John's University School of Law, author of Equal Education Under Law *and* Visions of Schooling

"In a clear, wonderfully personal voice, JoAnn Deak manages to get to the nub of dozens of cultural predicaments facing growing girls. Wearing her professional and personal experience lightly, she avoids utterly the poor-girls pitfall, instead laying out the real and wildly problematic realities facing our daughters and students. The practical advice is welcome and shrewd; the affectionate witness to the contemporary girl's situation makes one, well, want to do better."

—Richard A. Hawley, author of Boys Will Be Men *and* The Head-master's Papers

"Full of compelling insights about raising great girls. Parents who buy this book will raise girls who will be girls who have the strength of character to withstand anything that life throws at them. By focusing on 'crucible events' Deak and Barker give parents an exceptionally useful tool for understanding girls' development."

—Dan Kindlon, author of Too Much of a Good Thing: Raising Children of Character in an Indulgent Age *and co-author of* Raising Cain

"JoAnn Deak's *Girls Will Be Girls* is right on the mark. She celebrates girls and has a keen understanding of their intellectual, physical, and emotional lives. As an educator and psychologist, she gives practical and strategic advice to parents and teachers alike. Deak's goal for all concerned is that they offer guideposts girls can use as they navigate what she terms the gray areas in their lives. Whether at home, at school, or within a community, Deak urges us all to create environments in which girls will thrive. Cultivating competence, confidence, and connections is the bottom line at girls' schools and of this important new book as well."

—Meg Milne Moulton and Whitney Ransome,
Executive Directors, The National Coalition of Girls' Schools

every parent bring out the best in how we nurture and challenge our daughters. I wish I'd had it when my daughters were younger."

—*Nancy Gruver, Founder,* New Moon Magazine for Girls *and New Moon Network for Adults*

"*Girls Will Be Girls* is full of sound research and new information. Furthermore, Deak brings this new science to life with touching anecdotes about girls, their parents, and their schools. Deak's voice—rich with certainty and experience—encourages us all to be optimistic about what girls can achieve and who they can become when supported by caring adults."

—*Amy Lynch, Editor,* Daughters *newsletter*

"My daughters don't know it yet, but I'm a better parent now, having read *Girls Will Be Girls.* Its accessible blend of research, wisdom, and practical advice on all stages of girls' lives has helped me better understand exactly how girls thrive and how parents can help daughters thrive in this increasingly complex world."

—*Michael Brosnan, author of* Against the Current *and editor of* Independent School

"With characteristic brilliance and uncanny insight, JoAnn Deak shines a high, bright beam on the unique strengths and vulnerabilities of growing girls in the new millennium. You simply cannot read any part of this book without coming away a better parent."

—*Deborah M. Roffman, author of* Sex and Sensibility: The Thinking Parent's Guide to Talking Sense About Sex

"As I read Dr. Deak's book, I thought of my daughter: an African American young woman who traveled from childhood to adulthood with all of the attending possibilities and challenges that this book describes, and more. Through school, through college, and into the world of adult responsibility, she bore witness to Dr. Deak's 'science' of being a girl; a woman. As a father, I now have a better understanding of those inexplicable 'girl' moments that came without instructions. As an educator, I have a chance every day to support, nurture, and reflect on the ways that schools can be better places for girls, teenagers, and women."

—*Randolph Carter, Associate, East Ed and author of* Diversity in Action: Creating Change in Independent Schools

Girls

Will Be

Girls

Girls
Will Be
Girls

Raising Confident and
Courageous Daughters

JoAnn Deak, PH.D.
with Teresa Barker

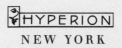

HYPERION
NEW YORK

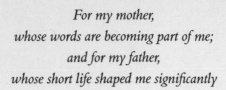

For my mother,
whose words are becoming part of me;
and for my father,
whose short life shaped me significantly

To Rachel and Rebecca with love
—THB

The quotes that appear throughout *Girls Will Be Girls* are authentic. However, most names and identifying details in stories have been changed to protect the privacy of the contributors.

Library of Congress Cataloging-in-Publication Data

Deak, JoAnn M.
    Girls will be girls : raising confident and courageous daughters / by JoAnn Deak; with Teresa Barker.–1st ed.
        p.   cm.
    ISBN 0-7868-6768-X
    1. Girls.   2. Child rearing.   3. Daughters.   I. Barker, Teresa.   II. Title.

HQ777 .D374   2002
649'.133—dc21

                                                            2001039247

Hyperion books are available for special promotions and premiums. For details contact: Hyperion Special Markets, 77 W. 66th Street, 11th floor, New York, New York 10023, or call 212-456-0100.

FIRST EDITION

Designed by Ruth Lee

10   9   8   7   6   5   4

Acknowledgments

This book is the result of twenty years of working with schools, parents, and children as well as having the benefit of the wisdom and feedback of colleagues, family, and friends. Rather than following that winding path, here is a more circumscribed flow of appreciation.

A school is more than a building. So, in acknowledging Laurel School, I mean the community and culture, the history and the present, the students and the staff. Barbara Barnes was the visionary head who inspired passion about education in all of her colleagues. Her successor, Leah Rhys, targeted that passion to the development of girls and thus began my work with the Laurel/Harvard project led by Carol Gilligan and Lyn Mikel Brown. And finally, the board of directors at Laurel gave me the financial gift of two years paid leave to begin my path of writing, researching, and consulting.

In 1998, when Dory Adams called from NAIS to ask me to

write a book that ultimately became titled *How Girls Thrive,* my course was altered from psychologist/educator/consultant to writer and author. She helped edit the book and continues to fertilize my thinking and writing and has become a very good friend.

A special recognition to three of the national organizations that make the positive development of girls their total focus, and who helped with their invaluable support of this book:

- The National Coalition of Girls' Schools: Meg Moulton and Whitney Ransome, the wonderfully committed executive directors.
- Girl Scouts of the USA: Marsha Johnson Evans, the courageous executive director.
- Outward Bound USA: Frances Rubacha as the wise board chair, and Robyn Reed as the charismatic leader of Girls on the Move 2000.

I have the best agent and the best cowriter in the world: Gail Ross and Teresa Barker. Their wisdom and talent made *Girls Will Be Girls* a reality. However, I would not have met them without the urging of Dr. Michael Thompson, and I am proud sometimes to be referred to as the female Michael Thompson!

Special thanks to Dr. Jeanne Simpson for her daily support and feedback; she keeps me writing through the gray skies of a typical Ohio winter. And whenever I needed a special story or family support, Dana; her mother, Barbara; and her father, Allen, were always willing to be there for me and always willing to share their family stories and their wonderful Tomato Face pasta sauce.

I wish my mother could be here to see how often her words crept into my mind and my writing. And I would especially like to tell her that they have become my words—the highest compliment a mother can receive.

And finally, a message for my brother: perhaps the third time is the charm, since you haven't read my first two books yet!

Please write to me via the website www.DEAKgroup.com. I'd

like to hear your thoughts about *Girls Will Be Girls,* and perhaps you can add your story to the sequel.

—JoAnn Deak

A mother's thanks to Rachel and Rebecca, for all the ways they contributed to the girls'-eye view of life contained in this book, to Steve and Aaron for the view from the other side, and to my own parents, Maxine and George, whose love and wisdom are present here; I am especially grateful to my family for their support and patience over time. I also want to acknowledge the generous contribution of insight and inspiration by all those who shared with us, with a special thanks to Susan, Beth, and Tobi Brown, Leslie Rowan, Linda Ellerbee, Leslie Whitaker, Holly Cohn, Martha Decherd, Judi Drew, Kathy Flaherty, Liz Leibowitz, Leah Nakamura, Eve Fine, Donna Patterson, Jamie Sullivan, Valerie Mindel, Nancy Moffett, Karen Wesolowski, Helen Shum, Linda Styskal and Linda Oliva, and all my girl sources. The book owes its genesis to Michael Thompson, who envisioned the collaboration that brought it about, and to our agent, Gail Ross, who tended the project like a mama hen. To them, and their daughters, too, hugs all around. Finally, I thank Leslie Wells and the Hyperion staff for their careful, thoughtful work to bring the book to our readers. And to JoAnn, heartfelt gratitude for the opportunity to collaborate and for the joy of our work.

—THB

Contents

Girls

Will Be

Girls

 **Introduction**

Most of us get one childhood to remember. I got two.

There was the picture-perfect one of my family: a mother and father very much in love, very loving parents to my older brother and me. We lived in a little town in the Midwest. My mother never worked outside of the home, but instead spent her days driving a station wagon, taking us, and all the neighborhood kids that could fit, to the public pool, the playground, and town. We even had a collie! That was my first childhood. It lasted fourteen years.

On a beautiful spring evening the Sunday before Easter of my freshman year of high school, my father suffered a fatal heart attack. Thus began my second life as a girl growing up, a life that began with an adolescence transformed literally overnight from a girlhood dream to a nightmare of loss and a new, bittersweet appreciation of life's nuances. Everything about my life changed, and with those changes came a heightened awareness of the gendered experience of everyday life for girls and women.

After my father's death, I watched my mother go to work in a factory; she was one of the few women there in the early 1960s. Since my brother was at college, I needed to get my driver's license as soon as possible because my mother worked the afternoon shift and was no longer there to drive me anywhere. An adolescent girl who drove herself to school, appointments, high school football games? I was not the only one, but—like my mother—I was one of just a few. What surprised and intrigued me the most was the way the rest of the world responded to the changes in our lives. My mother's best friend would become jealous when her husband came over to help my mother start the lawn mower. I proved quite able in my new life, yet without my father's enthusiastic endorsement, I felt smart but uncertain, more sensitive to what others thought, what others suggested, and what others assumed about me.

This second childhood was to become a particularly defining one for me for reasons that I would fully understand only later through my work as a child psychologist with girls. My father's death was for me a *crucible event*, a moment in which everything I knew and felt and *was* was put to a test. It was a trial by fire, and one through which I might emerge more fragile or more strong, or perhaps both. But whatever the outcome, I was changed. Without thinking consciously about it at the time, I've always separated my life into two parts: before and after my father died.

Subsequently, in my work with children and adults my sense of crucible events as the catalyst for emotional growth and development became a useful tool in helping others see the effects of life events on their own emotional development and their relationships with others. Through this lens of crucible events it is possible to get a better view of the inner life of girls. This I know from my work, and from my own personal experiences of moving from my family home out into the world. I would forever feel a particular empathy toward girls' emotional experience, and a strong desire to make sense of it for parents, educators, and girls themselves. But first I had to navigate those waters for myself, and it was a slow, deliberate journey.

My love of science and people drew me first to pursue an education in nursing, but I soon shifted my focus to teaching, earned my degree, and got the job. By my second year of teaching, when I couldn't figure out how to reach and teach some of my students, I took a day off to visit the nearest university, Kent State, to see which graduate courses were available to help me understand how the human brain worked. A serendipitous meeting and the discovery of an exciting doctoral program in preventive psychology prompted me to resign from teaching to resume my own education. With my Ph.D., I established a private practice and started a company with three other colleagues developing preventive psychological programs for schools. Soon one of our clients, the director of Laurel School, recruited me to serve as the staff school psychologist, a position I agreed to take for one year while we assessed their needs.

The next year Carol Gilligan, author of *In a Different Voice: Psychological Theory and Women's Development,* and her Harvard crew wanted to do a landmark study at the school. I had taken a course from her at Harvard; she now asked me to be an in-house interviewer for the next six years. How could I pass up the opportunity? I stayed on.

After the Laurel/Harvard study was completed, someone had to go to other schools and conferences to share what we had learned. Carol Gilligan was moving on to other studies and was too busy. Thus began my life as a gender expert. Laurel School graciously allowed me to take several days each year to do this. By now I was also experiencing the joys of being an administrator, having become director of the middle, primary, and early childhood divisions through another instance of serendipity. The previous director resigned in April one year, and the school was in chaos. What better person than the school psychologist to fill in the gap? It would only be temporary, the head of the school assured me. Well, it wasn't, exactly. Five years later, because of my speaking engagements around the country, and a growing list of requests for me to present gender equity workshops for parents, teachers, administrators, and students (girls *and* boys), I was asked by the National Association of Independent Schools to be on a national committee for women in independent schools. My already crowded calendar of speaking engagements and the growing demand for my gender equity workshops made my next career step clear: I became a full-time consultant, working year-round with schools, parent and teacher organizations, and students themselves in the United States and abroad.

Early in my career as a psychologist, after teaching for several years and then interning in a variety of settings, and with a variety of clients, from the very young to the very old, it was clear to me that for many clients, treatment was long, expensive, painful, and often ineffective. Being the idealist that I am, my core philosophy fit with the philosophy of prevention, and that is where I turned my attention as a specialist.

Preventive psychology is at the other end of the spectrum from the kind of private practice work most people envision when they think of a psychologist or therapist. I do counsel individual children and their families privately, but most of my time is devoted to what we call primary prevention. I evaluate factors in schools or families that cause mental health or learning issues and work to fix them, eliminate them, or modify an environment so those factors don't exist. As a public speaker and a consultant, I work with schools and communities around the country, conducting workshops for parents and teachers who want to create schools and families where children can thrive, and speaking with students about their concerns or issues of the day. My life and career have thrived in ways I would never have imagined in earlier years. I have made my way as many women do: on the winds of my intuition, a perfect model of affiliation motivation, influenced by people, connections, and gut feelings.

Wherever I go, I generally find thoughtful, caring, determined parents and school staff with a lot in common. They typically have high ideals, a desire for clarity, and a willingness to work at making their schools and homes places that support healthy development for girls. Parents always want to know in general how to be a good parent. Teachers want to be the one a student remembers fondly thirty years later.

But often, it is problems, issues, and concerns that motivate many of us to seek help, listen, and try to do something different. Sometimes it takes a problem to get everyone's attention, and then the task is twofold: Find a way to solve the problem and find a way to change conditions so it doesn't happen again. In these circumstances, I often encounter an undercurrent of fear, sometimes a kind of siege mentality, that prompts adults to respond to unwanted challenge by clamping down, nipping it in the bud. The prevailing attitude in that setting is that challenge or change are threatening and have to be quashed. It never works. Not for long, anyway. Not in families and not in schools. Not in politics or government. Not in nature. Growth *requires* change; how we fare with it depends on how we respond to it.

Girls face an extraordinary challenge in our changing world. They are dealing with more sophisticated issues than ever before, and they are doing so with less adult contact and guidance than ever before. Statistics tell the story of a population at risk both physically and emotionally: One in four girls shows signs of depression. Compared to males, twice as many females attempt suicide, and there is a sharp rise in actual suicides for females beginning at age ten and peaking at age twenty-four. One in four girls has been in an abusive relationship. When asked about their role models, girls only list one third of what boys list. Girls are five times less likely to receive attention from a teacher. Girls ages twelve through fifteen have the worst nutrition of any age group, followed by girls ages sixteen through nineteen. By age thirteen, 53 percent of girls are unhappy with their bodies; by age eighteen, 78 percent are dissatisfied with their bodies. Eighty percent of ten-year-old girls are on a diet, and the number one wish of teenage girls and adult women is to lose weight. Eight million American women suffer from eating disorders, and 90 percent of them are adolescents.

For parents, every day presents fresh challenges to tradition, and the future is unpredictable, shaped as it is by newly emerging influences from media, technology, peer culture, and a society in flux. Contrary to the days when mainstream society supported parents' efforts to protect, nurture, and guide their growing girls, today society itself is the high-pressure, high-risk realm where girls are more vulnerable than ever to the pressures for perfection and casual exploitation and experimentation, which can carry serious consequences. Parents often lack the information or insight to feel competent. It's easy to lose confidence in our intuitive wisdom, uncertain at times how much our judgment is clouded by ignorance or our own discomfort with social change.

Whether we feel ready or not, we are beyond the days of one-line answers to life's questions, or cookbook-style recipes for building self-esteem and smarts in girls. All of us—girls, parents, and teachers—share the same need for information, insight, and a perspective that enables us to make sense of the landscape and make reasonable day-to-day decisions that protect and promote a life of possibility.

A friend of mine says that as a parent, she often feels like the hapless character in the folktale of a bumbling farm boy, who repeatedly goes to town on an errand, and each time returns home carrying his purchase in such a way that it is ruined. He looks foolish. The first time, his mother scolds him and tells him the correct way to carry the thing, and the next time he goes to town, he follows her instructions to a T, but the circumstances have changed, the item is different, and he screws it up again! Dragging butter on a leash, carrying a donkey over his shoulder; each time, he's doing what he was told from the time before, but it isn't the right thing to do *now*. His intentions are good, but he is always one step behind in his ability to think and act effectively.

Parenting feels like that at times, and tidy lists of do's and don'ts fall short of helping us "*think* like a grown-up," as my friend says.

All of us want our girls to thrive. We want them to live lives in which they feel competent, confident, and connected to others, and to the grand scheme of life. That's not something we can give girls, or do for them. However, as parents and teachers and other adults who care, we *can* cultivate opportunities for girls to experience themselves this way. To do so, we need to understand girls better, develop our capacity to think like grown-ups, and expand our repertoire of responses to be effective in the moment and for the long-term, in the lives of girls.

One of the most gratifying aspects of bringing this book into being has been the opportunity to share the science of girls with parents and teachers who live in the laboratory of real life with them every day. Advances in neuroscience—the study of how the brain grows and works—are just beginning to shed light on fascinating differences between female and male brains. Research is also advancing dramatically in the study of hormones and other physiological and psychological aspects of growing up female. Every new scientific finding not only informs us about the true nature of girls—forget the hackneyed nursery rhymes or generations of stereotypes—but also underscores the need for parents, teachers, schools, and communities to see girls in a new light, and move more deliberately toward gender equity in all these realms.

In *Girls Will Be Girls: Raising Confident and Courageous Daughters,* I share this science and my guiding principles for understanding girls, understanding their hopes and dreams as well as their struggle and pain, and understanding what we can do, as adults, to create family and school environments in which they can find their best selves and live their best lives.

CHAPTER 1

The Search for Perspective

"It's pretty hard being a girl nowadays. You can't be too smart, too dumb, too pretty, too ugly, too friendly, too coy, too aggressive, too defenseless, too individual, or too programmed. If you're too much of anything, then others envy you, or despise you because you intimidate them or make them jealous. It's like you have to be everything and nothing all at once, without knowing which you need more of."

Nora, twelfth grade

My friend Clara calls me every now and then with one of her "bad mother" confession stories. Ostensibly it's to give me fodder for my talks and workshops, but just after she finishes the story comes the real reason: She needs some reassurance that she hasn't ruined her daughter for life. She's not a bad mother at all—just the opposite, in fact—but with a twelve-year-old daughter, her parenting judgment is always subject to criticism, and her confidence takes a drubbing.

The parenting dilemmas she describes are usually garden-variety, everyday episodes involving her daughter and school, friends, fashion, and responsibility. But sometimes even simple decisions—like whether to let her daughter buy the stylish but scanty swimsuit she wants—become more difficult in the high-risk, high-pressure context of contemporary life for girls.

Clara called one day, exhausted, confused, and depressed. She had just bought her daughter Robin the swimsuit of her choice. Of course, it wasn't as simple as it sounds. What had begun as an ordinary shopping trip had morphed into an episode in which Clara's parental judgment and values had fallen victim to a tiny two-piece bathing suit. As they walked from store to store, from mall to mall, from one slip of a swimsuit to another, it had become very clear to Clara that it would be almost impossible to find a fashionable teen suit that wasn't *extremely* revealing. Robin, ordinarily a modest sort, had begged to buy a popular style of two-piece suit, seemingly oblivious to the fact that it only barely covered any piece of her anatomy. Clara urged her to find something less revealing. Robin argued that in years past—before she "had boobs"—she could wear anything, and she felt that she should still be able to wear whatever she found comfortable and stylish.

Clara countered with a few predictable words about the way our clothes communicate something about ourselves. She said that while Robin might feel moved to buy such a suit because she felt stylish and fit and at ease with her body, the fact was that the males in the crowd would make their own interpretation of her clothes, her body, and her intentions, and their reactions had to be taken into account. She had to be careful "not to send the wrong message," Clara counseled.

But even as she spoke, Clara winced at the sound of her own words and the message they sent to her daughter—that Robin was not free to simply dress as she pleased for a day at the pool. She had to consider the possibility of undesirable consequences. That despite her girlish view of herself and the world, her body spoke of womanly potential, and *that* was problematic. Yet why should a girl have to view her blossoming body as a liability?

Robin objected and was furious. She didn't care what boys thought; why should she have to take them into account?

"The trouble was, on the inside, I agreed with her," Clara said. "I can't say that I honestly thought anything bad would happen to her at the pool. At the same time, there *is* a real element of danger for girls—you can't ignore the news stories of sex molesters, rapists—girls and women *are* preyed upon. But there was something else, too.

It was depressing for me to see her wanting to buy into this media image of girls as hot chicks, at twelve! She's this wonderful girl, with a great mind and funny sense of humor and a good heart, and I don't want people looking at her body and sizing her up that way. It's so demeaning!

"She's right—it ought to be okay for a girl to wear what makes her happy. Boys don't have to worry about what they wear, but the reality for girls is different. It made me angry to think about it, and sad to hear myself telling my daughter that she has to go by the same old unfair rules 'because I said so.' But I didn't want to go into much detail about my reasons because I didn't want her to have to think about the dark side of all this like I do.

"It was," she said, borrowing from the title of one of her daughter's favorite childhood books, "a terrible, horrible, no good, very bad shopping trip."

Eventually, though, Clara gave in. Every other girl in Robin's circle of friends had the same skimpy, stylish suit. To dress differently would have set Robin up for teasing and the most humiliating attention. Clara could remember the pain of that from her own girlhood; who can forget? There was also the fact that no other parent she knew had mentioned this as a source of worry, dismay, or a conflict of values. Maybe she was being unreasonable, too protective, too reactive. Maybe it really *didn't* matter anymore. She didn't believe that, but she wasn't sure that winning the bathing suit decision was worth the cost to her daughter, who would be the one to suffer the consequences in her peer group. Clara threw in the towel, so to speak, and accepted the inevitable. It was, after all, just a swimsuit.

"But I'm *still* upset by the principle of the thing," Clara told me. "Just because everybody's doing it doesn't make it right. There's so much that 'everybody's doing' that isn't right or healthy for girls. And how can I expect my twelve-year-old to make sense of things if I can't do it myself?"

Clara often feels like the Lone Ranger as she grapples with the issues of the day, but she isn't alone. In my work as a school psychol-

ogist, consultant, and speaker, I hear from thousands of other mothers, fathers, and teachers, and thousands more girls themselves, all of
whom share similar stories of their own struggles to navigate the rich
and risky contemporary landscape for girls.

From Silence to the Sounds of Success:
Unlimited Options, New Questions

Looked at from one perspective, it would appear that girls
have it all today. Studies confirm what we often see in everyday life.
Developmentally, girls are generally more emotionally literate, ver-
bally expressive, and socially facile than boys. At an early age, they
tend to have good "school brains" that enable them to experience success in the school setting. They revel in relationship and emotional
connectedness, the foundations of good mental health. In every facet
of their lives, their choices have grown as society moves slowly
toward gender equity.

Unlike girls a generation ago, they have access to sports and
educational programs that were once for boys only. In many other
ways, girls' lives today are illuminated by freedom of choice and
unlimited aspirations. They are growing up in the company of girls
and women whose natural talents are finding full expression in athletics, business, the arts and academia, and leadership and activism, as
well as in family life. They see stay-at-home dads and corporate
moms, and in countless other ways are witnessing transformations of
family and workplace to accommodate evolving gender roles for
women and men. They are beginning to realize their financial power,
both as earners and spenders, and their political clout, both as citizens
and leaders. And while boys still labor under the burden of masculine
tradition to be strong and silent, girls have social permission to be
tough or tender, and to be emotionally expressive.

At the same time, anyone who lives or works closely with
girls knows there is a darker side to growing up female. Research,
observation, and girls themselves document their continuing struggle

with alienation, anger, depression, eating disorders, physical and sexual victimization, teen pregnancy, and other health concerns.

Today, by the time they are ten years old, most girls have probably heard discussion of child abuse, date rape and other sexual exploitation, drugs, and AIDS, HIV, and other sexually transmitted diseases, either in the media, in conversations among friends, or in school health programs. A generation ago, parents and schools dryly dealt out the details of human reproduction and the occasional cautionary tale of *Reefer Madness*. Today violence and sexualized imagery have become a backdrop in movies, MTV, TV and computer games, and, sadly, too often in real life. The Internet has expanded opportunities for girls to access the world in exciting ways, but it has also brought pornography and stranger danger as close as the family computer through chat rooms and on-line activities.

It would be a mistake to say that *most* girls live just this side of anorexia, depression, and suicide, or that *most* girls are victimized by boys and men in their lives, or that *most* girls languish in schools. But it is no exaggeration to say that most girls are in touch with these grim realities as part of the context of their everyday lives. Whether it's through a personal contact, the news or entertainment media, or the Internet, girls of all ages have full access to the world, and every girl struggles to make sense of it.

Callie, a sixth-grader, described a litany of pressures that girls face: disrespect from boys, the unending demand to be perfectly pretty, the stupidity that prompts boys to judge girls by their breast size, the pain of periods, and the risk of pregnancy.

"Girls have a lot of things to worry about that can go wrong," she concluded.

Girls *and* their parents have a lot of things to worry about, or at least think about, and it's not only the risks that challenge our wisdom. Girls have access to opportunities we only dreamed about in our younger days, but with infinite options has come the competitive pressure to engage and excel at everything.

The mother of an athletic, happy-go-lucky fourteen-year-old

girl confided that she was worried that she was pushing her freshman daughter too hard to excel in academics. "But if I don't push, she'll be happy to make B's and C's, and she'll never get into a really good college with those grades—it's just too competitive out there!" She had pushed, prodded, and at times pitched in to see that her daughter's homework assignments were "A" quality, certain that other parents were doing the same thing, and motivated by the competitive environment and desire for her daughter's future success. Lately, though, she had begun to feel she had crossed the line between her role as a mother and a personal coach. She wondered if there is a line, and if there should or should not be a line.

"The competitiveness of the whole scene doesn't feel right, and that bothers me," she said. "But I honestly don't know which is better. Should I let her do her own thing and throw away her chances for these great future opportunities? Or if I do this now, will she be grateful twenty years down the road that I cared enough about her to be this involved? How does anybody know?"

Another mother echoed the desperation of so many parents when she told me, "I'm not saying that being a parent has ever been easy, but my parents had much more clarity about the world and what was acceptable and unacceptable to them, and society supported them. There's just no script anymore."

Yet nobody really wants a script anymore. As fast as change occurs these days, by the time we learned our lines, the play would already be three scenes ahead. Girls are pioneers in a landscape that continues to redefine terms of family, friendship, education, recreation, health, beauty, love, and sexuality in ways that create unprecedented opportunity, challenge, and risk for them. Even the traditional milestones of physical development are changing, as an increasing number of girls are beginning puberty at younger ages—often as young as eight or nine years old. The emotional passage from girl to young woman presents challenges enough; it has become even more difficult as girls' physical maturation has begun to outpace the developmental maturity they need to understand and embrace life as a maturing female.

Girl Territory: A Dizzying Picture for Everyone

It has been twenty years since feminist scholar Carol Gilligan first alerted us to the silenced voices of girls and women with *In a Different Voice*. Nearly ten years ago, Mary Pipher, in her book *Reviving Ophelia: Saving the Selves of Adolescent Girls*, brought those voices forward in the first candid portrayals of girls struggling in crisis through the most painful passages of adolescence. In the past few years, long-overdue attention to the ignored emotional life of boys has drawn public attention away from the unique challenges girls face as they struggle with the pressure to be "everything and nothing all at once." I am not suggesting that boys or their parents have it easy, but I have worked extensively with boys and girls, and with parents and teachers of boys and girls, and I believe the challenge of raising and working with girls is uniquely more complex. We'll look at the biological, social, and emotional reasons for that in the chapters to come, but suffice it to say at this point that when you combine the complexities of female development with the array of opportunities, challenges, and risks that life presents to girls today, it makes for a dizzying picture.

More Savvy, Yet More Vulnerable Than Ever

When I was five years old, I knew all anyone needed to know about milk: It came from a cow. It was good for you. And it was especially good with brownies after school. For most of history, that's all most people knew or cared about milk, especially if they were five years old. Today there is much more to know about milk, and a little girl set me straight on the details as we walked through the cafeteria line during my lunchtime visit to her kindergarten.

"Don't get the red milk—that's the bad milk," she said.

"Bad?" I replied. "Do you mean it's sour?"

"No," she said. Then she matter-of-factly explained to me the difference between "red, purple, and blue milk" and why it is bad to drink anything but "blue milk." The blue cartons contained skim milk, fat-free. Purple cartons contained milk with 2 percent fat. Red milk cartons contained whole milk.

"Red milk has the most fat, and fat is bad," she said.

I thanked her for her helpful explanation, and marveled silently at her decisive understanding of the subject for a five-year-old. Interestingly, she already had learned to think of whole milk as bad, despite such health benefits as calcium and other nutrients important for early growth. She had also learned to assume fat is bad. What she hadn't learned yet was that dietary fat, including milk fat, is part of a healthful diet; that fat is essential for the body to unlock access to certain nutrients in foods; and that there are good fats that actively promote health and prevent disease—especially in young children. Nor was she conscious yet of the way attitudes about fat quickly move from basic nutrition to punishing social judgments about body image, and that for many girls and women the thought that fat is bad becomes a personal mantra of self-hate and self-destructive eating patterns. She had used one fact about fat and milk to form an opinion and make her choice, but she lacked the fuller understanding necessary to put things into a healthful, useful, long-term perspective. Nonetheless, this early little bit of knowledge would shape her awareness and choices in years to come, and not necessarily in a healthful way.

Ironically, in a purely intellectual sense, girls are wiser today than we were at their age, and it is a mixed gift. They are thinking about things earlier, weighing issues, and making personal decisions far earlier than the generation before them. The time left for being a playful little girl has shrunk to little more than a moment in the march toward more sophisticated lives. And yet, in many significant ways, this early education in the wares and ways of the world has only made them more vulnerable. As girls get older, the topics quickly become more sophisticated and the stakes even higher.

Recently I was in Texas working with a group of high school junior and senior girls, ages sixteen and seventeen. I introduced myself as a gender expert, then opened the floor for questions. No one spoke. No one raised a hand. Gender issues were clearly not a hot topic of conversation here. Finally, I said, "Isn't there anything you'd like to know about boys?"

A girl raised her hand. "I want to know about erogenous zones," she said. "Is it true that the tip of a boy's penis is very sensitive?"

"Yes, it is," I said, "but why do you want to know?"

She replied that on dates with boys, whether the boys were officially boyfriends or not, "we're expected to do certain things." She and other girls went on to explain that oral sex is a common expectation. She said that it was not really considered sex or dangerous, and it was what girls were supposed to do in order to have a boyfriend. They weren't happy about the expectation, but they did feel compelled to get good at it. It was that, or be a loser in the dating circuit.

These girls weren't asking directly for ways to "just say no." They had mixed information about oral sex, and did not realize that AIDS and other sexually transmitted diseases could be passed along this way. Their initial concern was about this performance aspect of their relationship with boys, and they wanted to add to their knowledge base.

A five-year-old should not be looking at her food choices and worrying about the fat content unless there is a serious dietary issue and she is working with a professional. A junior in high school should not be worried because she doesn't like oral sex, and hence believes she won't have any boyfriends or will be socially ostracized. When I say these issues aren't "appropriate" concerns for girls of their age, I'm not just talking about my personal moral standard. I'm saying that developmentally, the brain is not yet ready to integrate this information with the judgment needed for a more mature perspective.

These kinds of assumptions and risks for girls today are so pervasive, and remain so completely unchallenged, that girls often accept them as a given. Destructive or high-risk behaviors that used to play out on the social fringe are part of mainstream culture now, and girls struggle to accommodate them. The effects are insidious, sometimes visible not so much in what a girl does but in how a girl thinks about herself and being female in the world. This compromise of core values happens over and over again to girls.

A couple of years ago in New York's Central Park, a group of women joggers was assaulted by a gang of drunken men partying near the jogging path. I was working with an inner-city group of mixed-age high school girls at the time, and when we talked about this incident, part of what they said was that the attack on the women "was their own fault."

"We're brought up to know that when there's a whole bunch of guys around drinking and partying, you put yourself at risk if you get around them," one girl explained. "Those women should not have gone into Central Park—they shouldn't have been there."

In news stories at the time, the women defended their right to jog as usual in this public park. One of them said, in essence, "I should be safe jogging on the jogging path I use every day, and just because there are a bunch of guys drinking beer, I shouldn't have to avoid the park where I run."

The girls were almost unanimous in their opinion that this was stupid thinking, that the women should have understood that drunken men could be dangerous, and they should have stayed away from the park. What surprised me in their firm declaration was that the frustration they expressed was directed not toward the men who had accosted the women, but toward the women, for "being that stupid" and "asking for trouble."

Typically, in my work with girls, when they have the time, place, and support to really explore their feelings about this kind of disturbing event, they eventually will say that they feel the situation is unfair to girls and women, and they don't want the world to be like that. But their experience of the world is that this is just the way it is for females. They take for granted that abuse by males is a distinct possibility for any female. Just as menstruation is a part of female life and opens you up to the risk for pregnancy, sexual assault, too, is a distinct and ever-present risk. Not a great situation, but an immutable way the world is set up.

In other ways, our contemporary culture has cast a new, harsher light on timeless patterns of development that girls once were able to experience unself-consciously. For instance, in the year and a half before a girl has her first period, she typically gains a little weight. This is a normal, healthy hormonal response in which estrogen kicks in and signals to the body that it's about to go through a huge developmental leap from childhood to the stage of being fertile and starting menstruation. The natural human female genetic code gives the go-ahead for reproductive maturity only when the body can achieve a certain level of fat sufficient (in primitive times) to withstand trauma and up the odds of survival; nature says a girl simply has to round out to move on through her normal reproductive development. This means that at around age nine or ten or so, girls naturally develop what might be called a pudgy look. When most of us were this age, prepubescent girls weren't expected to look like glamour models. They were left alone to be pudgy and outgrow it, as most girls do—or would, if nature were allowed to progress in normal, healthy ways.

Instead, the ideal of thin as beautiful has been communicated to an ever younger population of girls and their parents, resulting in an intergenerational panic when the pudgy phase begins. Today it's not uncommon for girls and parents to react with alarm at this girlhood weight gain and immediately set about to fix it with diets, weight-loss clinics, exercise classes, and a singular focus on losing weight. By doing so, they unwittingly upset the body's natural weight management system, which responds to an undesirable weight loss by storing fat more readily and burning it more slowly.

In some girls, the obsession takes a pathological turn, and in the effort to stave off menstruation, weight issues, and, perhaps, other complexities of life as a woman, they starve themselves or exercise excessively to keep their body fat unnaturally low.

What does a girl need to be told? She needs to hear from a credible source: "Just stay tuned. Trust me. In a year it will be different as long as you eat right, stay active, and go on about your life. If you fight it now, it will get worse because the body is driven to do this. The more you cut back on calories, the more the body adjusts downward and you don't lose weight."

What does a girl get instead? Thousands of marketing jolts a week from the media and our culture, and sometimes parents, about body image and how females are supposed to look—which is, of course, unnaturally thin.

Girls do have a lot to worry about that can go wrong.

When girls are confronted with attitudes or events they find unsettling, they are a little stunned; they go back on their heels and are quiet, and that's where the silence of girls begin. They can't figure it out; the world doesn't feel right, but everybody goes along with it. They don't talk about it because they don't have the words for it, and then they reach an age when they don't *want* to talk about it or think about it. Girls often tell me that they don't believe that their parents can see things from their point of view.

By about middle-school age, a girl begins to feel there are things she definitely doesn't want to talk with her parents about. She's assuming that her parents won't understand, or they'll overreact and blow it out of proportion, or they'll minimize what it is she's going through, or perhaps not even care, and who needs that? Many parents are unaware of the details of a girl's life that would be red flags for concern, or, even if they are aware, they don't know what to do about it.

In the past, parents were a fairly reliable source of information and advice, at least until a child reached the smarter-than-thou teen years. Today, even young children are more savvy about technology and popular culture than their parents. As girls routinely see adults react with alarm to new trends, they hesitate to turn to their parents with questions. The traditional parental litany of don'ts are not only ineffective, they widen the generation gap at a time when girls desperately wish adults could be thinking partners.

My aunt Anna comes to mind. Aunt Anna always seemed old to me, even when (as I realize now) she was a young woman. Life was one long series of don'ts to Aunt Anna. Don't jump off the porch step, or you'll break your leg. Don't go out in the cold, or you'll get pneumonia. Her anxiety didn't save us kids from ourselves. It just undermined her credibility with us, and dropped her from our list of available grown-ups we felt we could turn to with questions about this and that. Aunt Anna didn't lack in love for us. She just saw the world as a complex, threatening place, and her only reaction to that complexity was fear, retreat, and alarmist advice. Frankly, that was no lesson that any of us wanted or needed. When adults go into extreme fret mode over what they see in the popular culture, which they often do, girls are left even more adrift to fend for themselves and learn from their peers.

Eve, a fourth-grader, came to me with a dilemma. Her friend Caren had forwarded an e-mail to her that was a very sexually explicit poem that was meant for sophisticated adults, not nine-year-olds. Eve, still comfortable talking to her mother, shared it with her and asked what it meant. Eve's mother was shocked and upset by the e-mail and wanted the name of the e-mailer—Eve's friend—so she could call the girl's parents. Eve refused to give the name, and was now being punished. She was sorry she had ever talked to her mother. To make matters worse for Eve, she told Caren about the issue, and Caren was terrified her parents would find out. She was sure they would never let her touch a computer again in her life. Both girls felt trapped. They were miserable that this poem had caused so much uproar. They had parents who were understandably concerned, but totally reactive and unwilling to listen or to try to understand the situation. And, what was worse, Caren had shared the poem with Eve in the first place because she didn't understand it and couldn't ask her parents because she was afraid they would punish her.

Does it have to be like this? Does it have to be either/or? Girls who can't talk to their parents because they won't understand and will be punished—or girls who do talk to their parents but feel betrayed in the end? Do parents have to be overly strict authoritarians—or else parents who set no limits and aim only to be a daughter's easygoing buddy?

Chaos Theory and the Parenting Perspective

Physicists refer to "chaos theory" to describe the relationship between order and disorder in the universe, and our ability to see and understand it. This applies to everything from the birth of a star galaxies away to the genetic mutations that enable insects to adapt their diet to crop rotation in order to survive. I find that it applies perfectly to parenting, too.

Basically, chaos theory begins with the thought that everything in the universe fits into a pattern in connection to everything else. We have difficulty seeing the big picture because we are too close, or sometimes because we are focused on the wrong thing. NASA photos taken by orbiting probes in outer space, showing celestial patterns we previously have been unable to see from earthbound telescopes, add credence to this theory. When we can't see the forest for the trees, we recognize that it's a problem of perspective. In concrete terms, if you look closely through a magnifying glass at a fingernail (no matter what color it is painted), it fills your field of vision and seems to be a total singular entity. But if you move the lens back far enough to focus on the thumb, then you see the fingernail as only a part of the picture, and it is the thumb that becomes the whole—until you move the lens back far enough to see the hand. Then you can see that the thumb is just a part, and it is the hand that is the whole—until you move the lens back far enough to see the arm, and so on.

How does this relate to parenting specifically? Each and every day, many times a day, we look at a girl through our lens of experience and insight, and must decide how to respond to a singular behavior, a singular statement, or a singular decision. It's difficult to know where to put the lens, or whether you can back up far enough to have clarity about the whole picture. Everything is connected to everything else, and parenting perspective is not only limited, but also irrevocably tangled up with your personal morality and philosophy of life.

You may not want the world to be a place where a twelve-year-old girl like Robin must think of issues of safety and respect when she buys a bathing suit, but your broader adult perspective on the world makes you lobby for greater coverage. That bikini is like a laser beam shining on society's eagerness to treat a young female as nothing but a physical, sexual package. You don't want that for your daughter. You don't want her perceived in that way, and you don't want her to perceive herself in that way, believing that her clothes, weight, and complexion are her most important qualities.

Meanwhile, Robin, and every girl her age, sees the suit as a fashion statement and badge of belonging in the peer group world that absolutely fills their vision. Even if you articulate your concerns—point out the obvious forest you can see with the aid of adult awareness—they cannot see it, focused as they are on the trees. I don't mean that they are choosing to ignore you. I mean they really *cannot see it*. You might just as well ask your toddler to tie her own shoes. Can't do it; not just yet, anyway. And if we were able to flash forward ten years and talk to Robin at age twenty-two, and to her parents, chances are the choice of swimsuit that summer she was twelve would have proved to be of little or no consequence at all. (Unless she were forced to buy the suit that made her the target of teasing, and could still feel the sting of humiliation.) So why did it seem so important at the time? Was the conflict of the moment really about a swimsuit? Or was it moral values? Resisting peer pressure? Safety? Was it about parental control or about a girl's struggle for autonomy?

Each of us, at one time or another, finds it difficult, or even impossible, to move the lens back far enough to see the big picture. In the earlier story of Robin's search for a satisfactory swimsuit, even though she cannot see the issues through her mother's lens, it is still important for Mom to describe what she sees. It helps Robin at least have some understanding of why her mother reacts to situations like this with a different response. And, as she gets older, she'll remember these conversations and they'll start to make more sense. It is like reading a book when you are young and then thinking about it later. You get the more sophisticated concepts and points that you couldn't understand with less maturity. At the very least, when Robin becomes a young adult, she'll appreciate how hard her mother tried to be a good mother, or maybe that will only occur to her when she is the mother!

We also limit our perspective when we focus on one element of the picture to the exclusion of others. Some physicists suggest that light exists simultaneously in both particle and wave form, but we can't see both qualities at once. There are instruments that allow us to see light in particle form, and other instruments that allow us to see it in wave form, but we don't yet have an instrument that allows us to see both properties at the same time. In our relationship with girls, when we focus exclusively on one facet of the moment, our focus can blind us to other significant pieces of the picture.

Sandy, a third-grader, was arguing with her mother one day about dropping out of her advanced ice-skating course. The child had been skating since she was three years old, and had become quite accomplished in five years on the ice. Her coach called her a natural, and urged her and her parents not to give up now. Sandy wanted out.

"I just don't want to skate so much anymore," Sandy said, when asked to explain herself. "I want to do other things."

Her mother was exasperated. "I can't see you just dropping it now, after all your work, after all we've invested," she said. "I hate to see it all go to waste."

Sandy's mother had invested more than time and money in skating lessons. Her emotional investment of pride and expectation made it difficult for her to change the lens through which she viewed her daughter. Sandy's five-year experience of success as a skater might be viewed more objectively as an accomplishment, a training ground for self-discipline and determination she would carry with her for life.

Did her desire to try other things, at age eight, make her accomplished past a waste of time? Was she giving up, as her coach described it, or was she, perhaps, waking up to a wider world in which to express herself and develop her interests?

Chaos theory also teaches us about growth.

In everyday life, we typically think of chaos as undesirable disorganization. In fact, we generally think of all disorganization as undesirable in the orderly process we try to make of life. Chaos theory tells us that not only is everything connected in some larger pattern, but that chaos is a natural and necessary part of it. The essence of growth is change, and change requires reorganization and transformation, whether we are talking about the growth of a galaxy or a cell, an idea or a family or a school—or a girl.

We can see it in the physical growth patterns of children, and, as I mentioned before, in girls particularly as their bodies begin to round out in preparation for puberty. I recall Alexa, a sixth-grader, at age eleven glaring unhappily at her midriff one day. "I'm fat," she moaned, poking her tummy, which still held just a hint of that pot-bellied curve of younger days. But by her thirteenth birthday, she was delighted to see that the curves were in all the best places: nature's long-awaited but quite predictable reorganization of resources.

Change in terms of wisdom and knowledge and putting things together in the world happens that way, too. Your daughter grows, seems to be maturing and feeling comfortable in her thoughts, and then—*Boom!*—all heck breaks loose, but when the dust settles, she's at a new place in her development, she's made some gains, and life goes on. I'm reminded of this so often when I'm around exuberant young teen girls. One moment they'll be talking about makeup and what to wear to the big dance, and the next they're tucking their favorite stuffed animal in their pillowcase for the slumber party. One beleaguered father described his continuing state of confusion in communicating with his fifteen-year-old daughter: "Before I give her an answer about anything, I have to figure whether it's the five-year-old I'm talking to, or the twenty-one-year-old. I never know whether she's going to giggle at my attempts to be funny, or scream at me for treating her like a baby."

If we look closely at what's really happening in the midst of chaos, we can see that it is not so much dis-organization, but rather re-organization and re-forming that is about to produce a paradigm shift. If we try to close down chaos in an effort to provide structure and clarity, we run the risk of closing down creativity and stunting growth.

This seems to be especially true for girls. Ask teachers who have worked with hundreds of girls, and they'll tell you that girls tend to like arithmetic more than mathematics. In the educational world, there is a distinct and meaningful difference between the two: Arithmetic refers to basic calculations such as adding, subtracting, multiplying, dividing. If you work the numbers right, you get the right answer. Mathematics refers to conceptual thinking, problem solving. The traditional story problem is a good example of this. Or, geometrical theorems; you have to have a good mathematical mind to really understand them. If you're good at arithmetic, you can be a good accountant. But to be a physicist you must be a good mathematician. What we see in schools is that most girls typically prefer arithmetic. They like to know that there is only one right answer; not something you have to think about, struggle with, have no clarity about for a fairly long time.

In the next chapter I'll talk more about some patterns of neurological development as well as learned styles among girls that lead to this thinking. For now, I will just say that it is widely seen and accepted that most girls are far less open to ambiguity, and therefore risk-taking, than boys. Boys often see ambiguity as a game, a challenge, fun. To girls, more often it feels uncomfortable, unsure, unsafe. So it doesn't take much to close down a girl's divergent thinking, and the intellectual exploration and wading through the unknown that goes with it. Yet that is what living and growing and learning is all about. The nature of life is that it is unpredictable. Various permutations and varied situations come at us every day.

The most healthy and successful human being is one who can

deal with ambiguity, figure out how to negotiate situations where the path or outcome is not clear. Probably the worst thing we can do as adults, to handicap girls, is to encourage them in any way to want or need things in total order or control. They're already inclined that way. The best thing we can do is to help them learn to grow in a climate where chaos—internal or external—is always in the three-day forecast.

Beyond Black and White: Learning to Negotiate the Gray

Parenting is really all about helping a girl to negotiate the seeming chaos of life. I call this "negotiating the gray." The world has so much gray, and not very much black and white. Helping your daughter understand and negotiate the gray areas is what will help her be strong and successful.

What makes negotiating the gray such a challenge is the fact that most of us are helping our girls negotiate the gray at the same time we are negotiating the gray ourselves, both in our own lives and also in our role as parents or teachers of girls! Most adults I talk with are struggling with their own identity, priorities, and values. In addition, society no longer gives clarity about how to parent, where to draw the line, what to allow and not allow.

In some ways, it's back to the days of Columbus when there was no map to the New World. The maps in our new world are being redrawn and feel incomplete. So, how do we negotiate the gray?

The first order of business is to think about what you value most and what you are willing to go to the mat for. This will become the foundation for your reasoning as you and your daughter negotiate the gray. In the case of a two-parent family, this is a joint venture. It is really the cataloging of your values as a family, and coming to compromises when there are differences. This is better done before parenting crises arise.

But then again, parenting crises bring on more discussions

and push you as parents to identify more and more of your values and goals.

Negotiating the gray is a process. Just as those thorny math problems require reasoning, and not simply calculations, there are as many possible strategies for negotiating the gray. You may not know exactly what to do or how to help your daughter, but you need to be as sure as you can be about the bottom line, the core value or philosophy you have as a parent. After that, you need to *really* understand the problem. The only way to do this is by engaging, connecting, interacting with your daughter.

We often assume we understand what the issue is, and move immediately to the consequence or the "fix it" mode. Instead, it is important to hear and try to understand the complexity of the situation as it is perceived by your daughter. Helping her to think about the issues, to identify options, to weigh cost factors will better equip her to handle unforeseen and unidentified situations in the future.

More than "responsive" or even "empathetic" parenting, I think of this as "connected" parenting. It involves seeking to understand what she is saying, asking questions to get the full perspective, validating her feelings, discussing options and best next steps. Certainly, adding your parental values and wisdom is an important part, but only a part. The pioneer girl brings a knowledge and perspective and wisdom to the moment that you need, too. Parenting conversations are really that; conversations between you and your daughter, with both parties making valuable contributions that enrich and add meaning to each other. Connected parenting doesn't negate the need for parents to mete out consequences for unacceptable behavior. It just means that the process is more complex, and that understanding your daughter and what she faces, and deciding the best course of action, requires less reaction and more interaction.

Chaos theory for parents also suggests that there are many times you let her live with some chaos and ambiguity and struggle on her own. By figuring out something on her own, she not only grows wiser, but she also develops the kind of competence and confidence that will help make her a strong and resilient human being. You can help by clearly communicating your family values, setting limits, and generally supporting her efforts. But if you do too much, help too much, or even try to talk through things too much, you can interfere with the experience that will teach her to cope with the chaos of life.

Jessie's School Crisis: Process as Rx

Pat was on the tail end of a crisis of sorts. Her daughter, Jessie, just starting eighth grade, had walked in the door from school on a Friday afternoon, one week into the school year, and announced that she could not, would not go back. "Please don't make me," she begged Pat. "I *can't* go back!"

Their family had just moved to this community the year before, confident that the highly rated public school, though large, would serve them well. It was a fine school, but Jessie had been slow to make friends, not surprising given the cliquish world of junior high school and Jessie's quiet, reserved personality. Over the summer, Jessie had attended a small girls' camp where she had made friends quickly in her two-week stay, and now she was desperate for the same feeling of acceptance and camaraderie in her school life. She explained precisely that to her mother and father and pleaded to be either home-schooled or allowed to attend a smaller, private school. Her parents had never seen her so desperate and unhappy about school, and they pressed her to be more specific about the problem. Had someone said something? Done something? No, Jessie said, there wasn't any one thing, it was *everything*. The situation was hopeless; she'd rather *die* than go back. Pat called the school, but counseling services offered little response.

Not wanting to succumb to her panic, but not wanting to ignore her feelings of desperation, they agreed to explore alternatives. Three intense weeks later, after following their exploration through admissions applications and a few school visits, the time had come to make a choice between her public school and several other options.

Jessie had brightened at the warm welcome she received from students and teachers at the other schools, and she had remarked on the individual friendliness and more personal feeling of community in the smaller school settings. Her final choice? To stay where she was. Her explanation? "Everything's fine now."

Her parents were incredulous. How could "everything" have changed in three short weeks? But in fact, it had. The anxiety of the first week in school had given way to a more comfortable sense of belonging. Enough friends from the year before had turned out to be friends again. Teachers had begun to show some personality and warmth. Classes weren't so bad, and after-school activities offered some potential for fun. Even the cafeteria food had its good days. It was hard to believe Jessie was talking about the same place that only a short time before had been portrayed—and experienced—as such a hellhole.

Pat was relieved that Jessie was now comfortable with her situation, but she was exhausted and disconcerted by the whole frantic episode.

"What was that all about?" she said wearily. "I'm glad it ended well, but I'm left wondering if we could have handled it differently and avoided all that commotion."

This was not a crisis on the order of anorexia or attempted suicide, but it offers a good example of chaos theory and negotiating the gray with one of those normal issues of growing up: how a girl feels in an environment and how her parents can help her to negotiate the daily context of her life. It is extremely difficult to watch your daughter experience discomfort, pain, or conflict for even a moment, let alone for a period of weeks. Given all that has been said about the importance for girls to experience ambiguity, to learn to deal with the gray of life, it is perhaps the hardest parenting task of all to know when to intervene, how much, or whether to intervene at all. We'll revisit this aspect of parenting in later chapters as we discuss the vulnerability of girls to negative emotions and the possible short- and long-term effects. But for now, this story represents the classic parenting dilemma: How much do you let your daughter struggle and how much is enough, signaling the need for parental involvement? Remember, the days of quick fixes and scripts are gone. How do you negotiate the gray?

Step 1: Consciously stage or layer your responses with active involvement. Don't jump in the deep water; wade in and see how far you need to go. By simply being open to Jessie's concerns, her parents established the process that would eventually take them, step by step, into a deeper exploration of Jessie's feelings and, with that as a foundation, a resolution that ultimately needed only a little more time and patience.

Step 2: Listen without judging and without rushing to identify a fix. Listening and acting as a sounding board can always be part of the equation. That doesn't prevent a girl from figuring out things and handling them on her own. However, this listening phase is often compromised by parents when they move into the advice and fixing mode too early in the process. What's needed is what we call "active listening." When Jessie said, "I'm miserable and I don't want to go back to school," our immediate knee-jerk reaction might be to move directly to a discussion of options and solutions. Sometimes it is enough for a girl to just have someone hear her thoughts and feelings and acknowledge her situation. It is sage parenting in the first round to say something like: *"I'm so glad you talked to me about this, and it must be really hard for you to go back to school right now. But I promise we'll keep talking and figure out what to do if things don't change at school."* Mission accomplished: The verbal and emotional upset has found a safe outlet.

Step 3: Continue to listen, and guide her understanding of the situation. If the feelings and perceived situation continues without some reduction in force, so to speak, then you continue to move along the parenting continuum of negotiating the gray. Now it's time to listen and to guide her understanding of the situation. *"When you said that you hate school, you mentioned some things, but could you help me understand by giving some examples?"* It's important to help Jessie understand what has happened, what set it off, what's causing her to feel this way. During this phase you're taking the next step in negotiating the gray: pulling apart all those noodles that make up this bowl of I-hate-my-school spaghetti. Getting her to see things more clearly is the goal.

Step 4: Discuss strategies for action. If the situation continues, then exploring options and techniques for remedying it is in order. Her options and techniques should be explored first. *It is important at this phase to not be too judgmental of her thinking.* For example, if she says that a viable option is for her to drop out of school, bite your tongue, refrain from saying that is a stupid option, and instead explore with her the pros and cons of that option. The goal here is to let her practice thinking of strategies and weighing their potential for success or failure. You short-circuit the process by giving her the answer. It's very much like guiding her through the steps of a math problem in which she must do the work herself. Only *after* she's exhausted her repertoire of possible strategies do you offer some of your own thoughts of possible options. If you do that first, she will stop thinking on her own and rely on your thinking and your interventions. It's what happens in a classroom when one bright student always supplies the answer to every question. Everyone else soon stops thinking about any question asked and waits for her to answer it. If a parent always jumps to answer the question or solve the problem, the end result is the same: A girl just stops working on how to negotiate life and lets you do it for her. Or worse, she stops talking and sharing because she doesn't want you to take over her life.

Once you're into the strategy phase, this is where your knowledge of the world or of your family's assets and constraints can be shared. Your daughter may not know that there are five other schools that she could attend in your district. Your daughter may not know that the family finances are such that you couldn't afford the $14,000 tuition to the independent school in town. Your knowledge and wisdom base comes into play here.

When choosing which strategies to try first, keep in mind that it is not a contest to try to be successful in the first round. If your daughter chooses a strategy that she thinks will work and you feel is doomed, let it happen, unless the consequences are very high. That is how she will learn to make successful choices in the future. It is also important to understand that just taking an active approach in dealing with a situation is an important lesson in negotiating the gray. In Jessie's case, visiting another school gave her the sense of having some control over her life, taking some action, having an alternative and not being trapped. It also bought time by alleviating some of her desperation in searching for a way out. That allowed her to relax more, to continue to go to school each day, and to let the "new shoe" feel of her public school become more comfortable.

Step 5: Resolution through action or acceptance. The final step becomes obvious. The situation either dissolves over time, or you gradually move to resolution by choosing action or by choosing acceptance of the situation. This is a continuing and perhaps time-consuming process, but if you continue as an active listener and a guide through the process, resolution will come.

Throughout the process of negotiating the gray, no matter what step or phase, don't hesitate to make value statements about your core philosophy or moral standards. This is not the same as telling your daughter how to solve her dilemma. For example, if she says that she should just trash the lockers of the girls that are being mean to her, speak immediately to share your values and rules about not damaging others or their property. This is not the time to talk about pros and cons of such an action! Some things are not negotiable in child rearing or in life, and drawing the line clearly is important. Since so much of the world is gray, it is critical for children, *and it is a relief to them,* to see the areas that parents know are black and white.

Negotiating the Gray with Parents and Teachers

The same process of negotiating the gray applies to all of us: as parents, as teachers, and as others invested in creating environments where girls can thrive. When we embrace the process of connection, listening, and sharing strategy, we create opportunity for genuine growth in our girls, ourselves, and our institutions.

As an administrator and consultant in schools across the country, talking with teachers and parents has been an ongoing, consistent, and integral part of my job. In the last several years, as news stories and our own experience began to point to an increasing incidence of earlier physical maturation among girls—e.g., menstruation at an earlier age—at the Laurel School, we knew we needed to tailor our attention to the issues in a new way. There wasn't any formal research literature to guide us; as pioneers, along with our girls, we had to negotiate the gray. We developed a careful process for responding to the issue. The school nurse was most often aware of when girls began to need supplies. We talked with parent groups in the primary and middle school, and consulted pediatricians. All sources pointed to earlier and earlier physiological development of our girls and, therefore, the need for earlier conversations with them.

Ten years ago we had what was dubbed "the hormone talks" beginning at fifth grade. The nurse and school psychologist would spend several sessions talking to the girls about the physiological and psychological aspects of hormonal changes and the beginning of menstruation. Five years ago we had to move the curriculum down to the end of fourth grade because enough of our girls were starting their periods then. Three years ago we moved the curriculum into the beginning of the fourth grade. Two years ago the idea was raised about moving it to the third-grade curriculum.

The decision about when to begin to talk about all the realities and ramifications of a maturing female body is not frivolous or easy. Like many other aspects of life, talking about serious issues too early, before a child is ready and mature enough to handle all the details, can cause negative side effects. Traditionally, too, there has been a heavy focus on the dire consequences of sexual activity and pregnancy, and not enough focus on physical maturation as a normal, healthy process for girls. Specifically, girls may feel fear, frustration, or a desire to avoid growing up, which can lead to anorexia in an effort to keep the body small.

The onset of earlier physical development does not seem to be correlated with earlier emotional development and decision-making wisdom. The conundrum is that girls are becoming physically more like a woman, more attractive to boys, and able to become pregnant at very early ages. On the other hand, most of them are not ready for the sexualized attention they receive, the clothing provided by the fashion industry and promoted by the advertising industry, the push for earlier dating and such. We continue to negotiate the gray on this important aspect of girls' lives, addressing the need for information and guidance not only for girls, but for parents and teachers alike.

Fortunately for girls and the rest of us, when we negotiate the gray, the results don't lock us into a five-year contract. Quite the opposite. We are all learning on the job, and ours is a negotiation of life. It allows us—all of us—unlimited opportunity to continue a dialogue, open new topics for discussion, make mistakes, improve our skills, and do better the next time around. In Chapter 2, we'll explore the way that give-and-take works in parenting young girls, and how that process shapes a girl's experience of herself and the world around her in lasting ways.

The String of Pearls

I like to think of basic insights about girls as pearls of wisdom. You may receive them from someone like your parents or friends, or you may discover them yourself, as I know every parent and every teacher does at one time or another. No matter how perfect those pearls are, though, singly they don't have much effect, but when you string them together to make a necklace—then you've got something!

When we talk about life for girls, and life with girls, our insights are useful only to the degree that we bring them all to bear on the moment. One at a time, they are information and they can expand your understanding. Strung together, they have a much more dramatic effect. Here is your first box of pearls, designed to string with your daughter—a gift of interaction you can give to her yourself!

Pearls for Parents and Pearls for Girls

- It's okay to be a gatekeeper. Try to screen out at least some of the very toxic messages of society by limiting access to some websites, TV shows, etc.
- If you can't beat 'em, *balance* 'em. Try to balance out what isn't screenable with consistent and periodic family discussions.
- Hold on to your values and rules, even when you hear: "But everyone else is doing it!"
- Get smart about sneaky advertising! Order a subscription to *Adbusters* or *New Moon* for your daughter. These periodicals will help her see how the media and advertising work on her perception of herself as a female.
- When negotiating the gray with her, get used to starting out with phrases like: "Could you explain? I'm not sure I understand . . ."

CHAPTER 2

The Formative Years: The Layering of Nature, Nurture, and Life Experience

"What I like most about being a girl is that usually when a class gets in trouble, they blame it on the boys. Also, being a girl, you get to do more fun things with your friends than being a boy."

—Ilana, fourth grade

My grandfather had a favorite saying, his version of a famous old German adage: "Too late smart." His English translation, with a slight Slavic bilingual influence, made it stick in my head even more. It is so apropos in any discussion of parenting and the frantic race to stay one step ahead of our children on life's learning curve! I've often thought it would be good to have a practice child to test out our child-rearing skills, to be able to make mistakes, to learn and to adjust; in sum, to become a wise and talented parent before the task begins in earnest.

However, parenting seems to be more of an internship: learning in a real-life situation. Every parent will make a myriad of mistakes, will often spend time with clearer hindsight than foresight. Parenting situations and decisions happen so quickly and so often, there is just no way to be adequately prepared when your first baby arrives. And, just as you feel somewhat stabilized as a parent, two things often happen: Your child enters an entirely different phase, and you feel that you are on totally foreign terrain *again*. Or, you have a second child that is different enough from your firstborn so that the techniques and strategies that have served you well as a parent are no longer nearly as effective.

And so it goes through these all-important formative years, from birth through about eight years of age. The term *formative years* could just as accurately apply to the development of parenting as to the development of the child. As parents often lament, their small new human does not come with directions or a child-rearing manual. And whether a child is your biological child or your adopted child, instinctive parenting rarely seems to be enough for parents to feel secure in their wisdom for the multitude of situations and decisions they face each day. From crawling to talking to walking to reading, as children go through classic developmental milestones, we all heave a sigh of relief, feel a little more confidence as a parent, and hold our breath for the next milestone. We have good days, we have bad days, and some days that just race by, and it is the cumulative effect of them that, over time, builds our competence and confidence in ourselves as parents.

I used to think back to my first year of teaching and how many mistakes I made, and how I would do so many things differently now that I was "too late smart" as an educator and psychologist. I hoped that those thirty lively eight-year-old boys and girls I had that first year were okay. Then, fifteen years later, I went back to visit my old school when they had an open house and reunion before tearing down the old building. Five girls from among my first-year students were there, and they ran up to me and began recalling stories of our year together. They all burst out saying it was the best year they had ever had in school.

I asked how that could possibly be, and began telling some stories of my own about the mistakes I had made or events that had seemed disastrous at the time—like falling down a flight of stairs the first day of school and having the entire class see my underwear. Each girl, in her own way, expressed the same simple sentiment: "You cared so much about us. We knew you wanted us to be the best we could be, so we tried and learned and grew that year."

I'm still not sure about the math and reading skills they accumulated, but it is only one of many stories that children have shared with me that confirm the core, baseline child-rearing premise: While you're progressing along the learning curve to becoming a wise and effective parent, your daughter's learning curve will stay high and positive as long as she knows how much you care and that you are trying your best to help her grow and prosper. Translation: Children forgive us for having to learn how to be parents as long as we show that we take our parenting responsibility seriously, we care, and we keep trying. In the same way, it is the cumulative effect of nature, nurture, and life experience that shapes a child, and it does so in some special ways from the very beginning when that child is a girl.

Strudel Theory: Building a Life with Layers of Experience

For children, the major developmental task during the formative years is discipline, and by that I mean defining and setting their behavioral and moral patterns. We'll look more closely at discipline later in the chapter, but first we're going to examine some aspects of female body and brain development that create, in each girl, the unique internal environment in which those patterns will develop.

Every time we see a little boy turn to the box of blocks as his female playmate heads for the dress-up corner, we see the backdrop for the "nature versus nurture" debate: Are gender preferences the result of genetic hardwiring, or of socializing influences in the environment? The answer is still hotly debated in some circles, but only in terms of how much. Now there is consensus: An individual is shaped by nature and nurture. How much of each, and in what ways, appears to fluctuate with the individual gene pool and the force and volume of life experiences interacting upon the child.

So from a parenting point of view, from the inception of the fetus, the layering of experiences and happenings each minute of each day has a shaping effect. That is both reassuring and scary. We can and do influence what our children become, although to some extent it's not entirely understood or even knowable. By the same token, every parent knows that within the same family, with the same parents, with the same environment, children turn out exceedingly different. When we look specifically at girls, new information about gender differences, hormones, and other brain and body science sheds a useful light on the way girls experience the effect of nature, nurture, and life experience, especially in their formative years.

It's easiest for me to illustrate this with my Strudel Theory of child development. Basic Strudel Theory says that each of us is born with the main ingredient (nature), but it is the layering of that with other ingredients (nurture) and the interaction of them all together (life experience) that creates the finished product.

To take the illustration just one step further, think about your daughter's personality and let's call it either sweet cherries or tart apples. Starting with that main ingredient, now let's imagine adding a cup of sugar (representing your loving attention, of course!), some salt and spices (friends and family interactions), a pastry crust (home and school environments), and some heat (the pressures of everyday life) to bake it all together. No matter how carefully you measure or mix those ingredients, each strudel is going to turn out a little differently, depending on the characteristics of those apples, cherries, and spices, and the chemistry that occurs in the mixing and baking.

And now you have the fanciful explanation of why individual development is so complicated, and why there is not an exact way to extract how much is nature and how much is nurture, or predict with certainty how it will actually turn out. On the other hand, the mixing and layering effect means that every single layer is tempered by the presence of the others.

In human terms, Strudel Theory says that whatever qualities a girl's basic nature brings to the mix, her life experience becomes the layering that will shape who she becomes. It also means that we can and must layer experiences over time, which helps her grow strong and resilient. With that in mind, let's examine what research tells us about the nature of girls and the distinctly female development of the core neurological system, which includes thinking, perceiving, feeling, and movement.

Girl Brains: In the Beginning

A few simple points about brain development help set the stage for understanding the female experience of life and learning from the earliest days of life.

We are each born with an existing pattern and number of neurons, or nerve cells, that conduct impulses throughout the body and to and from the brain. However, with each experience and with layered experiences using the same sets of neurons, two things happen:

First, the axon, or nerve cell body, becomes thicker with added coats of the myelin, a fatty covering on a nerve that, as it grows thicker, conducts an impulse faster and more effectively. The entire neuron grows thicker through this process we call myelination. In other words, as a neuron or set of neurons is used, it gets bigger and better.

Second, the dendrites, which are like little branches that connect one neuron to the next, also grow bushier with use. With no or little use, dendrites do not grow and, with time, are naturally pruned out of the system. Neurons with more dendrites conduct impulses, or thoughts, more effectively and efficiently. So we want to grow dendrites and have "bushy" areas in many parts of our brains.

From birth to about age three, the human nervous system is primed for growth. Just like a tree, it grows quickly during this early stage, and that growth establishes the basic pattern for continuing development. Those areas that develop the most branches (dendrites) and the sturdiest branches will be the strongest part of the tree, or in this case, the brain.

We now know that this process of dendritic growth can, and does, happen all through life. However, just like the tree, it is harder to prune large branches, or habits, than smaller branches, such as learning incorrectly that two plus two is five. So once something is learned or felt for a long enough period of time, it is harder to change. It is also easier to grow bigger branches early in the tree's life than later, when the patterns of growth have already been established.

There is not enough definitive research about myelination, or the thickening of the nerve cell, to be as clear about the implications of that growth as we are about other aspects of brain growth, but at this time, myelination appears to be enhanced by use and experience and age, and it certainly facilitates the use of the neuron. Less clear, but very interesting, is some evidence that myelination may also be related to readiness. It is possible that, with beginning reading, for instance, the hearing of vowel sounds may be related to when that part of the auditory nerve center is myelinated or ready for use. This development may differ by gender, though the evidence thus far is only circumstantial. For example, it is clear that most boys are not ready to begin phonics or to sound out words as early as most girls. If this is related to the physical growth of the neurons, which we call cognitive maturity, then beginning phonics too early may be, at the least, frustrating, and possibly damaging to the system.

This readiness of the system, not just psychologically but in terms of the hardwiring of the brain, is very important in thinking about the earliest parenting responses to girls. Females and males seem to have differing time lines of physical and brain development, especially during the formative years.

In terms of phonics or spelling readiness, girls can and do move into reading earlier than boys, often up to two years earlier. Boys are able to do spatial tasks—building those Lego models, for instance—much earlier than girls are. We used to think that this was due to experience, toys, or other influences that were gender stereotypic. Brain research now clearly shows that the structure of the female and male brain is different at birth, apparently the result of estrogen or testosterone shaping it in utero. In other words, female brains have more neurons in certain areas than male brains as a result of having more estrogen bathing them during fetal development.

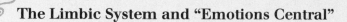

The Limbic System and "Emotions Central"

Now let's consider the lower or mid-brain, called the limbic system. You'll be hearing a lot more about the limbic system because it is the center of the emotional system. More specifically, an almond-sized portion of the midbrain, called the *amygdala* (pronounced ah-MIG-de-lah), is the home of our emotions. The amygdala, small as it is, nonetheless has a powerful influence on all thoughts and behaviors, especially in the female. Females seem to have a very sensitive and active amygdala. The thought process in both the female and male brain intertwine the activity of the cortex (the pecan-shaped gray matter, which is the center of rational thought) and this amygdala, the emotional center of the brain. This tells us that there is no such thing as totally rational thought; our thoughts always have amygdala involvement. However, research indicates that the female brain usually has more amygdala involvement than the male brain under the same circumstances. Research has not yet discerned an explanation for this, but scientists who think in evolutionary terms suggest that there must be a survival advantage for the female of a species to be hardwired to feel some emotions, especially negative ones, more frequently and more intensely than the male of the species.

What does all this mean? To use our Strudel Theory metaphor, the female strudel is very different from the male strudel at the most basic level. The combination of different ingredients by gender and by individual mixed with the experiences layered over time exert a strong influence on the way things shape up and turn out.

So what are little girls made of? What is the nature of girls?

- Most females are slightly predisposed by their estrogen-bathed neurological hardwiring in these cognitive areas: language facility, auditory skills, fine motor skills, sequential/detailed thinking. Simply put, estrogen seems to enhance the neurological functions housed on the left side of the brain.

- Further brain research also indicates that, in comparison to the male brain, the female has a more decentralized brain that uses many parts for a singular task; a more integrated brain, which uses both hemispheres for most tasks; and a more developed corpus callosum, the bridge between the left and right hemispheres that allows communication back and forth and enhances the integration of those brain activities.

- The limbic system, which houses the amygdala, the emotional center of the brain, appears to be more sensitive and more active in females. That is, females' thoughts are integrated with the emotional system more frequently and more intensely than most males' thoughts. For example, females can feel depression at much higher levels than most males; some researchers claim up to five or more times as much. In everyday activity, a girl views the moment with both the rational and emotional parts of her brain, so that seemingly unemotional situations contain an emotional component for her.

The infant girl comes into the world with the above three predispositions as a result of her female-differentiated brain. Eventually, she will probably talk sooner, learn to read faster, form written letters better, and remember how to tie her shoes better than her brother. She may also take a bit longer to think through a task, and may also be more sensitive to the tone of her parents' voices than her brother.

That is the pure interpretation. But nothing is 100 percent pure. There is a range of female characteristics, not a set amount of each characteristic for every individual. So there are differences within the population of females. And there are some males who have neurological systems more like a female's. In his book *The Owner's Manual for the Brain: Everyday Applications from Mind-Brain Research*, Dr. Pierce J. Howard refers to a segment of males who have female-differentiated brains and to a segment of females who have male-differentiated brains. Dr. Howard suggests that about 80 percent of females have female-differentiated brains with the above hardwired three predispositions, of course with some variation; about 20 percent of males have female-differentiated brains with the above three hardwired predispositions. About 80 percent of males have male-differentiated brains and about 20 percent of females have male-differentiated brains.

The terms *male-* and *female-differentiated* refer to learning style, not necessarily to gender or sexual orientation. It appears to mean that these neurological systems had a tad more of the other gender's androgens (estrogen and testosterone) in utero. There is some evidence that a dramatic preponderance of the other gender's androgen can have an effect on gender orientation, but that research is still in the preliminary stages regarding those extremes. Generally speaking, a stereotypical male learning style in a female does *not* signify that she is a lesbian; nor does a stereotypical female learning style in a male indicate that he is gay.

In terms of cognitive predisposition of the brain at birth, the world can and does intervene. Early experiences can exacerbate these slight gender predispositions or modify them in the other direction. During the formative years, what is done has significant impact on the wiring of the brain and the development of the personality. For example, in a coed preschool, if children are allowed to choose how to spend their time, you will see choices made mostly by gender. Keeping the 20 percent crossover minorities of each gender group in mind, for clarity I'll refer to those groups as the "20 percent" boys or girls.

Observations show that boys will tend to spend a great deal of time in the block corner, along with the 20 percent girls. Girls will spend a great deal of time in the dress-up corner or the writing/drawing center, along with the 20 percent boys. Certainly there is some other gender crossover some or all of the time. But the overall pattern in choice of activity reflects the neurologic predispositions listed above.

Keep in mind that use increases the dendritic branching and neuron growth; that this growth improves the facility of thinking in the used area, and that the formative years are the high neurologic growth time. This means that boys who are whipping together those Lego models use their spatial neurons because they are good at it, and there is a brain comfort factor with this activity. As they engage in this kind of play, they are growing even more dendrites and making these particular neurological connections even stronger. Girls, on the other hand, are spending hardly any time in the block area and are therefore not only *not* increasing dendritic growth and neurologic strength in that area, but are probably pruning back the number of dendrites there because of little usage. This is the area of the brain that deals with math and logic-based problem-solving later in life. So it is a critical area of development of the female brain in terms of later success in school and in life in general.

"Logging In" for Optimal Brain Growth

I refer to usage and time spent in a particular skill area as "log-in" time. It is important for girls (and boys) to spend log-in time in areas that are counter to their neurologic grain. Translated, for optimal lifelong neurological balancing and growth, girls generally need to spend a lot of time in the block corner and boys need to spend a lot of time in the writing/drawing corner. Provided in an enjoyable way, these early against-the-grain gender experiences help create a well-balanced brain that is better equipped to handle the range of tasks and challenges the brain will have to contend with all through life. This concept can be expanded to many areas. Young girls need to be spending time in all of the areas that they are not as hardwired to choose early on of their own accord:

> **Gross motor tasks:** skipping, riding a bike, climbing
> **Spatial tasks:** puzzles, tangrams, carpentry, orienteering
> **Strategy and problem solving:** team games and sports, checkers

Risk taking: doing anything that takes a bit of courage on a particular girl's part.

This can range tremendously by individual.

If you have a 20 percent girl, then she needs to spend more time on:

Fine motor tasks: painting, drawing, tying, zipping

Auditory tasks: books on tape, rhyming, reading poems and stories aloud

Sequential and detailed thinking: hidden word puzzles, jigsaw puzzles, putting things in order, alphabetizing

Connecting with others: cooperative play, volunteer work

In a visit to a girls' school one day, I heard screaming down the hall. Naturally, I ran to investigate and found several kindergarten girls kneeling down in a dark corner. Their screams were really squeals of joy: They had spotted a millipede and were trying to catch it to take it to the science lab because "Mrs. Farrell will think this is cool." One girl emerged triumphantly with the millipede in her hand and they all took off down the hall. One of the new girls to the school, unfamiliar with hands-on science study like this, remained standing in the hall, her face ashen white. She looked at me and said: "How can they touch that terrible thing?"

This certainly speaks to the importance of role models like Mrs. Farrell for girls, but also to the effect of early and consistent experiences. The excited girls had had lab science since they were three years old, and were used to finding previously scary creatures to be very interesting scientific specimens. Clearly, if we could see those brains in action, we'd probably see quite different dendrites in the cortexes and amygdalas of the excited girls, compared to those of the distressed girl standing in front of me!

Crucible Moments and Events:
The Layering of Meaning

Now that we have a sense of the layering effect of nature, nurture, and life experience, and the particularly female aspects of that mix, we're ready to move on to a closer look at the experiences that are the most profoundly influential ones in girls' lives. I call these "crucible events and moments."

The dictionary defines "crucible" first as a vessel or melting pot of some very refractory material such as glass or clay, and second as something that tests, as if by fire. Crucible events or moments are what help forge the emotional vessel of a human being. This forging makes our vessel stronger or more fragile, or both; but crucible events and moments do not leave us unchanged.

I use the words *events* and *moments* to describe the two dimensions of the crucible experience for girls. An event connotes something larger or more important than a moment, and that is what it means here. A crucible event, in this context, is something that happens at some time in almost everyone's life, and it has some significance. For females, these crucible events often are related to connectedness or relationships, but not exclusively. Examples include change, friendship, discipline, risk-taking, death, and loss. Although clearly unpredictable, trauma, too, is a crucible event because it carries such emotional power. For instance, rape and other physical or sex abuse are crucible events that continue to define or color a girl's emotional life, long after the event is over.

The word *moment* connotes something smaller, more transient, of possibly less significance, and that is what it means here. A crucible moment is something that can happen several times a day or a week. They just happen, they are not anticipated, and, in the scheme of life, seem to be unimportant. However, it is the accumulation of crucible moments over time that is like the accumulation of the fine layers of phyllo dough in the strudel of life: They make a difference and actually shape us as significantly as crucible events. As we look back on life, it is often the crucible events that stand out vividly, and we forget the slow accumulation of the crucible moments. But all told, they are just as important.

Crucible Moments: It's the Little Things

So let's start with the often overlooked, or at least underestimated, crucible moments. Every parent and every teacher has stories like these, but here's one story that captures this reality quite well.

A teacher stood on the side of the playground watching her preschool children at recess. One of the little girls came up to her and said, "Joey won't let me slide down the sliding board!" At first she looked at the teacher with some anger in her eyes, but as she saw the teacher hesitate, the tears began to form. I think most adults are somewhat programmed either genetically or environmentally (I would say both) to have an instant response to this kind of situation: one of protecting the underdog or fixing the situation. In this case, the teacher understood the concept of crucible moments very well. She said, "Hannah, why don't you go over to Joey and use your big-girl voice and tell him that it is your turn to slide?"

Hannah looked at her quizzically for a moment, then turned on her heel, marched over to Joey, and said in a loud voice, "It's my turn!"

Joey, somewhat surprised by this change in Hannah, stepped aside. At some later point, we will talk about pendulum shifts and how this new act of assertiveness initially led to Hannah being a bit of a bully herself, requiring some intervention to bring her pendulum back into the middle. But for the time being, it is a clear example of a crucible moment helping to forge a girl in the direction of being independent, able to take control of her own needs. Just picture the layering in the other direction if the teacher had responded only with sympathy and gone over to deal with Joey herself.

Parents have the opportunity to fine-tune the lessons girls learn each day in this way. For example:

Do we recognize and use her questions as a way to help her see and think about the complexities of life's situations? So often, parents and teachers think that questions are merely something to answer. We need to drop our "Q and A" mind-set and view questions as an opportunity, an invitation to step into her world and explore the complexities of life. A question is a gift.

Do we routinely admonish her for making a mistake, or do we use it as an opportunity to practice negotiating the gray? Again, the important thing about a mistake is that it offers us a window into her world, an opportunity to join her in the process of thinking and reasoning through the moment. This is connected parenting, and it transforms a moment of "failure" into an opportunity for growth.

Do we routinely assign her tasks because we think of them as girl jobs, or do we rotate household assignments and use that subtle layering effect to counter the not-so-subtle layering effect of stereotypical attitudes in the world outside home and school? If you crack the gender stereotypes routinely at home by assigning all tasks to girls and to boys, then you provide your daughter (or son) with the experience that builds competence, confidence, and an expectation of fairness. You give them the lens to see stereotypical attitudes elsewhere for what they are. You can lecture till you're blue about gender equity—or about anything—but if they never have the experiences that provide those lenses, they can't see it. It's the routine layering of doing and feeling from an early age that creates the eyes of experience that allow them to see.

Crucible Events: Life's Major Defining Episodes

A crucible event is one that parents and teachers often have more luxury of time to think about, since most of these events will happen to most human beings sometime in life. It is important that we contemplate how best to respond to a girl in ways that will forge her and thus make her stronger, more capable and resilient, and better prepared to successfully negotiate all the other events of life.

As we saw earlier, most females are predisposed to take relationships very seriously, to feel connections to others very deeply. It is not surprising, then, that many crucible events for girls cluster around these relationships. Friendship and loss are two very clear examples of crucible events in the lives of girls. The whole area of social development and stages will be covered in a later chapter. So, in a condensed way, for the purposes of friendship issues that are crucible events, let me just say that most girls have a very high need for a close friend during the ages of about nine to fourteen, and sometimes, depending on the personality of the girl, much earlier than that.

Dana and Kathryn: Friendship Loss and Gains

Dana and Kathryn's relationship began at age two as next-door neighbors whose mothers were friends. As the years progressed, they ended up attending different schools, yet still lived next to each other, spent their free time together, and became true pals. Their friendship was an anchor in the sea of life. For each girl, the other was a person who could be trusted, confided in, counted on for commiseration and support. When Kathryn's father was transferred to a job in another city and they had to move, it had profound effects on both ten-year-old girls.

Dana's parents were confident that their daughter would adjust, but they were also sensitive to how it must feel to lose your longest, closest friend at that age. They respected Dana's need to grieve and feel miserable as part of the process of growing through the experience.

Quick assurances ignore the need for the internal emotional process. "You'll find other friends." "Life goes on." "You can still talk to each other on the phone and see each other sometimes." It's not that these statements are false, it's just that initially they don't help and they don't acknowledge how loss of friendship can affect a girl.

Dana's mother was superb in her handling of the situation. Each night she would encourage Dana to talk about her day, to share with her what she would have talked to Kathryn about. They signed up for Internet service so that the girls could e-mail each other and have immediate responses. The girls could talk by phone every other day to begin with, then twice a week. The parents bought each girl a calendar and they made visitation dates for long weekends and vacations.

Just as important, Dana's parents talked to her about being able to have friendships with other children at her school. They acknowledged that others would not take Kathryn's place, that it would be hard to reach out to others, that her tendency was to stay home and feel lonely because she had lost her one and only best friend. But they made a bargain. If they, as parents, were going out of their way to transport the girls to see each other frequently, paying the phone bills and such, then it was Dana's task to invite someone new over once a week to play, do homework, or go somewhere together. So all of the assurances I mentioned above came true, eventually, without saying them at a time when they couldn't be accepted or effective. Her parents' responses enabled Dana to learn how to deal effectively with loss *and* expand her friendship skills and experience.

Crucible events like this are common throughout our lives. Several categories of crucible events will occur in the life of every girl. We know our daughters will experience issues of connectedness: loss, death, painful friendship difficulties, issues of discipline, and issues of risk-taking and maturation. And what's more, we have faced some variation of all of these issues ourselves in our lifetime. So it stands to reason that we should have a reservoir of experience and wisdom from which a calm, premeditated script comes forth whenever a crucible event comes along. I have yet to find one parent who feels this way. Why? Why is it that when crucible events occur, we feel so unprepared, so blindsided, so unsure of how to respond?

Because we care so much. This isn't just some objective problem to be solved, it is our own little girl. Seeing her hurt or upset interferes with our cognitive processing. I'll make the case later that at high levels of emotion, we find it hard to think clearly. In addition, it is instinctive in the animal kingdom to protect our young, to want to stop their pain or frustration right away, not to prolong it or continue to live with it for any period of time. In essence, we have to go against our genetic and emotional grain to deal effectively with crucible events, and it is incredibly difficult to do that.

Because we want it to work out better for our daughter than a similar situation did for us. Can't she learn from our mistakes? Did we gain wisdom for nothing? We apply the data from our lives and situations to hers, and it is impossible to have an exact match. We are not the same identical individuals in the same identical situations. The world isn't the same, and similar situations are really different enough so that it feels like our dated road maps are just that, dated. The old road maps don't work, and we can't decipher the new road maps without our daughter's help. What an impasse! You want to help your daughter, but you need her help to do so.

It seems easier to control the external aspects of the event than it is to deal with the internal—intellectual and emotional—aspects of it. It takes much of our time, much of our patience, and all of our wisdom! In the example above, it would have taken Dana's mother three seconds to say, "Life goes on; find some new friends." It took years to stay on-task as a parent through this crucible event, and to layer in all of the things that would make her stronger in the end. It feels like climbing a mountain.

The more complicated something is, the more unsure we are of how to tackle the problem. There are too many steps, and we're not sure of what each one is, let alone how to sequence them. It is like the difference between arithmetic and math. We can add two plus two, but that awful story problem of one train going 50 mph for three hours and one going 30 mph for ten minutes, and where they meet—parenting sometimes feels like math anxiety!

So what can we do to help our daughters negotiate the gray in the crucible events of life? Connected parenting suggests we engage her in the process and respect the complexity that can only unfold with time. Time is a key word. My first bit of advice is to take some time to think, to talk to your spouse or partner, to seek advice and wisdom from other sources, to give yourself some distance to gain perspective. When we slow down and take the time to listen and reflect, we offer a powerful model for our girls, even if the process doesn't produce a quick fix—and it shouldn't. My mother taught me that one memorable evening, and the "Green Blanket Story" remains one of my most favorite anecdotes about her.

The Green Blanket Story: Mother Knows Best!

My mother called it "puppy love." I thought that was a weird choice of words: Jay wasn't a puppy. He was this redheaded boy in the other first-grade class. I thought he was wonderful. The highlight of my day was recess, when we would walk around the playground together holding hands and talking about interesting things. Jay thought I was neat! It really had nothing to do with his being a boy and my being a girl—we were pals. Then this blond little girl moved into town. The next day, when recess time came, I ran outside and looked for Jay. He was talking to *her*! I was forgotten. And so it continued for several weeks.

Now, my parents knew something was wrong. I'm a morning person and I loved school, but I stopped jumping out of bed and racing to school. They asked what was wrong, but I just couldn't bear to tell them that I must be ugly or something else must be wrong with me because Jay liked *her* now. The joy was gone from school, from me.

One night, at tuck-in time, my mother sat on my bed. She pulled my blanket—my father's green army blanket—up to my chin and said, "Now, will you tell me what's been bothering you?" I was tired, I was sad, my defenses were down: I confessed my ugliness and unworthiness. I will never forget that look on my mother's face as she said: "You're the most beautiful first-grader in the world. And I'll think about this and talk with your father, and maybe tomorrow night we can all talk together. No matter what, you know we love you, and we'll help you to feel better."

I don't remember the details of my broken heart's recovery, but I will never forget the feeling of that green blanket and my mother's words.

So my sage advice is simple. Dealing with the crucible events of life can be hard. First, provide your own version of a green blanket. Second, buy yourself some time. Third, give your daughter a sense of hope that there is a light at the end of the tunnel. Fourth, seek help and counsel. Fifth, keep talking and being there enough to try some things, or to weather it together.

Discipline: Teaching a Way of Life

Moral thought and behavior is the major developmental task for a child in the formative years, and that, for parents, translates into discipline, or shaping the behavioral and moral patterns of a child. Discipline is so much more than punishment, but that is what most people think about when they hear the word *discipline*: punishment. The two are not synonymous. It is like saying a hand and a thumb are the same thing. Discipline is the whole hand; punishment is the thumb, just one part of it. Discipline is really the total system of teaching a child what is appropriate and inappropriate, what we value, and what we believe to be right and wrong. As adults in the lives of children, we use punishment and consequences, certainly, but we also use praise, love, rewards, discussions, and other ways of affirming what we like. It is all of it, the carrot, the stick, and everything in between.

That is why rigid formulas that say "If you do A, then B will happen" don't work. They don't take into account the total situation, what would best teach the child how to handle similar events in the future, and turn experiences such as this one into an opportunity to learn and grow. It is also very dangerous for young girls to begin to view the world as black and white in terms of good and bad. As we will see in Chapter 8, girls seem to have a high need to conform and please. If there are set consequences for every perceived transgression, it discourages the young girl from healthy risk-taking in the formative years, hurries her down the path of being a pleaser, and often makes her view of herself and her self-esteem dependent on the world's reactions to her.

An example of this was a situation that arose with the fourth-grade girls at my school. It had become cool to use extreme profanity, frequently and prolifically. However, being clever girls, they never did this within earshot of the teachers. This began, however, to change the climate of the fourth grade from one of feeling friendly and secure to one of being tough and somewhat mean. Girls who didn't want to talk tough were receiving great peer pressure from the in group to participate or be ostracized. The tough language gradually grew into tough behavior, and the climate of our division started to change. Fourth-graders were really the seniors of the primary division and, as such, had a modeling effect on the younger students.

So, as the director, I pulled the thirty-six girls of that grade level together one day in a class meeting. I explained what I knew was happening and what I thought was happening to our school, our special place, our sanctuary. I explained that I knew they weren't doing this to be bad or mean, but that their actions were hurting others. I drew the line in the sand, so to speak, and said that *any* continuation of profanity would be dealt with severely because it was important that our school remain a sanctuary from much of the junk that we all have to face in the rest of the world.

You guessed it! I had barely left the room when Sylvia, one of the natural leaders in the group, turned to all of her classmates and said, "Dr. Deak can't do a [expletive deleted] thing about this."

Standard school policy would have been to tell her that was bad and wrong, punish her, and make this a clear message to the other girls. Yet, however inappropriate it was, Sylvia was also exhibiting some of the chutzpah that made her the leader she was. When young girls are punished too publicly or too much early on, without the overall discipline/learning part, it often leads to diminishing their spirit and strength. On the other hand, there are social standards and the needs of the group to consider. Discipline often involves many more steps than simply handing out consequences, which is why there cannot be many effective formulaic responses for inappropriate behavior, especially for girls.

Sylvia was suspended for one day. But in a private meeting, I also said to Sylvia that I had always admired her strength, like the time she had stood up for her friend on the playground. A similar message was given to the class: Sylvia was a great potential leader and a good person, but she had made a misstep on her leadership road. I fully expected her to continue to be respected by her class.

One of the most important pieces of my response for girls is what I call my Alzheimer's speech: Everyone makes mistakes, and there is too much in my head to remember it all, so tomorrow, I would totally forget it and still think of each of them as a great human being. Finally, it was important for me a few days later to smile and talk to Sylvia, and give her an important public task to do, and to make it clear that life goes on and we learn from our mistakes.

You can see that punishment is only a small part of the disciplinary paradigm. Discipline is the total system of shaping a child's character and behavior. Punishment is a small part of that system that refers to the negative consequences of an action. Just as important in shaping character and behavior is the flip side of the punishment coin: reinforcement or praise. In fact, the research suggests that reinforcement and praise are incredibly powerful tools in shaping character and behavior with less negative side effects than punishment.

However, in the last few decades, the importance of reinforcing and praising children has been raised to Mt. Everest heights. In an article in the *New York Times,* the author recalled seeing parents at the base of a hill yelling to their sled-riding children how wonderful they were for riding the sled down the hill. Had this been the first run of tentative children, it would have been very understandable. But this yelling of praise continued for over an hour.

The point is that if every little behavior or action of a child is praised or reinforced, it not only loses its impact, but it gradually leads a child to believe that anything she does is great or that everything she does is equally good, from scribbling on a piece of paper to writing *War and Peace*. You can just imagine all of the possible ramifications of this: from no internal motivation, to needing everyone to be superlative, to becoming angry when there are negative responses.

If excessive praise carried a warning label, it would read:

Excessive praise can lead to the development of:

A very selfish child who wants reinforcement from everyone for everything;

A very needy child who can't function well without constant adult feedback;

A very complacent child because everything is responded to in the same way;

A very angry child because she/he will inevitably interact with people who are not effusive about her/his every behavior or will set the bar higher for obtaining praise;

A very confused child because her/his outside world is not the same as her/his home world;

A very lazy child because the littlest effort is rewarded.

My mother used to say: "Let the punishment fit the crime." I would add: Let the praise fit the deed.

In the school world, teachers are also being guided to provide specific praise for specific pieces of work. An example would be saying: "I like the way you used graphs to highlight the comparison of heights of girls and their mothers," instead of "Good job!" The point with specific and earned praise is the same for specific and earned punishment: It gives the child the clear feedback to understand her behavior and be able to use this information to consider the choices and ramifications of future behavior. And, ultimately, it is a significant part that leads to the overall belief system and morality of this female person.

The whole issue of praise and reinforcement relates strongly to gender. For example, Myra and David Sadker's *Failing at Fairness:*

How Our Schools Cheat Girls and many other researchers have identified clear differences in feedback given to girls and boys in school. Girls often receive positive generalities—"Good job." Boys often receive specific feedback, such as: "You need to write legibly so I'll be able to read your good thoughts." We know that girls often respond to criticism or negative feedback by being hurt, feeling that you do not like them. Boys, on the other hand, seem to take the negative feedback more in stride. The end results, conclude many researchers, is that adults are often unduly positive with their feedback to girls and very specific, with constructive criticism, in their feedback to boys. This allows boys gradually to improve their performance or behavior because they are given the kind of specific messages that allow them to do that. Girls learn early on that the bar is lower for them and they either become dependent on praise or it loses its validity.

Teeter-Totter Parenting: Bringing Balance to Our Responses

In the rest of the animal kingdom, other species seem to have instinctive knowledge of how to raise their young. Lions know instinctively what to do when their cubs stray too far from home. Seals know when their pups are ready to learn how to swim, and they know how to teach them. What about us? I think that much of parenting can be quite instinctive, at the basic level. We are programmed to protect our young, to feed and shelter them. There are certainly parents who are thin on instinct, but the vast majority has this inner drive and knowledge base. I often say to parents, when in doubt, trust your instincts. But then, the lives of human beings have evolved to such a state of complexity that there is no possible way to be programmed for each eventuality. Also, among animals, there is survival of the fittest that helps streamline parenting complexity. If there is an ornery lion cub that just won't obey, that cub will stray and be eaten. When we have an ornery child that just won't obey, it isn't that stark or that simple. So I offer the Teeter-Totter Theory of parenting to help us cope at a conceptual level with all of the eventualities that each of our offspring brings to us.

Simply put, the Teeter-Totter Theory says that you adjust your response to your daughter depending on her personality, temperament, sensitivity, and the situation, to name only a few of the variables. It is a yin to her yang, responding in a discerning way to match the intensity and tone of her needs. Teeter-Totter parenting is about balancing your responses.

Psychologists and parenting experts always advocate consistency, so the idea of a teeter-totter, or the movement and flexibility it implies, might appear to be contrary to this advice, but it isn't. Consistency really refers to consistency of values and philosophic stance, not necessarily the same consequences to particular actions. Our legal system reflects this in the way it metes out vastly different consequences for the same behavior. Motives matter. Ignorance may not be an excuse, but it can be a mitigating factor.

The word *obsession* leads nicely into a subset of Teeter-Totter Theory. It is not only a responsive theory, but it can also be viewed, in a way, as a state of being for a parent. This is tricky, since all parents have their own temperament and personality. I'm not talking about being a different person with each child, but perhaps adjusting our emotional being and responses to each child's situation or personality or temperament. An example would be responding to a child who gets upset easily, cries easily, and gets excited easily. In most situations, the place to sit on the teeter-totter is a bit back, to bring some balance to the steep emotional pitch. It only exacerbates most situations when a parent responds with high emotion or energy to a young child's or teen's high emotion or energy. Easier said than done, but well worth the effort.

This type of situation often makes having two parents a luxury. It can allow the more even parent to be on the other side of the teeter-totter. The parent who is not quite as even has a great role also, and will often be the one who absolutely understands the rapid ups and downs and is available for green blanket needs.

Enough said. You'll see this part of Teeter-Totter Theory embedded in all of the following chapters and examples. Now let's take a look at two aspects of our personality and temperament—identity and control—that come into play in everyday interaction with our daughters. Identity and control color our parenting style, shape it from the inside, and affect the way our responses offer discipline and balance—or sometimes fail to—to the girl on the other end.

Identity: Remembering Who's Who and What That Means

Erik Erikson was not the first psychologist to talk about bonding and trust between infant and parent, but he is probably the best known and remembered. He made the absolute statement that touching, holding, loving, and bonding were critical during the first few months of life for a baby and a significant adult, usually one or both parents. It is this feeling of physical safety and emotional well-being and connectedness that allows the developing person to trust the world and the people in it enough to grow, to reach out, and to explore. As with most concepts or characteristics involved with humans, this identification falls somewhere on a continuum. And, as with most concepts or characteristics, there can be too much or too little. It's the too much that can often be an issue with daughters, and that can lead to some issues with identity and with what I call *identity enmeshment.*

Let me first say that loving a child deeply cannot help but lead to some identity overlap. This is your child, a part of yourself, someone you have the biological and/or moral responsibility to care for, provide for, and raise with the best of your ability. It is only logical that you would periodically blend your feelings about decisions with what you think are your child's feelings. Or you might occasionally and unwittingly blend your goals with your child's goals. It is normal, will happen frequently, and, in the long run, is perceived by your child as what parents do. However, when this overlap becomes too enmeshed, parents need to pull back a little and think about identity enmeshment and identity separation.

In these formative years, the identity issue is potentially more thorny with mothers and daughters than with fathers and daughters, for some obvious reasons. Mothers and daughters are both female. A mother often knows, in the deepest meaning of the word, what it is like to be in the situations her daughter lives through. We know what it is like to want to be liked, to fit in, to watch our bodies changing and growing as young girls do. We've been there, and often either want to shorten the learning curve for our daughter or make sure she has or does things we regret we didn't have or do as a girl.

In addition, females have a high need for connection and are predisposed by nature to care about others, especially offspring. Whether from a Darwinian perspective, a social biology perspective, or a learned perspective, the female of the species—a mother—has this connection. The umbilical cord is both a literal and figurative connection. Combine this with the fact that a daughter is a female, too, and you have a high need on both sides for connection and identification. In short, it is just very hard to separate our emotions, needs, and dreams from this smaller, albeit different, version of ourselves. It can also be difficult to separate theirs from ours. We're cold, so we ask our daughter to dress warmer. Our daughter is devastated by a friend's hurtful remark, and we feel incensed.

I know a woman who is staunchly independent, and who cares deeply about gender equity and the capability of females to do anything. When she had her little girl, she had visions of her being outgoing, outspoken, and forceful. My friend was, instead, blessed with a shy and tentative daughter. On the neighborhood playground one day, she watched with dismay as her daughter cried because she wanted to go on the swings with the other children, but she wouldn't venture forth. In frustration, she told her daughter that she needed to just go over and do it! Her daughter said that she couldn't, and cried even harder. My friend's frustration grew, and she ended up blurting out to her daughter: "What's wrong with you?!" Naturally, this resulted in more crying.

It was a moment of identity enmeshment. My friend believed females should not be "shrinking violets"; she was not one herself, and she didn't want *her* daughter to be like that. She forbade it! Her vision of her daughter conflicted so deeply with her vision of herself and what kind of girl her daughter should be that she was unable to pull back enough to see that her daughter needed help to develop the skills and confidence to overcome situations like this.

While it is normal for a parent to want a child to be independent so that facing the challenges of life will be easier, the depth of what a parent feels and believes herself can distort the message. In this case, if my friend could separate her deep philosophical view of females from what her daughter was experiencing, she could have thought of alternative ways of dealing with the situation. For instance, she could have said something like: "Playing on the swings can be really fun. How about if we both go over and I'll push you on the swing for a while?"

The next time a similar situation arose, my friend tried this wading in approach with her daughter, and she discovered that with just that little booster, her daughter developed confidence quickly. Over time, she needed her mother's hands-on support less and less, and left behind her shrinking violet phase.

A quick way of knowing if you are falling into the identity enmeshment quagmire is to listen to your own words. As the frequency of sentences that begin with "I want . . ." increases, your ears should perk up. "I want my daughter to get good grades." "I want my daughter to take gymnastics." Again, it is normal for parents to say "I want . . ." in relation to their children. However, when you hear yourself saying those two words very frequently, it might be a good idea to ask yourself why.

"Why do I want my daughter to take gymnastics?" If the answer is that you want her to be physically fit, there are many other choices, and her interests and body may lead her to be more interested in playing soccer, for instance. If the answer is that you always regretted not taking gymnastics lessons, well, begin to think soccer, or some other sport, unless gymnastics is your daughter's dream, too.

Control: Rein Her In or Turn Her Loose?

"Go to hell," said the six-year-old as she kicked me, her principal, in the shins. She had been sent to my office because she had done the same thing to her teacher when she was told she had to share the Magic Markers with a girl she disliked.

When I talked with her parents, they certainly didn't approve of her behavior. But at the same time, they had done little over the years in setting clear limits on such responses. Their motives were good. Both parents felt passionately about raising a daughter who was strong, would stand up for what she believed in, would not lose her voice. They didn't want her to grow up to be a pleaser, like so many girls who silence themselves, marginalize their own needs, or measure their worth by their ability to win the approval of parents, teachers, friends, and others. However, their free rein, coupled with their daughter's temperament as a girl who would push the limits, had spared us a pleaser and produced instead a little tyrant.

Control is the other key concept in the formative parenting years. There are entire books written about this topic, both from a psychological and a sociological perspective. Relax, we won't go down that entire highway! But there is part of the road that is important to map out for the formative years. To put it simply, a child grows and develops to the broadest, most positive extent when there is neither too much nor too little control. Here we are, negotiating the gray again!

Some parents have a greater need for control than others, and should be aware that this personal quality of theirs can unfairly color their view of their daughter and affect the way they practice discipline. For girls, the issue traditionally has been one of too much control. Girls are expected to exercise control from an early age: to be nice, to laugh discreetly, to sit and stand and look just so, to control their anger. Girls are not supposed to behave in ways that suggest lack of control, or risky ways, whether that is climbing a tree or speaking their mind in a challenge to authority. Control, boundaries, guidelines—where is a parent to draw the line? For girls, too much control leads to early dependency and/or later wildness. However, too little control leads to early wildness and later dependency.

Certainly the Teeter-Totter Theory of discipline holds some hints about how to proceed. But the proactive and preventive setting of *just enough* guidelines, limits, and boundaries is something for parents to consider, discuss, and decide before this baby girl becomes very mobile. A study that came out of Harvard several years ago, dubbed "Raising the Water Level," is a very basic example of allowing as much freedom within set boundaries as possible.

"Raising the water level" referred to moving things that are dangerous or fragile or inappropriate for a child to a level higher than the child can reach. So during the crawling stage, the cut-glass bowl can remain on the coffee table. As soon as she can pull herself up and stand by the table, the cut-glass bowl moves to a shelf that is about adult eye level and is replaced with a plastic container of plastic flowers. When she can climb, the cut-glass bowl moves into the locked china cabinet. In addition, movement is also very important. So instead of putting her in a constraint like a playpen or seat, blocking off stairs with baby gates is a less controlling alternative. The research found that children whose parents practiced this strategy in their home the first few years of a child's life were brighter, more inquisitive, and better problem-solvers than children whose parents did not do this.

The first thing many parents say upon hearing this is, shouldn't children be taught the concept of *no*? The answer is *yes*, but there are so many things to say *no* about every day, and movement and exploration without constant control and hearing the word *no* allows for much greater learning and growth (remember that growing dendrites is dependent on use!). Everything has its limits: pulling your brother's hair gets a *no*, because making him bald to "raise the water level" is not in the plan.

The Last Word on the S-Word: Self-Esteem

Self-esteem is a term that has been so overused that it has lost any clarity of meaning and, worse, it has become an easy label that is used as an explanation for all female questions and issues. I've heard it used as a single-word diagnosis of everything from eating disorders to speech problems. As a catchword, it lets everybody off the hook by eliminating the need for us to pull a problem apart and deal with the complexity of it.

Self-esteem implies confidence and satisfaction in oneself; if you have good self-esteem it means you have a good opinion of yourself. Self-esteem is a crucial piece of a girl's internal life, an ingredient in the strudel that gets layered in again and again. However, self-esteem isn't just one thing. Researchers who study self-esteem describe and debate about the various components that blend together to create this internal state. My view is that three pieces are critical to self-esteem: competence, confidence, and connectedness. If any one of these three C's is absent, it is impossible for a girl's self-esteem to be high.

You can't *give* a girl self-esteem. She has to get it the old-fashioned way—by earning it. Competence, confidence, and connectedness can't be taught or improved by discussion. They have to be experienced, and the earlier the better, given what we know about brain development in the formative years. In terms of Strudel Theory, we can't control whether girls will have negative experiences that layer in—negative experiences are part of life, after all—but we can consciously create opportunities for girls to experience each of the three C's enough to enhance self-esteem. One very dramatic experience can be life-changing, but typically these experiences will be layered over time.

It's also important to think about the synergy of the three components. All three need to be present and about equal to generate the highest level of self-esteem. For example, a girl who has a high level of connectedness, but much lower levels of confidence and competence, will be less likely to take risks or to face conflict than if there are higher levels of all three C ingredients.

There are many ways we can provide opportunities to girls to experience the three C's in everyday life at home and school. We'll explore them in chapters to come. But for now, it's important to know that we can't assume that a particular experience builds all three. Our assumptions and a girl's experience can be worlds apart. I'm reminded of a little girl in first grade who made straight E's (for excellent) on her report cards. She was smart, responsible, and well behaved: a perfect student and happy child at home.

Kate was nearing the end of her first-grade year when, one night during a bedtime chat with her mother, she began to cry about the prospect of moving up to second grade in the fall. She was a very bright child, and could easily have skipped second grade altogether and not missed a beat academically, so her mother was astonished at this sudden wave of anxiety. When she asked Kate why she was worried, Kate replied tearfully, "Everybody says second grade is hard, and I've never learned how to *do* anything hard!" Her fears were unfounded, but they were real, and her competence was no match for her lack of confidence.

It is in the *doing* that the layered effect of experiences in the formative years creates a basis for new dimensions of growth as girls move from the "little girl" world into the fringe area of adolescence: the "tween" years.

Pearls for Parents and Pearls for Girls

- Draw the line. Some things require no process and you just have to be an unpopular adult and draw the line in the sand. Your daughter may make you pay for that, but she needs that help in setting the parameters of her life now.

- Tell her the green blanket story, or your version of it.

- Use both "What do you think?" and "What do you feel?" when discussing things, so she gets used to analyzing her thoughts and her feelings.

- When discipline issues arise, explain about natural consequences for actions.

- Take up yoga or some type of stress reduction activity; you'll need it through this and the next stages!

- Begin to cultivate and keep a small group of adult peers as a sounding board and support network for the thousands of times you'll doubt your judgment or question what to say or how to handle something.

- Remember—your daughter is watching! Two critical words: ROLE MODEL. Look at yourself in terms of what you say and do through her eyes.

CHAPTER 3

Betwixt and Between:
The Preadolescent Years

"What's good is you're not a little kid anymore, you know stuff about the world that little kids don't know, like about having your period. But you aren't a teenager yet, either, so you don't really have to worry about a lot of that stuff, like boys and college and driving a car—yet."

—Rebecca, ten

When I was a kid, we used to spend our spring afternoons wading in the clear, rocky creek near our house, for fun. We'd catch minnows in our cupped hands, and then let them go. We'd lift rocks to surprise the crawdads and watch them scoot to the next rock and vanish into its shadow. Along with these quick pleasures of creek exploration was the slower treat, day-by-day, of watching a gelatinous mass of toad or frog eggs transform into tadpoles—we called them pollywogs. From nothing more than a black dot in some slimy, shimmering goo, over the course of a few weeks, the pollywogs would emerge, some sooner than others, and grow into independent little swimmers. First the feathery gills would bloom, and then the tiniest of legs, which continued to grow larger as the tail began to shrink. On any given day, we might see a cluster of pollywogs bobbing around a floating leaf, or we might have to look harder to find them hidden in the flickering shade of a creek plant. If we were lucky, we got to see the tail end—

literally!—of the metamorphosis, a nearly "done," perfectly formed frog or toad no bigger than a lima bean. And then they were gone, off to live their secret froggie lives in the creek and surrounding woods.

Tweens are the pollywogs of homo sapiens. When we look through the lens of chaos theory, it makes perfect sense. When you're a parent in the middle of the tween experience, this age between little girl and teen girl is a period of constant change, and the tension and exhilaration that comes with it is so different girl to girl, day to day, and even hour to hour! That changeling energy makes a girl seem alternately goofy, sweet, serious, crabby, distressed, and defiant. One moment they're playing make-believe, and the next they're making unbelievable developmental jumps in the direction of adolescence. I've heard the tween years described as the "terrible T's"—terrific, turbulent, and trying. If you pull your viewing lens back and look at the big picture, as chaos theory instructs us, what else could this be but the pollywog stage of life? The body, including the brain and the limbic system, the center of emotional development, is literally reorganizing, growing, and transforming itself in a very complex way. What appears to us to be chaos is a period of reorganization, which will then allow this organism to propel itself into an almost completely new being.

Coming of Age: From Cartwheels to Camouflage

We used to call them preteen or preadolescent girls, an easily overlooked transitional culture of girls defined primarily by what they weren't yet—teenagers. At the same time, there was a silent acknowledgment of what they were no more: little girls. Clothes were often hard to find: the girls' sizes were either too small or too cutesy, but the junior teen sizes were too big, and all the dresses and blouses (long before tube and tank tops!) had those funny little dart seams that assumed there was a developing chest to accommodate. Remember training bras? Training for what?—we might ask now. But back then, and for a few decades to come, everything about being a preteen was anticipatory.

Today we call them *tweens,* a term popularized by the advertising and marketing industry, which was perhaps the first to recognize and celebrate them as a distinct and powerful population—of consumers. Money has a way of commanding attention in the adult world. Girls in this preteen age group—anywhere from eight to thirteen years old—spend allowances and their parents' money freely, on everything from doll clothes to pop CDs. This infinite range of consumer goods includes magazines, posters, stickers, candy, gum, T-shirts, backpacks, lip gloss, and just about anything that carries a pop icon or looks cute or funny. Ralph Lauren and other high-end fashion labels have started lines for tweens. Popular stores like Gap and Limited Too cater almost exclusively to this clientele. In our consumer culture, tweens are no longer *pre-* anything—they have arrived!

In all sectors, our society is struggling with the definition of this age group of girls, their interests, their wallets, their fashions, and their bodies. For parents, teachers, and other caring adults, there's a collective cry, a protective, and even angry, protest that I hear everywhere I go, and that is this: Our girls are *more* than consumers and MTV wanna-bes. They are individuals of infinite promise, and more than anything else, we want to nourish their hopes and dreams, and guide them through their own struggle to become confident, capable, and connected young women. Not that we always voice our heartfelt ambitions quite that way, or meet with applause anywhere but in our own minds, of course. Quite the contrary.

The tween girl litany features these familiar refrains:

Stop treating me like a baby! I'm old enough to . . . [go to the mall by myself, go on a date, set my own bedtime].

You expect too much of me—I'm only _____ years old! (This is the pollywog perspective.)

No one else's parents . . . [are so strict, so weird, so nosy, so mean]. (A key signal preparatory to bargaining.)

I have no . . . [friends, clothes to wear]. (Symptomatic of the "I can't measure up" dilemma.)

In the parallel universe of parents, the tween litany echoes in questions like the ones parents have asked me:

Is it reasonable to let my twelve-year-old daughter go to the mall with her friends and no adult supervision? (Everyone else is . . .)

We watched the movie Erin Brockovich *at home, and our ten-year-old loved it because the woman character was so strong and was fighting to help others. But her best friend's parents won't let their daughter see the movie because it's rated R. Did we make a poor choice? (Is she old enough to . . .)*

A girl in my daughter's seventh-grade class invited her to a party at her house, but we don't know the girl or the parents. Should we let her go? (We're uneasy about this . . .)

My fifth-grader wants to use her one hour of TV allowance to watch a popular program that shows music videos that I think are too suggestive and crude, especially for a young girl. All her friends watch it. Am I too protective? (I'm not sure of myself . . .)

Are girls that start dating in their tweens likely to become sexually active at a younger age? (I don't know enough . . .)

Should our middle school host a Friday night dance for fifth- and sixth-graders? (I'm unsure . . .)

The tension in this "is she—is she not?" and "should I—should I not?" continuing dilemma permeates life with tweens precisely because they are, by definition, changing and so changeable, every day. Tween girls often look like they are ready for this stuff, but are they? The reality is that girls' bodies are developing sooner, and the world is dressing them and treating them like—well, not like children.

One elementary school administrator described the dilemma

as she sees it in her own school, where girls begin to wear bras and develop curves as early as third grade. "I know what they hear and see on television, and I would think that becoming sexual beings at eight or nine, and delaying marriage until age thirty, or later, would pose some problems, even though birth control is around and available. How much can an eight-year-old understand about sexuality? How many little girls think that kissing, touching, and such leads anywhere else but to kissing and touching? How do we talk to a young girl about the fact that the way she dresses affects the way boys and men look at her? Our first-graders in miniskirts have no idea how to sit . . ."

We are all in new territory. The creek of my childhood was a quiet, unspoiled one, surrounded by acres of woods that sustained a world of indigenous plants and wildlife, including my pollywogs. Over time, that environment has been altered dramatically by thousands of new homes, malls and other commercial buildings, and the accompanying traffic, litter, and decline in air and water quality. The creek is there, but I haven't seen anything as healthy as a pollywog in it in years.

The landscape for preadolescent girls today has changed just that dramatically. If they once were ignored, they now are the targets of sophisticated marketing strategies and other come-ons from a world that is more interested in their bucks or their bodies than in their health and well-being. In this way, our challenge is greater today than it was in our parents' day. In this highly exploitative environment we have to work with what we have and what we know, and only sometimes what we remember from our own preteen years, to understand our tweens and what they need in order to thrive in their transition from girlhood to adolescence.

Camouflage: The Code of Conformity for Tween Girls

Before tweens were defined as a marketplace phenomenon, researchers in the field of female psychology had identified this age period as one of critical significance, though hardly studied and not well understood at all. Feminist scholar and author Carol Gilligan, in a 1993 study with several colleagues, noted that girls are deeply affected by their experience of these years "at the edge of adolescence," but that this transformational period was often overlooked or ignored, in part, because the object of concern—girls themselves—seemed to almost intentionally fall out of focus, disappear by choice into the crowd.

In this study and related ones, researchers said, they found that seven- and eight-year-old girls "were quite commonly outspoken and courageous, willing to say what they felt and thought, even when this made others uncomfortable, and were able to resist outside pressure to relinquish their own perceptions, feelings, and judgments." However, they said, by about age eleven and twelve, "these psychological capacities in girls seemed to become endangered" and girls struggled "to stay with what they felt and knew, to authorize their own experience, and to hold on to authentic or genuine relationships."

This was the developmental point at which girls "lost their voice," literally and figuratively, Gilligan said.

Like the pollywogs that drifted in and out of scrutiny into the dappled shadows of the creek bed when I was young, girls this age move psychologically into what I call *camouflaging*. The psychological equivalent of adaptive coloration, camouflaging means you just slip into an attitude—fake it, if necessary—to blend in with the crowd and avoid being singled out as different in any way. If you're a tween girl observing this code of conformity, you might say you're interested in boys even when you really think they're stranger than strange, or you might give the brush-off to a boy you secretly like, just to quash any rumors of a crush before they get started. You might act interested in makeup, or even wear a little, even if you aren't really excited at the idea. You might hide your glasses in your pocket because "they look nerdy," even though you can't see the chalkboard in the classroom without them. Or you might wear clothes that are more revealing than you like, simply because to do otherwise is to draw attention to yourself as different.

While we might not think of camouflaging as an event, it is a predictable, identifiable, crucible event of the tween years, a cumulative experience of countless crucible moments—camouflaging moments—in which a girl decides if, when, and how much to modify herself or hide her feelings. Camouflaging isn't inherently bad. In one sense, camouflaging is positive in that it indicates some social savvy; it's a sign that you're able to read social cues and you're willing to adapt a bit. That's part of healthy social and emotional development. It's the same for any of us. If we ignore or fail to pick up on routine social cues, we suffer the consequences when others make fun of us or distance themselves from us. A fifth-grade boy who makes fart sounds with his armpit gets big laughs from his pals. If a fifth-grade girl did the same, it would be social suicide. She could, however, squeal excitedly over a cute, cuddly kitten with theatrics that no boy could get away with in a group of his peers.

I worked with one girl because her teachers and mother were seriously concerned about her social isolation. When observing her in the lunchroom, I noticed that everyone avoided the seat on either side of her. It didn't take long to see why. She visibly picked her nose. Not only was that disconcerting to the girls in general, but it was really hard to take during lunch. This girl appeared oblivious to the social cues and therefore helpless to analyze what to do to change. She didn't seem to have a clue of what the concept of camouflage was all about, and she suffered social isolation as a consequence. That's the downside of not camouflaging at all.

But there is also a problem on the other end of the continuum. If you do it too much, then you close yourself off to new experiences and honest self-expression. It can create a temporary stagnation of the developmental process. In an effort to blend in, girls risk losing touch with the truth of their own experience; the genuine knowledge of their own feelings and beliefs. They can lose the courage of their convictions, so to speak, the willingness to resist conformity and to honor their own deepest held values, hopes, and dreams. This becomes increasingly relevant as they move into their teen years and the need to define and grow themselves with confidence and courage. Girls in their teens have told me that they've been playing the part for so long, they've lost any sense of who they really are and what they really believe in. As one fifteen-year-old girl said: "I don't know if I like myself or not anymore. I don't even know who 'myself' is. Am I this person who pretends this and acts that? Where's the real 'me'? Who am I?" Often, grown women ask the same question, and when they think back to the time they began to lose sight of themselves, they typically go straight to these tween years, when the pressure to blend in first became so all-important to them, and their moment-to-moment efforts to camouflage became a way of life.

As parents and teachers, we're torn by trying to decide how much of a girl's camouflaging at this age is positive and how much is negative; how much to allow and how far we let it go before we deliver the "be yourself" lecture—*again*. It's a difficult judgment call: Especially with preadolescents, if you push too far in either direction, it can have negative consequences. Intervene too much, and your daughter can lose social status and friends, and it undermines her self-esteem and willingness to form relationships. Going back to the girl in the lunchroom I just described, in a discreet conversation with her, I was very surprised to learn that she was well aware of her nose-picking behavior and its effect on others. However, she had heard so often in her formative years to "be yourself" and "be an individual," and she had taken it so literally that she did much of what she wanted to do without any social filtering.

On the other hand, if you don't intervene somewhat, or discuss the issue, a girl can grow too dependent on the no-risk safety of camouflage, and delay coming to understand her own strengths and weaknesses. When she camouflages, she hides herself not only from others, but ultimately from herself.

A parent came up to speak to me after one of my presentations when I had talked about camouflaging. She was obviously the proud mother of a bright and vivacious tween girl. Just that week her daughter had gotten her long hair cut short, which both daughter and mother thought was very becoming. Then at school the next day, some boys commented, "Only lesbians have short hair." Now this mother was concerned that her bright, strong, beautiful daughter would let this kind of pressure dictate what she did with her hair, instead of simply wearing it the way she wished. We talked, this mother and I, about whether her daughter should opt to fit in with longer hair in the future, in order to diminish some of the social pressure, and put her energy elsewhere; or whether she should keep her hair short if she liked it, and fight this battle. Her mother left, appropriately undecided, and went home to have a conversation with her daughter about camouflaging, and whether it was worth it related to this issue.

At the other end of the continuum, where the concern is of too much camouflaging, a mother called concerned about her daughter's obsession with how she looks. "She won't even go outside to play in the yard without makeup, fixing her hair, and making sure she has on the right clothes." This mother went on to describe someone who spent her life reading the landscape of tweendom and blending in so perfectly that the army would do well to imitate her camouflage techniques. This tween and I had some long conversations about why it was so important to her that she look and talk and act just so. Over time, she began to take some minor risks, like no makeup when at home. I longed to give her my issue of O magazine in which Oprah Winfrey allowed herself to be photographed *before* the makeup, hair, and fashion artists began their work on her. Actually, her mother bought the magazine and left it lying around for her daughter to happen upon. Sometimes you just can't be too direct with tweens—but you can get your messages out there, nonetheless!

Like all crucible events, the camouflaging of preadolescence is inevitable, and it can provide an opportunity for self-discovery and growth. How a girl learns to use it, and what we can do to affirm and encourage her through this period, will depend on the nature of her tween landscape. That context is shaped by her physical, intellectual, and emotional growth; in her relationship with family, friends, peers; in her vulnerability to the wider world of media and popular culture; and in the future she sees for herself as a woman.

Menarche: More Than a Milestone, the Main Event

In the real life of a girl—not the one defined by words or numbers or spending habits, but by the natural development of her body, her mind, and her life experience—the tween years represent a passage between childhood and adolescence, characterized by somewhat of a mismatch between outer growth and inner maturity and wisdom. Most girls experience their first menstrual period during the tween years now, not the teen years. Menarche, the beginning of physical sexual maturation, is the most obvious crucible event of the tween years, marking the start of what amounts to a complete physical transformation over the course of just a few years. These changes will affect every aspect of a girl's life, from academics to athletics, from the shape of her body to the shape of her thoughts, from her most social moments to her most intimate relationships, including the relationship she has with herself.

During this developmental period, a girl's entire body shape changes, from one that is fairly boxlike to one that is very rounded, from head to toe. As an example, the face actually becomes more rounded in a very refined way. Most mature female faces end up being somewhat heart-shaped: rounded cheeks and a more narrow, but rounded, chin. Studies of males responding to female faces have found that males are much more attracted to this type of face than any other type. (If you don't believe it, look at the faces of the women who have become supermodels!) Tweens begin to have the narrowing in the chin line, but the molding of the cheeks really continues into the teen and sometimes early adult years. This beginning shaping of the face signals boys to all of the other changes, even before girls' breasts begin to develop noticeably.

The internal and external organs are also evolving. Increased estrogen production is beginning to cause the mammary glands to grow and round out from the budding of early tweens to the I-need-a-bra stage of the later tweens. As with the development of the face, this is a process that comes to total fruition later in the teen or early adult years (or any time later in life, thanks to breast enhancement techniques!). Estrogen also has a profound effect on the uterus and ovaries. Everyone assumes that menarche or the onset of menstruation marks the beginning of fertility. Actually, a tween can be fertile prior to menarche or slightly later than menarche, but menarche visibly marks this evolutionary change in girls. Estrogen has caused the ovaries to change from their semiconscious state to fully productive egg machines.

Brain Science: Hormone Happenings

Continuing to the top of the body, the brain is changing in very important ways. The limbic system, the lower part of the brain that houses the emotions, is changing to include the hormonal effects of stimulation and excitement. Although these feelings can and do happen during childhood, especially during periods of hormonal production, it is the shift into a much larger hormonal production and infusion throughout the body that heightens sexual interest and stimulation. While this may not happen until later tween years or even early teen years, preadolescent girls find themselves pushed by society, and sometimes their own parents, into coed interest and dating much earlier than this limbic development normally occurs. To make matters more complicated, the frontal lobes, and the part of the brain that deals with judgment, are very immature and not fully developed during the tween, or even the teen, years. This means that there is a mismatch between feeling and concrete thinking and the ability to make mature judgments. Wisdom truly comes with age and with the maturation over time of the frontal lobes combined with life experiences.

Moving up to the top part of the brain, this area is referred to as the gray matter or the cortex. The cortex is divided into two halves. The corpus callosum is the fibrous bridge between the right and left hemispheres of the brain. Just like the ovaries, the corpus callosum has been there all along; it just hasn't been particularly functional. Sometime during the late tween or early teen years, this part of the brain also develops and begins to work more. This happens earlier for girls than boys, sometimes up to two years earlier. In girls and boys, though, the maturing of the corpus callosum varies with individuals. For girls, this physiologic change happens sometime between ages ten and twelve. Prior to this time, the brain acts more laterally. That is, the two halves don't act in coordination very well. The left (analytical) and right (creative) hemispheres really act and think separately and don't communicate effectively with each other. One of the end results is that higher-level abstract thinking doesn't occur well before the maturing of the corpus callosum. Teachers will tell you that sometime during middle school, girls write better essays, are better problem solvers, and think more complexly. For boys, this change may not manifest until the late high school years.

Living in Feelings

It is stereotypical to talk about females as being caring, "touchy-feely," or emotional. However, often I find that stereotypes, although often exaggerated beyond recognition, also start with a grain of truth. In this case, current brain research is beginning to support the view that most females experience their emotions more frequently and more intensely than most males. Why this is so is unclear, and probably will be open to speculation forever. Evolutionists declare that caring and nurturing, and therefore emotion, are programmed into the females of the species so that the offspring will be cared for, insuring survival of the species. I'm sure that other mind and body experts have some different views, but whatever the explanation or cause, the idea that females are more emotional—feel emotions more acutely—is gaining more and more scientific validity. Although this would relate to all female life stages, it is perhaps more visible or characteristic of some stages than of others. The beginning of the hormonal onslaught is one of those times.

I always tell parents of girls in third, fourth, or fifth grade that they can expect to see more tears and more of an emotional roller coaster than at any previous time in their little girl's life. I save them the worry and headache of searching for a cause at home or at school. One mother of a ten-year-old girl called to get my recommendation for a good psychologist. I asked what the problem was, and she described her daughter as a generally upbeat girl who previously had skated blithely through life, but who now came home and often cried for no apparent reason. When asked, her daughter was puzzled also: School was positive, things were smooth at home. It was clear from her age and her physical development, the absence of other causes, and the rapidity of the emotional swings, that most likely body chemistry was having its effect. More attuned, and more informed about, the mood swings of preadolescence, both mother and daughter were able to relax a bit and let nature take its course.

A good deal of tween tears are this emotional expression of the physiologic surge of female hormones. The latest research even correlates the amount of estrogen in the female monthly cycle with the amount of tears the eyes produce! This is not to say that tweens are emotional wrecks, but they do typically experience more, more intense, and more fluctuating emotions than the previous stage of development.

Anxiety is usually rated by laypeople and professionals as the worst emotion to experience. Most psychologists hypothesize that anxiety is programmed into the system to be highly uncomfortable in order to motivate action. If you are not clear about a situation—whether there are people-eating tigers about, for instance—anxiety causes you to try to find out or leave the vicinity. The tween years are either the most anxious years of development, or a tie with any other period. It is the time period that is most ambiguous. Our bodies are not the same, but we still don't know what the end product will be. Our emotions, somewhat due to hormones, somewhat due to the world, somewhat due to our amphibious pollywog state, are volatile, and the line between laughing and crying is very thin indeed. People unexpectedly, it seems, treat us as children when we're not, or as grown-ups when we're not. We're far less comfortable with the opposite gender than we were in childhood and are miles apart in at least physical maturity. All of this adds up to plenty of tension, plenty of uncertainty, plenty of anxiety.

Middle School: A Is for Adjustment

My mother used to say: "If I had a nickel for every time . . ." In my case, it is every time I've heard a girl worry about middle school—about starting it, or about life smack dab in the middle of it. A girl worries about the unknown, and worries that she is the only one worrying, that everyone else seems calm and collected; that this move to middle school is "no big deal," as so many of the adults say so confidently.

Fact: It *is* a big deal. For girls, the change from primary grades or elementary school to middle school seems especially stark. Because of this, I've spent a good deal of time working with schools to help build transition bridges, smoothing the gap from one division or one building to another.

Why is middle school such a challenge? First, part of it has to do with the structure of the elementary schools and middle schools and the structure of girls. The word *connected* best captures what the research literature says about females. Our connections with others are the cornerstone of our lives. With girls, this translates into close relationships with teachers and classmates, as well as feeling more comfortable in a small, connected setting like a classroom—the description of a typical primary or elementary setting. Middle schools, on the other hand, by their very structures, are less connected and more impersonal, with multiple classes, multiple teachers, and different classmates in many of the departmentalized classes.

We know from brain research that females can and generally do feel more anxiety, even in response to seemingly purely intellectual aspects of school, than do their male counterparts. So, in general, change and the unknown are often more unsettling for girls. They think about it more and worry about it more. The self-contained classes of the primary grades, with one basic homeroom teacher and the same classmates all day, had become very familiar and predictable; a very comfortable setting for most girls. Now middle school looms with an incredible number of changes each day. Elementary school is a favorite pair of comfortable old sneakers. Middle school is a stiff new shoe that pinches all over.

Second is a conceptual shift between the primary and the middle school years. The primary years are designed for what we call learning-to. That means learning to read, learning to write, and learning to calculate. In the middle school, the shift is rather dramatic, to the application of the skills, or using what has been learned. This means moving from learning-to to doing to learn: reading to learn, writing to express yourself, calculating to solve problems. This shift is huge! The learning-to thinking is more sequential, more detailed, more exact. The application thinking is more complex and not always sequential, and often there are many ways of doing the same task.

Going back to the brain research, it is clear that there is another gender difference that can make this shift more difficult for girls. Although it is not known why, the fact is fairly well established that estrogen has an enhancing effect on some areas of the left hemisphere of the brain, and testosterone has an enhancing effect on some areas of the right hemisphere of the brain. This means that most girls are slightly predisposed, and therefore more comfortable, with sequential, detailed, language-based factual tasks. This is a fine fit with the learning-to tasks of primary school. Most boys are slightly predisposed, and therefore more comfortable, with problem-solving, nonsequential tasks, and visual and spatial tasks. This is a fine fit with application learning. It is not that girls can't do application tasks, or that boys can't do the learning-to tasks; it is just that there is more of a fit for each, and the obverse task is just a bit more of a stretch. It is one proposed reason why girls do better in primary grades than boys, and do less well and are less happy with school as the grade levels increase. Boys, on the other hand, report less satisfaction and more trouble in the primary grades (boys comprise 80 percent of remedial group students) and then begin to get better as the grade levels increase into middle and high school.

Add to all of this the tween girl's budding self-consciousness over her body image, her body functions, and boys in general, and you can see why, if I had that nickel for every girl who worries about middle school, I'd be a very rich woman indeed.

One school I worked with decided to withhold letter grades for the first trimester of fifth grade. It just seemed too much to worry about all those grades when all those changes were happening. This way the focus could be on helping new middle-schoolers adjust to a departmentalized schedule, numerous teachers, assignment notebooks, more homework, higher achievement standards, more independent work, and the myriad of other things thrown at them.

Birds, Bees, and Body Basics: Protecting Girls from Innocence and Ignorance

Sexuality is the ubiquitous theme of the marketplace and a casual piece of the everyday landscape for most of us, and especially girls, the targets of so much sexualized advertising, marketing, and social pressure. Human sexual development is a different conversation, however, most often addressed in a biology lecture. Individual developmental timing, in the context of our highly sexualized culture, raises some new issues. Even in this new millennium, health classes and parent talks still focus on the physiology of changes and the paraphernalia of menarche. With earlier onset of menarche, this poses a real dilemma. The early-maturing girls are ready for the biology talk as early as third grade. For the later-maturing girls, this is a bit early, and can be something to think and worry about for years. It's tough wondering when you're going to have your first period, what it will be like, if it will happen in the middle of class sometime. And, for later-maturing girls, if you've had the hormone talk in third grade, you're sitting with these thoughts, waiting, with the added level of anxiety that accompanies uncertainty, for three, four, or maybe five years! All of this plays out in the context of imagery and music that celebrates sexuality, and often exploits it, to a new and naïve audience of girls.

Talking to tweens gently, but openly, about more than body changes is a high need, given the sociological backdrop for most girls. The "slut look," the push to date or have a boyfriend as early as possible, miniproms at fifth grade, all combine to make this conversation critically important. The reality is that sexual activity is part of the social conversation as early as tween years, and even part of social expectations among some. In this era of AIDS and other sexually transmitted diseases, if we avoid the subject of sexual activity because we don't want them to engage in it, we leave them only more vulnerable to the social pressures, and ill-equipped to make wise choices. An age-appropriate objective: to give them a comfort level with discussing these matters, to give them enough information to dispel the mystery, and to help them manage the uncertainty without excessive anxiety.

When it happens, this openness and willingness to discuss awkward issues is magical. After many discussions together, a group of coed seventh-graders ended up airing their complaints about kissing. One girl bravely said that when boys kiss, "all they care about is themselves, not about us." Encouraged to explain herself, she said that boys' kisses were just too rough. I turned to the boys, who wiggled but weren't ready to talk yet. So I jumped in and talked about the gender difference in sensitivity of the face: that a female face was about four times more sensitive based on the neurology of the face than a male's face. "Perhaps boys just need to kiss harder to feel it at the same level of girls." That opened the floodgates for boys, and they began to all talk at once about how they didn't want to hurt girls, that it was just another example of how they are blamed for stuff that's not their fault, etc. Kissing was the vehicle, but we had a great discussion of how girls and boys don't communicate well about sensitive (skin or emotional) issues, and how that leads to all kinds of blunders, confusion, and misunderstandings.

Can We Talk About It? Kind of, Sort of, Maybe...

You might think that with all these changes and challenges to manage, and a female propensity for relationship and verbal expression, tween girls would just talk everything over, bare their souls a bit, and be done with their worries and willies. As teenagers, many of them will do just that. But they're not there yet—we don't call them preteen for nothing—and the idea of talking openly about these new feelings and changes is unimaginable for them. That's why you—or any well-meaning adult—can sit down to have a frank, open discussion about some aspect of tween life and find yourself talking to— yourself!

It *is* possible to have these discussions, but to do it, you have to be willing to do it on their terms. That may mean you have to take the scenic route, talking about something else and eventually get around to the original point. Or you may want to try asking the question directly and see where that takes the conversation.

For instance, in my first months on the faculty of a girls' school, as we headed toward our first coed dance for the seventh- and eighth-graders, the girls were very nervous about the whole thing, anxious about the great unknown—boys! Most of these girls had little contact with boys in everyday activities, and they really just didn't know much about how boys think. So I began our discussion—which eventually became a questionnaire—by asking them: "What do you think boys like about girls your age? What attracts them? What repels them?" Then I went to a couple hundred boys at another school and asked them to give us the answers. I also asked them the same questions, only about girls. What did they think girls liked? Disliked?

As it turned out, the accuracy rate—girls and boys who had a pretty good sense of the other—was only about 10 percent at my girls' school. Surprisingly, however, when I used the same survey at coed schools, the accuracy rate was about the same. Even when they went to school together, they didn't necessarily have much greater knowledge about each other!

Rather than chatting with girls about issues or sharing words of wisdom—suspect because I am, after all, an adult—I was able to look at the survey responses and give them the facts:

"You girls think boys like makeup and popular girls," I said. "Boys say they're scared of that." We talked about the three things girls do that make boys uncomfortable (according to boys). If girls stand in large groups, whisper, and giggle, a boy will not come up. Why do boys not like that? Because if they make a mistake, there are fifty girls to laugh and giggle instead of just one.

I didn't tell the girls they should or shouldn't do this. We talked about why boys are this way, and why we are this way, and framed the whole thing in terms of choices and strategies. We asked the question: For the brief time period of the dance, is it worth it to change yourself for half an hour, to stand with one friend instead of the group, to encourage a skittish boy to come over and talk?

The girls went off to the dance and made their choices. Some stayed with a big group because they didn't want the boys. Others chose to stand with one friend.

Now, instead of being cut off from a learning opportunity because they chose camouflage and conformity just to "play the game," the girls had accurate feedback and could use that as a tool for deciding how they wanted to spend the evening: Automatically hiding out in the group, choosing the camouflage moment, they had a conscious choice and some understanding that served as a tool for decision making. They could all play the game at the dance; they knew that talking to only one friend was a temporary choice for that event to increase the probability of getting to know a boy. This made them less susceptible to adopting this kind of do-whatever-boys-like as a consistent theme of their life's behavioral repertoire.

If you listen to girls, they will offer a multitude of comfort cues that invite the conversation they are prepared to have. In the context of that comfort zone, girls can talk in some way about virtually *anything*.

The sixth-grade class had a camping trip coming up, and girls were real nervous about it, but it wasn't because they feared the great outdoors. In this sixth-grade class, like most, the girls were clearly at different points in their physical development, with hair growth in new places, and budding breasts. The girls were aghast at the prospect of this extended sleepover with no certain privacy. They couldn't talk about it with one another, or even confront it visually, which means that sixth grade is the peak time for learning to undress without anyone seeing any body part.

We had a planning meeting, these two dozen girls and I, and they talked about what to bring and worrying about bringing the wrong things. Then one of the girls said, "And don't forget your beach towel!"

All the girls snickered. Well, I knew there was no beach or swimming.

"Beach towel?" I said. "Why?"

Amy, who had quite a bit of chutzpah, said, "Dr. Deak, don't you know? Beach towels let you get undressed without anybody seeing anything."

"Oh, really?" I said. "How do you use a beach towel like that?"

Amy went on to describe The Bunk Bed Routine. In this routine, you are on the bottom bunk and you use the top bunk to tuck in your beach towel, and that gives you a little dressing room with total privacy. Woe be to the girl in the top bunk, of course!

"Does anybody else have ideas about how to get undressed without showing anything?" I asked.

Then it was fun. Everyone knew The Sleeping Bag Routine. One girl boasted: "I can take off a whole outfit and put on another whole outfit in my sleeping bag."

They just went around the room then, talking about it and having a great old time. Before that, they couldn't talk about it, even though it loomed huge in their minds. By approaching it that way, everybody knew everybody else had the same fears, experienced similar feelings, and they weren't the only ones. It was incredibly relieving for them.

Tween Rx: Fun, Family, Friends, and Focus

A mother shared with me the comment her nine-year-old son made to her one day when she was searching frantically in the clutter of their house for the keys to her car.

"Mom," he called out, in a sprightly voice. "Remember the F-word!" She blanched before she caught his follow-up: "Focus!"

I like to use a few other choice "F-words" when I talk about the experiences that strengthen girls in a special way in their tween years, or avenues we can use to reach them: fun, family, friends, and, yes, focus. These are the layers of experience we can purposefully encourage and expand to enrich girls and support them through the challenges of the tween passage.

Fun

Early tween years are just a hop away from formative childhood, and because of this, fun is somewhat self-explanatory. I'm really referring to the concept of play. Emerging from childhood, young tweens are still very playful and lively. The freedom and encouragement to "just play" is vital for them, as is the need to be able to talk about anything and everything, and to be able to voice their opinions without censure or the obligation to please others.

Whether it is young lions or monkeys or dogs or children, a prolonged play stage is what helps develop thinking, coping, interact-

ing, and strategy skills. For girls, this freedom to be expressive physically, intellectually, and emotionally continues to build and sustain
their self-esteem, grounding them more firmly for the predictable
crisis of confidence that comes with the changes ahead.

Too often today, for our pioneering girl, the days of simple
fun and play are quickly curtailed by the onslaught of fashion, beauty,
and social expectations, competition in school and in sports, over-
scheduling in organized after-school activities, and peer pressure to
mimic teen interests.

"You just sort of know who doesn't *play* play anymore, and
who does," explained Lianna, who, at ten, knew precisely which of
her friends she could still invite to play with her Barbie dolls and
Beanie Babies, and which ones might think she's odd for still playing
with dolls. Lianna wasn't ready to give up her younger, playful self,
but she was developing the social savvy to know when, where, and
with whom it was safe, in the social sense, to be herself this way. Her
mother made a special effort to protect that kind of playtime, so
opportunities with those playful friends didn't get crowded out by
shopping excursions, TV time, or other social busy-ness. She also
kept materials for simple activities, like drawing, clay work, and playing cards, handy on the table in the family room, where Lianna and
her friends, as well as other family members, could gather to relax—
and to play.

Other parents tell me they've protected play space in their
daughters' lives by making sure they continue to play games as a family, by asking their daughters to be part of noncompetitive sports
teams, or by being with younger cousins or neighbors who are still in
that play mode.

Family

For girls this age, fun is still very much related to the second
F-word: family. They talk a lot about family events and travels—and
travails! In fact, it is really the last time, for many years, that girls place
family in the top three categories of what is important in their every-

day lives, along with bodies and buddies. Although family may remain an important anchor in the sea of life, through adolescence it seems to drop into the background in terms of everyday priorities. One of the crucial points here is that family time together, family events, family conversations, and family rituals need to be maintained and even enhanced, whenever possible. Ideally, family time has been a priority all along, but, like fun and playfulness, it needs to be extended as long as possible. Family really is one of life's major anchors, not only in the turbulence of the tweens and teens, but for the rest of our lives. A wealth of studies point to strong family connections and time together as being most important in the prevention of a host of childhood problems, including drugs, delinquency, school failure, and pregnancy. The time to build and strengthen that solid foundation is now, before the natural pull away from family in adolescence.

One seventh-grade girl, when asked what she would change about her parents if she could, responded without hesitation: "I wish they'd spend more time with me. I know they love me, but they're so busy, and we hardly ever get to do things together."

Most of what we hear about limited, but potent, quality time is a myth. There is no substitute for quantity. Families that spend a lot of time together bond, know one another, are able to see and predict when issues arise, and have better communication. Meaningful relationships take time and emotional investment. The more time you spend with someone, the more opportunity you have to get to know him or her better, and to share moments that create closeness and underscore caring. Of course, the quality of that time is important, and of course, working parents cannot always spend as much time as they'd like to with family. However, in many families today, parents excuse themselves from too much of their children's lives, and the children suffer the consequences.

Last month in the airport waiting for a delayed flight to take off, I watched two families, both with two tween children. One father was reading a book, his leg loosely resting on the lap of one of his daughters, who was also slouched on the uncomfortable airport chair reading a book. The mother was talking to the other daughter about her shoes. Farther down the aisle was another father on a cell phone making nonstop calls. His tween daughter and younger son sat staring out the window. This may have been just one of those times that Father #2 had to make calls. Or it could have been a family pattern.

All I'm saying is that Father and Daughter #1 looked like they did this a lot: hung out together, not always actively engaged with each other. My point is that time together in some kind of connected way is quality time, and it needs to happen with enough quantity.

Friends

Friends, connections, and relationships have been and will remain a central force in the lives of females for a lifetime, but the focus changes with the age and stage. In the early tweens, girls are just coming out of what we call the transitory years. Those were the formative years of friendship, the fickle years; the years where you're invited to my party one day, but not the next. Transitory friendships are an important part of growth; they let a child learn about a variety of people, and they extend her knowledge base, as well as her wisdom, about forming relationships and interacting with all types of people.

However, by the early tween years, the pattern changes. The Baskin-Robbins theory of social development for girls is the order of the day! Now that she has sampled all thirty-one flavors, she knows what she likes, and she's done dabbling with the rest. We'll explore how this works across the age continuum more fully in Chapter 7, "The Galapagos Islands of Girls' Social Development."

Early tweens discriminate more, and don't interact as fluidly with as many people. These friendship clusters are not quite the same as the clique stage of later tweens and teens, but a more fluid and playful precursor. These clusters are still somewhat permeable by new members, and subject to movement between groups, depending on the activity or situation at hand. Friends haven't yet replaced parents and teachers in the hierarchy of a girl's attention and loyalty, but they are inching their way along that road. The friendship clusters of ages eight and nine evolve into the "best friends" category by about age ten.

If you walk down the hall of a school, you can tell what stage/grade the girls are in very easily. Third- and fourth-graders walk in loose clusters of three to six girls, all talking together. Fifth- and sixth-graders tend to walk in duos, the sure sign of the BF (Best Friend) era.

A girl's need for a best friend is almost a palpable drive. Psychologists suggest that this is a very critical phase related to practicing intimate relationships for later partner choices. Perhaps this accounts for the depression and anxiety experienced by many girls who have not found their tween soul mate. This is a fairly short-lived, but very intensive and emotional, phase that lasts a year or so. What is a best friend? That's one thing every tween girl agrees on!

"She doesn't reveal your secrets, she's honest, she is always there for you, and she doesn't care if you do something stupid or weird, she isn't on-and-offy, she confides in you, and she is kind, thoughtful, and funny, and a little silly."

"She is someone who is forgiving and someone who does not brag, and treats you with total respect. Also, she is caring and says she's sorry when she hurts your feelings. Also, she understands your feelings. She likes you for you."

"She can keep a secret, or if you are sad, then she comes over to you and asks if you want to play. She is full of respect instead of ignoring you and walking away."

Carol Gilligan was really the first one to talk about what she called *authentic relationships*. She said that it is important to be able to give negative feedback to a friend or a loved one; that is part of what makes a relationship. There really is no friendship or relationship if you only say nice things to each other. Having a relationship means being able to be honest and disagree and get hurt. That's how you learn to trust someone and really know that you are friends. That's what makes a relationship or friendship different from an acquaintance or someone you just hang around with.

Most girls panic when a classmate disagrees with something.

"Are you mad at me?" is the frequently heard refrain. On the other hand, best friends can be heard arguing and disagreeing for longer periods without someone saying "Are you mad at me?" because they know their best friends won't just walk out of their lives.

It's also important to discuss with your daughter that things don't always turn out peachy with friends. There are many girls who have a hard time hearing something negative about themselves, and it can signal the end of that relationship. This can especially happen once boys enter their field of vision. One girl lamented that her best friend liked boys and couldn't understand why she didn't, and now her best friend was hanging out with the "boy-crazy crowd" more and more. There is a stressful schism between the girls who are physically and/or socially mature and those who are not. It's as if they're in different worlds. There are sixth-graders or seventh-graders still playing with dolls, and others who are fondling boys. This is a gap the girls don't know how to bridge. Often it causes abrupt changes in friendship clusters and cliques. If your best friend in fifth grade suddenly finds boys enthralling, and you still think of boys as just too weird for words, suddenly you've got a lot less to talk about, and two divergent life views that are hard to bridge. Temporary developmental gaps like these can blast apart friendships that have been good and solid. That's when you, as a parent, are also there to lend your shoulder and support for finding new friends!

Focus

Mary Pipher calls it a North Star. I call it an anchor. I'm sure there are other terms in the literature that attempt to label this important concept. *North Star* or *anchor* refers to something that guides you, keeps you stable, or serves as something to hold on to in the stormy seas of life. And there are storms in every period of life; they just often seem more like typhoons to girls this age.

You help search for, and hope your daughter finds, her anchor, but it doesn't have to be her anchor for life. In her middle-school years, it might be one stabilizing interest: horses and horseback riding, or collecting pictures and everything ever written on puppies, for instance. Then, in teen years, it may stay the same or translate into an adult-based interest. Often, even though the interest changes, the new focus taps familiar skills or qualities of character.

I knew a highly self-motivated and disciplined girl who was devoted to ballet from an early age, and throughout her early tween years. Then, in eighth grade, after sitting out a season due to a foot injury, she suddenly declared that her dance-centered life was too limited, shifted her interest and energies to science, earned high marks through high school, and went on to a stellar academic and professional career in medical research. The discipline she had honed as a dancer served her well as a scholar and, later, as a scientist.

Another girl was a horse lover in her elementary school years, but, unable to afford to ride, she drew pencil sketches of them in every margin of her notebooks and test papers. She turned to making and selling hand-painted jewelry boxes during her middle-school years, then put her paints away in high school and turned to fiction writing instead. She went on to study art history in college, then returned to writing and eventually became a successful author. All through her school years her parents had worried about her reluctance to stick with any one interest, but, in fact, her focus was on creative expression, and her serial interests each represented a facet of her creativity.

Whether a girl's attention turns to horses, or gymnastics, or drawing, or music, or reading, it is important that she pick her own anchor, and it is important for her parents to respect her choice, recognize it as an important developmental step, and resist the temptation to turn it into a source of pressure to achieve or measure up. The best you can do is open up possibilities, keep offering the associations or opportunities to get involved in something, and when something clicks for her, you can get excited and back it financially, or with time or whatever support you can give it. Just remember whose anchor it is; if your daughter is ready to lift anchor and explore other waters before settling on a new interest, celebrate her curiosity and willingness to try new things. Those are qualities that will serve her well throughout life.

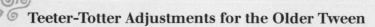

Teeter-Totter Adjustments for the Older Tween

Just as parents and teachers get used to the early tweens, girls transition into a slightly different animal: the older tween. Still short of bona fide adolescence by a bit, the older tween nonetheless is different from the younger tween in a few significant ways. The first thing most parents notice is that they and other parents suddenly become dumber than doorknobs—at least in their daughters' eyes. Some girls are more polite or kind about this than others, but the conclusion remains the same: Adults are clueless about the things that matter most to tweens; their experience is outdated, and their interest is suspect. As much as you may want to argue the point, don't bother. Once you accept this lowly assessment as the tween truth, and let go of any assumed superiority, you're actually in a better position to listen, learn, and influence your daughter in new ways. We'll get to those in a minute, but first, we'll examine the other telltale signs of older tween behavior, a shift in attitude on the three F's to the telltale B's: body, buddies, and boys.

B Is for Body

One thing is very clear: Older tweens can no longer look in the mirror and believe they are children, and that changes everything. It begins to matter what boys think, and it matters that they're looking with a new kind of interest at girls' bodies. Most ten- to twelve-year-old girls respond to their blossoming bodies and newfound male attention with one of two basic and opposite responses: by "draping and slouching," wearing baggy clothes and sporting stooped shoulders to disguise any chest changes; or by "chin up and chest out," wearing clothes and a posture that accentuate their new curves. It's hard to predict which way a girl will go. It is certainly influenced by temperament and personality on the extrovert/introvert scale. Draping is classic for introverts, chest out is classic for extroverts. But the social group, the culture of the school or geographic area, and expressed parental or religious values can all influence a girl's style. One mother was thrilled when her thirteen-year-old daughter came back from an Outward Bound–type camp experience and announced that she no longer had any interest in her once-favored slinky tank tops and such. She preferred the sturdier "outdoorsy look."

The best advice is to not make too much of where your daughter is on this continuum, because it is almost always a temporary phase. Just like friendship patterns at this age reflect the Baskin-Robbins sampling syndrome, this is the time for "See how I look as . . ." sampling, with the added overlay of responding to social pressure and fashion trends. One exception to that relaxed rule of response would be in the instance that your daughter adopts any extreme habit or behavior that goes against your family values or moral standards, or if she suddenly shifts from one extreme to another. Any sudden or extreme changes—in friends, fashion, grades, appearance, eating, you name it—always merits at least some observation and investigation. If your shoulders-back girl suddenly becomes a serious sloucher, it may be a response to something that needs to be further addressed. For instance, a quick move from chest out to serious draping can reflect some painful body or emotional incident. If it is related to something like harassment, it needs to be addressed. If it is merely the result of slight embarrassment because of sudden chest growth, then you can just let it slide.

Menarche and hormonal fluctuations add to the complexity of the older tween's experience. Given current research, there's not much doubt that for most girls, their moods and emotions are strongly influenced by this new twenty-eight-day menstrual cycle that rules their bodies. It is a hard time for adults to know how much to try to discuss body issues and how much to be laid back and not underscore the myriad of body issues that permeate our culture. This is often a time when mothers can share some of their history as a way of opening the door to conversation. For example, I was still a bit of a neophyte in understanding this monthly cycle stuff when I asked my mother to get me a thicker kind of pad when she went to the store. She said, "Oh, I forgot those beginning years." And that prompted her to share a story about when she first started to menstruate. Her mother had never talked to her about it, nor had her health or science teachers in her Catholic school. So when it happened, she ran to her older sister to see what could be wrong. Her older sister, in one of her ornery moods, said, "See what happens when you eat too much jelly?" We were able to laugh together, and it somehow made it easier to have these "girl" conversations. It didn't hurt that she said it meant a lot to her that we could talk like this.

So letting her know that you understand her feelings, being able to talk about it matter-of-factly, and letting her know that it matters to you is the best a parent can do. She'll take it from there and let you see her boundaries very clearly!

B Is for Buddies

Relationships with peers take on a new, overriding, and almost overwhelming importance for older tweens. Actually, "overriding" is a good term for how the girls view the new role of relationships. "Overwhelming" typically fits the parents' and teachers' view. Girls talk on the phone or use chat lines during every free minute. They try never to be seen alone, they walk down the hall in amoeba-like clumps, and they pass notes in class, instead of hanging on to every precious concept or word of wisdom being shared by teachers. My psychologist friend calls this the "trendy tribe" stage. Others refer to cliques.

I like to think of this as the wet butterfly stage. Prior to this time, girls have been in the cocoon of their families and surrounded by other protective adults (teachers, relatives, clergy) from whom they accepted decisions and/or words of wisdom.

With the onslaught of the just-too-dumb view of adults, the older tween is left cocoon-less. It is certainly exciting, but it also is an incredibly scary and shaky time. It is exactly analogous to the butterfly emerging from the cocoon, with wet and fragile wings, about to fly. The issue with wet wings is that if they are touched before they dry, the butterfly is damaged for life and flight is either very curtailed or does not happen at all. Tweens, with their wet wings, surround themselves with a buffer against the world that might hurt them during this fragile stage. That protection comes in being surrounded by other wet butterflies. They cluster together and need to act alike, talk alike, and look alike for the protective camouflage it provides. It reminds me of a Discovery Channel program about running zebra: The stripes made them all blend together so that any predatory animal would have a hard time singling out any one zebra. Viewing buddies and cliques as a survival technique helps adults understand the rabid devotion to friends at almost any cost.

B Is for Boys

I remember one parent seeing her four-year-old daughter on the playground with another four-year-old, a boy, saying to her in a teasing manner, "Oh, so you have a boyfriend!" The world suggests to girls, practically from Day One, that they should have a boyfriend. And yet, genetically and developmentally, the real interest in boys is more in alignment with menarche, for obvious reasons. Hence, girls often fake their interest in boys so that the world doesn't think something is wrong with them. The problem sometimes is that an individual girl may think something is wrong with her because she is not interested in boys in early tweendom. All of this begins the game of not being truthful about boys or to boys.

Whether or not there is a little lie in the history of her attitude toward boys, most girls, by about age twelve or so, develop a genuine curiosity, if not downright rabid interest, in boys. It's important to remember that there is a continuum from some interest to total infatuation. It was the older tween group that made the movie *Titanic* and sweet stud star Leonardo DiCaprio the titanic hits they became. Older tweens often do become infatuated with stars, or distant individuals, before that spotlight of emotion lights on one real and known boy. It is a nice, safe, socially acceptable, and exciting way to genuinely show interest, without having to deal with a real relationship. Girls so often are teased about this harmless infatuation behavior, but it can be a very healthy stage—one to hope for and prolong in your daughter! So many girls have maturing bodies without the emotional maturity and cognitive wisdom to manage real-boy attention. This virtual courting that can be shared with one's group can help a girl wade into the coed interaction stage.

As for early dating, what's a parent to do? Delay your tween daughter's dating as long as you can. The developmental purpose of boys and girls being together at this age is to get to know what the other gender in our species is all about, how he is the same and different from a female, from a girlfriend, etc. The developmental purpose of boys and girls being together at this age is not to begin the selection process of a mate, and that is what one-to-one dating, simply put, is all about. Sitting in a dark movie theater or putting bodies together at a dance is not an effective way of getting to know the other gender. It is an effective way to facilitate a physical relationship. And physical relationships are too complicated and too costly at this young age. This point was so poignantly made in my discussion with eighth-grade girls, as previously discussed, when one brave girl asked why boys liked oral sex so much and why it wasn't much fun for a girl. Most of the girls nodded sagely, having either experienced the pressure to perform or heard about it from other girls.

Dating and dances can wait until later high school years. One group of schools in the Cleveland area sponsors middle-school socials: sled riding, skiing, hiking, movies with discussions afterward, pizza parties, and the like. Groups of girls and boys interacting around some kind of activity is the healthiest relationship mode for this age range.

Negotiating the Gray and Teaching Tweens to Do the Same

When I travel and speak to audiences of parents and teachers, I always ask the women how many of them would want to be in middle school again. Over the years, and out of thousands of women, a total of three have raised their hands. The others can feel that uncomfortable in-between feeling like it was yesterday. They almost wriggle in their seats. It was uncomfortable for most of us when we were going through it, and it can be doubly hard to watch the girl we love be uncomfortable—uncomfortable with school, with her body, with her friends, or with her self. For parents, it's really double jeopardy: a daughter's experiences layered on our less-than-favorable memories, and our very real concerns for her well-being.

How can we help our daughters negotiate the gray of tween life if we can barely stand to confront it ourselves?

Some parents don't. They can't wait for their daughter to get out of this ambiguous pollywog stage, and they are one with the crowd that fast-forwards the tween into teenage life—dances, dating, unsupervised parties, few limits, lots of freedom, and high expectations. Some avoid the uncomfortable gray by trying to keep their girls young and dependent, trying to stall the developmental moment as long as possible. (Which only backfires, I might add.) This stage really underscores our insecurities as parents and other adults in the lives of these pollywogs.

Negotiating the gray in this amorphous tween environment is made harder by the fact that there is so little shared history in dealing with contemporary tween issues. Those who would exploit these girls as consumers are way ahead of the rest of us in their research on the mind and behavior of tween girls. While they've invested millions of dollars to learn what makes preteen girls tick, as consumers, scientific research and general parenting literature specifically on tweens is scarce, though growing slowly. Parents of tweens also don't find the ready social supports that helped them network with other parents when their girls were younger; they feel isolated, and sometimes handicapped in reaching decisions they wish to be grounded in good parenting practice and reasonable contemporary standards. Finally, girls themselves feel pressured to grow up (but not too much, or too fast) and mimic the teenage quest for autonomy, without the additional years of emotional growth and life experience to temper their impulses. Be your daughter's listening post; hear what she says and thinks is going on, and talk to her teachers to get a better perspective. Your goal is not to help her make the grade, socially or academically, but to help her figure out how to negotiate these new school expectations.

Pearls for Parents and Pearls for Girls

- Your tween will believe you have no wisdom, but keep acting like you do.
- Your daughter will pretend she isn't listening to a word you are saying, but keep talking, because she is.
- Call her a tween one day and when she asks why, lead into a discussion about negotiating the gray of pollywog life.
- Play basketball, jump rope, or jacks with her: Help prolong the part of her that is a child.
- Tuck her in at night like she's a little girl, but treat her as a semiadult during the day, especially when others are present.
- Try desperately hard not to embarrass her in public, but know you will be somewhat of a failure at this.

CHAPTER 4

Everything and Nothing:
Sharing the Adolescent Girl's
Struggle to Be and Become Herself

> *"There are a lot of double standards out there. We're looked down on as inferior, even if we are equal or excel. We're taught to be quiet and submissive, and at the same time they tell us we can do anything! I wish I were happier."*
>
> —Sharon, seventeen

> *"I love how I am so brave about all my family problems and life. There's a certain amount of inner power that comes with being a girl, a strength we have to possess in order to survive. We're stronger simply because we have to be."*
>
> —Oona, fifteen

If you were an explorer from another galaxy and stumbled upon earth in your search for the most exciting life form in the universe, you would call off the hunt and celebrate "mission accomplished" the day you discovered teenage girls. The complexity! The intensity! The energy! The volatility! The extraordinary physical, intellectual, emotional, spiritual, and intuitive capacity and creativity! The elaborate facades and the incredible depth! In the next few moments, after your breathtaking discovery of teenage girls, you would note the second, oddly interesting species that clearly shares their space and seeks to interact with them, yet, mysteriously, often seems dazed, frantic, confused, or depleted by those very interactions. Further, you would note that the relationship between these two life forms is often marked by tension or conflict, yet, for the most part, they seem compelled to remain engaged. Perhaps most curious of all, this alternately contentious and collaborative connection appears to be a critical component in the vitality of the girls' continued growth and development.

Welcome to the universe of relationship in which adults and adolescent girls live together, each species with its own point of view, shaped by completely different innate developmental tasks to accomplish. Adolescent girls are compelled by nature to push away from their parents. Parents (and teachers, by virtue of their roles) are compelled to hold on, to continue the guiding and shaping tasks as long as needed. Everyone is after the same objective, however, and this mild tug-of-war allows us to maintain a bit of tension in the rope, to enable the teen to move gradually away while the adults are gradually letting go. An abrupt pull or letting go on either end results in too rapid a shift for both parties.

We may lack the detached perspective of an otherworldly visitor. However, when we pool our observations, the pictures tell the story of that challenging passage, for girls and parents alike:

"The minute you think you know a teenage girl, she does or says something that completely shatters your illusions," one mother says.

"Living with a teenage girl is like looking at a beautiful rock," says another of my favorite "mother sources," implying that there is a hidden facet that is always surprising and often startling during those rare glimpses of what is hidden under the rock.

"You often find yourself simply crossing your fingers and hoping they will make the right decision, but not having nearly the control or influence you would like . . ." a father says.

"Hold on to your hat!" As a colleague of mine puts it, referring to the dizzying list of challenges that we psychologists identify as givens in female adoles-

cence: "hormonal changes, gender and sexual identity issues, balancing the process of individuation with the need to be part of a group, conformity vs. non-conformity, coping with increasingly intense academic pressures while developing other talents and abilities, the never-ending tug-of-war between the desire for short-term gratification and sacrifice for long-term gain, the development of character and the ability to hold on to one's values when in situations that put them to the test, the rising importance of friendship and the need to differentiate oneself from family in preparation for adulthood, the ability to adapt to a rapidly changing global, cultural, and technological environment, and the human yearning to endure and make one's imprint in a world that often seems overstimulating, temporary, superficial, and disposable." (Somehow all of those words without a pause for breath really captured the essence of teendom.)

A sixteen-year-old girl puts all that in more succinct terms: "boys, dating, rumors, reputations, sexual activities, etc." (That "etc." covers a lot of territory!)

If you have been on this planet in the last decade, you know all the ways it can go wrong. Books, articles, talk shows, and scary stories from other parents all have described or commented on the state of adolescence. Almost all of those messages suggest a time of great upheaval and huge conflict between parents and teens, and, for girls, a psychological minefield ready to explode should she take one step out of line.

Drugs, sex, depression, suicide, eating disorders, and other self-destructive potentialities are clearly a part of the teen world (see Chapter 9, "Parents Under Pressure"). These issues surround them in the media, in their schools, with their friends, and sometimes in their own lives. And, as we discussed in the tweens chapter, all of this is happening at earlier ages for girls. Who would ever have thought, even just a few years ago, that trends in dating behavior would lead to the need to talk with teen and tween girls about the AIDS-related risks of oral sex?

The pitfalls for adolescent girls are real, and the concerns of parents, teachers, and other caring adults are valid. But we do girls a disservice when we let our fears for them—and sometimes our fear *of* them—obscure the extraordinary gifts of mind, body, and spirit and the basic, normal, everyday developmental needs that define the lives of most adolescent girls. It is similar to the way the media hypes crime and keeps social fear of crime alive, despite the fact that felonies have dropped more than 30 percent in the past few years. The real essence of teenage girls is one of high hopes and high expectations for themselves and the world.

However, so much recent literature on girls focuses on the pain and pitfalls of adolescent girl life that we overlook the other reality—that this generation's girls do not see themselves as victims, but as eager pioneers in the changing landscape of female adolescence. Every generation has said and felt this somewhat, but for girls today, there truly has been, in the space of one generation, a seismic shift in the landscape of life for females in our culture. This has produced unprecedented choices and challenges in life, education, and careers, and an entirely different context for a girl's engagement with the world, her most intimate relationships, and her deepest experience of herself.

Our best hedge against the risks of adolescence is to fortify our girls with a sense of their own value, their own power, and their own capacity to meet what they will deal with in life, and make wise choices for themselves. They need to know the difference between a stupid risk—for instance, getting in the car with a drunken driver, or engaging in unprotected sex of any kind, risking AIDS or STDs—and a good risk that challenges them to learn, stretch, and grow stronger. If we want to cultivate this survival savvy and other self-affirming qualities that will help our girls thrive, we need to recognize those very attributes and capabilities in them, understand the process through which adolescent girls grow and develop, and exercise our own continuing role in purposefully layering experiences that encourage girls to discover and develop feelings of confidence and competence to handle the world.

Crucible Events in the Big, Bold, Beautiful Chaos of Girl Teendom

If we adjust our chaos viewing lens once again, we can see that the turmoil, the conflict, the experimenting, the view that parents are not as bright as they used to be, is, though difficult at times, altogether normal. By that, I don't mean that it's just typical, or common, as in, "everybody does it." I mean that it is a normal part of healthy psychological growth and development. It all makes perfect sense. In simple terms, learning and growing fully is a continuous upward, lifelong gradient. However, in adolescence it specifically leads to adulthood, that pinnacle of development that, in every teenager's eyes, represents the finish line—freedom at last! (It takes an adult to know that's only the beginning!)

Each developmental stage has many aspects to it, but also represents an overarching developmental task or focus. For a girl in early childhood that means learning about herself and others and negotiating the gray in that terrain. In the tween years, it means experiencing the pollywog stage of a changing body and learning what that means to her and the rest of the world. At the end of the tweens or the very beginning of the teens, menarche signals that she is seriously along the path to adulthood, and her physical development makes that quite visible to her and to the rest of the world. Just as significant is the emotional and intellectual growth that is transforming a girl's interior life. The global task of adolescence is fairly well agreed upon by most adults: figuring out how to leave the nest, physically, emotionally, and practically. But a girl's experience of this transition emerges from three key crucible events of adolescence:

- Core building—her interior work, often carried out behind a facade of "cool" or even indifference.
- Measuring up—how she feels about herself in relation to others in every aspect of her life. This includes grades, looks, friends, family,

material possessions, qualities of character, and potentially everything in her life.

- Sex and sexuality—every girl develops a strategy for dealing with
this inescapable need to negotiate the natural impact that an adult
female body has on its observers and on relationships with the other
gender.

The Adolescent Girl Interior: Brain and Body Basics

The expanse from age twelve to nineteen is too wide and
diverse to talk about in any detail as a total entity. So, just as I referred
to younger and older tweens, depending on some developmental
measures within that preadolescent age group, I'll refer to girls
between twelve and fifteen years old as young teens and girls from
about age sixteen to nineteen as older teens.

The early teen years are truly as gray as it gets. Barely out of
that pollywog stage, girls are very fuzzy about what they think and feel
and want and need, and so are their parents. At least in the tween
years, a girl has the luxury of following her friends or clique, and
melting in with the group. Friends are still as important as oxygen,
and it is still important to blend in, but somehow, the thought is
emerging for the early teen that it is time to grow up—somewhat,
some days. That means that girls begin to seriously ponder if they are
normal. They wonder what the finished product of their growth spurt
will turn out to be (most girls are full grown by the end of the early
teen years). They become more attuned to moral issues, and are
thinking in more mature ways about moral dilemmas and what is
worth standing up for. They may or may not act on any of these
thoughts, but the perking has started in earnest.

As brain growth and development continues, one of the most
important areas of cognitive maturation usually occurs during the
beginning teen years. Most of us have heard talk of right-brain and
left-brain thinking, often in terms of personality styles, but this par-

ticular aspect of brain science becomes a significant piece of girl thinking in adolescence. The thinking part of the brain is divided into the left hemisphere, associated with analytical thought, and the right hemisphere, associated with creative thought. In the middle of these two halves is a sturdy and fibrous bridge known as the corpus callosum. This is a critical connecting piece of the brain that allows the two hemispheres to send messages back and forth and coordinate and synthesize the kind of thinking that happens on each side of the brain. During the early teen years, this part of the brain becomes mature, and therefore allows the brain to work more fluidly and allows us to think more abstractly and with much more complexity. So, for a young teen girl, often some of the clouds will part in some areas of school that had been a bit fuzzy to her. At home, she is able to argue her case in much more depth!

A basic understanding of this cortical growth spurt can also come in handy when you're confronted with circumstances or decisions about course work at school, when you need to decide whether your daughter will be better served by one option than another. For example: What if your daughter has the opportunity to take algebra sooner rather than later? Unless she has clearly and significantly advanced mathematical talent, it is better to give her the time for that additional corpus callosum maturation before taking algebra, even if she is fairly bright and gets good grades. This increase in facility with both hemispheres will help ensure that she learns algebra in a meaningful way, rather than the memorizing approach that many girls employ.

Core Building: The Power and Promise of Teen Girls

The camouflage of tweens is a protective device a girl uses to blend in and not cause more waves and conflict than she feels she can handle. The camouflaging gives way, in the teen years, to what I call the adolescent facade, which serves as more of a screen or retaining wall. From the teen years through to, and perhaps including, the young adult years, a girl uses the facade to keep the world at bay while she continues the construction of her core self with a bit of privacy. It keeps the world from really seeing her until she's ready. Meanwhile, she's building and refining that interior core; getting more clarity on what she thinks and believes; building her strength and keeping all of that growth process from being tampered with too much by outside influences.

A girl can look out from this facade and continue to see the world, and keep collecting the data, wisdom, and experience that allows her to mold the construction process of that core. So the inner side of the facade has a retaining function, and the outer side has a viewing function and a reflecting function: letting her view the world without letting the world view her inner core, and reflecting the temporary image she wants to show the world while she's finishing her master project.

Sometimes the building project goes on unabated and, as the core nears completion, she begins dismantling the retaining wall, brick by brick, slowly or quickly, depending on whether she thinks this core self can withstand the light of day and be safe in, and respected by, the larger world. Often, however, late teens or young adults call a halt to the building of the core when it is almost finished, and they don't dismantle the wall. Instead, they adopt the facade for many years, virtually forgetting about the core and how it differs from the facade.

This often happens because as they continue to view and size up the world, many women see that their facade is a better, more acceptable, and easier fit in the eyes of the world than is their more authentic core. So they just stop building and set that work of art aside until later in life, when the world's opinion is diminished in importance to them. I can't tell you the number of women hovering around the age of fifty who have said things like:

> *"I only wear comfortable shoes now, not what is high fashion—I can't be bothered . . ."*

"I don't go to cocktail parties anymore—my time is too precious to spend it chatting and smiling all night with large groups of people . . ."

"My husband says I've changed—I used to be so agreeable, so easy to get along with. Now I say what's on my mind."

Some girls are ready to say that at age sixteen. Most aren't. Regardless, most teenage girls possess a remarkable complexity and growing strength and vision, core qualities that become the building blocks of this behind-the-facade interior project.

Core Qualities: A Girl's Interior Building Blocks

I went to have my hair cut last week, and the hairdresser's eighteen-year-old daughter was there helping with cleaning. She looked the teenage part: tight spandex pants and a body-sculpting shirt, the latest shoes. She was very shapely, very pretty. We talked about school and her friends. Then her mother told her I was a psychologist, and that I was writing a book. She gave me a sizing-up look, then became fairly quiet. I told her that I really needed to hear from girls her age, about what it's like being a teen today, and I asked her if she would help me understand it from her experience.

She paused and looked thoughtful, I think to decide whether I was just making conversation or if this was serious and important. I must have passed.

"Well, I'm probably not the one to talk to," she said. "Inside, I'm not like most teens."

I asked what she meant. Again, the scrutiny.

Finally, she said that she was in the process of figuring out if she should have breast reduction surgery. Now she really watched my reaction.

"It must be a hard decision," I said.

She cocked her head and looked at me like my dog does when I do something unexpected. I passed the test again, and she went on to say that it really wasn't a hard decision. She was experiencing back and arm pain, and it was getting to be almost unbearable. She talked about how supportive her mother was, and how much that helped her. She said that at first, most of her friends told her how crazy she was; that "most girls and women pay to have their breasts enlarged to look just like mine!"

She explained that as she had held her ground in those conversations and talked about what it was like to have uncomfortably large breasts, her friends had become supportive, too. She also knew enough not to talk to her boy friends about this issue. She said that in general, boys were less mature than girls and really couldn't talk about breasts with any real understanding or empathy.

I was impressed with her maturity and good sense. Here she was having a very serious conversation with another adult that she didn't know well. She was exhibiting some real insight in sizing up others and deciding how far to wade into this discussion with her age-mates.

This conversation reminded me of the study that was done at my girls' school, with Harvard researcher Carol Gilligan and a team of interviewers. I had the good fortune of being one of the on-site interviewers, and I interviewed many ninth- through twelfth-grade girls. I was always so surprised by what was "under the rock" of these high school girls. Girls I had known for years, who never seemed to talk about very serious subjects, suddenly talked in-depth on a variety of philosophical topics; girls who had the reputation of being airheads weren't. Girls I thought of as real followers had serious thoughts about how they would leave their mark on the world. If I learned one thing about teens during this five-year study, it was not to judge a book by its cover. What a teen shows her friends and the adults in her life may be and usually is quite different from what her core is all about.

Depth and Thoughtful Complexity

I am always moved by the depth of teenage girls' thinking. I reflect back to my own teen years—could I have thought those thoughts at age sixteen or eighteen? I don't think I was there. I didn't think about world issues, or issues of where I was heading in life, and whether I'd be successful, or whether marrying early or late, or at all, was important. I hear the same thing from other people I talk with, and most significantly, from other women. Anyone who spends any time with teenage girls on a school or community project walks away so impressed with the quality of thinking and the intense idealism that is there. In a world that, in many ways, still pushes them around, limits them, and causes some real headaches, most teenage girls are incredibly idealistic, caring, and forgiving.

I know, because I've been on the blundering end from time to time.

At one high school, I was asked to talk to some of the black students who were segregating themselves at lunch. They weren't sitting with the other girls. I sat down with the older girls in this group, juniors and seniors, and told them why I was there.

"The administration is concerned," I said, "because we want an integrated, inclusive school, and at lunch you sit by yourselves. We don't know what to make of that. I'm here to see what I can do so that you'll feel comfortable sitting with the white students."

Big mistake! I assumed sitting separately meant they didn't feel comfortable. . . . They looked at me, kindly, and they were genuinely forgiving of the school and my naïveté and failure to understand.

"Dr. Deak," said Olivia, one of the senior girls, "if you went to China and you were the only English-speaking person there, and you were there for a long time, and one day you went out to lunch in this Chinese cafeteria and there was a table there with Americans, who would you sit with?"

I admitted that I'd most likely sit with Americans.

"For some of us, sometimes it feels foreign here," Olivia continued. "We can walk the walk and speak the language of this school, but we also need the sustenance and feeling of community that we get being together at lunch. It's like not having to wear your makeup all the time. We do sports together with everyone, and classes together with everyone. When it comes time for lunch, we just want to relax and be with each other."

They didn't hold my question or my ignorance against me. They tried to help me see through their eyes. They were sweet about it. Other adults who work with teenage girls see this quality in them, but parents don't always see that sweetness and forgiveness.

Resilience

I admire teen girls' resilience: Every day they get up and cope with a very consuming and intense world and it takes a good deal to quell their enthusiasm and interest in things. Even if boys make fun of their answers in class, they hang in there and get better grades. The resilience part of it is finding a way to survive and keep going, regardless of what obstacles are put in the road. That's impressive. For example, in the academic world, if they don't get called on in class, they find another route, like stopping in to see the teacher during a free period. It may be indirect or perceived as going underground, but this resilience is far healthier than the stereotypical stoic behavior of some boys.

Caring and Connection

The world often focuses on the cattiness and uncaring behavior of girls. The other side of that, which is just as powerful—perhaps even more so—is the caring and connection with friends, or others who touch their heartstrings. Some of that goes along with being the female of the species and an innate urge to be nurturing.

I remember standing in the hall admiring an art project of one of the eleventh-grade girls, a lion's head made out of papier-mâché and painted beautifully. The proud artist said that she was going to hang it in her bedroom. I said, rather wistfully, that I wish I could do something like that; I loved lions and I loved beauty, and this was both rolled into one piece of art. I meant it as a sincere tribute to her talent. At the end of the year a package arrived at my house: the lion's head. Attached was a note that said, "You don't have to know how to make a lion's head, you just need to know how to touch the heart of an artist."

If you touch her heartstrings, a teenage girl responds with everything she's got, and that's incredibly wonderful. Even the cattiness is, in a perverse way, about caring about somebody; it usually reflects some anger over somebody that she cares about, or the need she feels to protect a friend or her group. Flip side: It's also what makes these girls so emotionally vulnerable, and it's why we feel concerned at times that this quality will be exploited by others.

 Savvy

Another core quality I see in girls is savvy. Most of them are savvy about what is expected of them. In my days as a school psychologist, when I would sit down with girls and talk with them about a teacher's concerns, they would know chapter and verse what that teacher wanted, what that teacher thought, and what would placate that teacher. It's always so interesting to hear a girl talk about how she handles her mother or father. Many girls have a finely tuned intuitive sense. In the early years, they become extremely good at reading faces. Later, they assess the total person fairly well. I will never forget watching some kids doing skits about adults. They have a way of seeing us that is so perceptive and so on target. Boys tend to see the tunnel picture; girls see the nuances.

At a rainy camp experience, in frustration to come up with yet another indoor activity, we did skits, and the girls portrayed various

members of the faculty. One girl imitated me. It was worse than looking in an unforgiving mirror; it was like being viewed under a microscope! When they combine their caring with their idealism and savvy,
what a powerful combination! This is why I think that wars would
cease in the world if women were the majority of members of all
negotiating teams.

Now, whether girls as teenagers combine these incredible
characteristics into synthesized action is another thing. All of that layering and building goes on inside at a much higher rate and faster
level of maturity than we think, because the outside package doesn't
lend itself to our seeing it.

Looking Under the Rock

Parents don't always see these finer qualities because when
girls are at home, they're engaged in a different kind of struggle to
define themselves in the family, and the tactics look quite different.
It's the one place they can let their hair down and show their irritabil-
ity and childish behavior, and not have to keep up the facade. Educators can lose that fuller perspective at times, too. All of us jump to
conclusions too often about teen girls' intentions and motivations.

I was asked to consult at one school when the entire varsity
field hockey team had mutinied and refused to play in that afternoon's critical game against their number one arch rival.

Off to the coaches' office I trotted. When I asked what the
issue was, I was told that, basically, the girls didn't like the coaches'
decisions about who should be on the team, and they wanted the
decision to be overturned.

That was "the rock," at a distance: immature girls wanting
their own way. What we think is under the rock is usually much more
complex than its surface appearance, but if we don't listen or ask—or
worse, if we let our fear or discomfort rule—then we don't get close
enough to see what's underneath. In this case, what was beneath that
rock was much more complicated than what the coaches thought.

Off to the girls I trotted to find out. The newly formed but nonplaying varsity team agreed to meet with me over lunch. "I hear you're not going to play the game," I said.

Their response amounted to: "You're damn straight we're not playing, and you can't make us."

"I'm not here to make you do anything," I said, "but to figure out what's going on and see if I can help you. What can I do? What's going on?"

They glanced around their circle of players.

"Do you know what happened?" several girls asked.

"Not really."

They lifted the rock and let me see what was underneath:

"It's not fair!"

"It's not right!"

"The coaches don't care about us!"

"We shouldn't have to play for a school that treats its students this way."

Maybe the coaches were right; maybe they were immature. . . . But then they went on to tell the rest of the story.

The last two weeks in August was field hockey camp. All of the interested girls spent ten days doing drills, playing practice games, etc. That next Monday, the girls returned to school to see the varsity team list posted on the bulletin board.

Two senior girls, who had played since seventh grade, weren't on that list. They were the only seniors who did not make the team.

I asked the girls if these two were, in fact, good enough to be on the team.

They acknowledged that they weren't great players, "But still, it's not right," one girl said. "They're devastated, and we're not going to take it. The coaches just care about winning. It isn't just about winning."

I asked what it was about, and they said it was about caring and being a team. With discussion they acknowledged that the definition of a varsity team was that they were the best players. They reluctantly agreed that these two girls had always played in all nonvarsity games because those teams were designed for girls learning to play, or for girls who just liked playing.

They saw the garden path I was leading them down.

So that got down to the essence of their anger. The list had been posted on the bulletin board where all could see, without first notifying the two girls who hadn't made the team. The girls had run up with all their friends, and found out the news in that awkward moment. The girls on the team felt that someone should have handled it personally.

When I lifted the rock in this incident, what I found was not snotty girls who didn't like the coaches or the idea of performance standards. I found a group of concerned girls looking at an important moral code. Whether we adults agreed with it or not, their motivation was as good as we could ever want it. It was a purely moral stance, and it showed incredible courage on their part to go against the system. They didn't want to lose field hockey games, especially this one. But they were putting their feelings about their peers above their need to win and play and be on the team.

I talked with the coaches about the girls' feelings, and then about their own, and why they had handled the process the way they had. By posting the results, instead of making the news known in a more personal way, they had hoped to avoid "an emotional reaction"! I'm not sure if they meant on the part of the girls, or themselves.

Then it was time for me to get out of the middle. The girls and the coaches met instead of having a practice time before the game. They worked things out, and the game went on. I don't even remember who won, but I do remember the coaches apologizing for their insensitivity, and the girls saying that they understood why varsity teams need to be selective.

As for the girls, I had to congratulate them on their strategy and courage, connection and caring, loyalty, all of it. The girls had known about the team selection for a week, but hadn't declared the standoff until the morning of the game, when the pressure was high.

They knew that if they had any leverage, they had it that day. And they used it for the highest purpose. Caring, savvy, resilience—I love seeing what's under the rocks!

I know some teachers who won't teach teenage girls. They'd rather go into the roughest inner-city school than teach seventh-through twelfth-grade girls. When a group of teenage girls wants to go up against anything, it's very hard to beat them. No wonder most adults run the other way screaming. I doubt if such girls understand how formidable they are. Now, you can look at that as a negative quality, something to be punished or discouraged. Or you can see it as a magnificent resource that girls have, and look for ways to groom it and guide it.

From Facade to Freedom: Inviting Your Daughter to Be Herself

In the face of what the fashion industry, boys, the media, and their friends seem to see as the image of a teen girl, most teen girls will go to great lengths to keep a low profile behind that image, because those who don't are considered a bit weird, or downright geeks. Just like camouflaging can suggest social savvy in a preteen girl, in some ways, having a facade that holds the world at bay is wise and mature, and allows for comfortable living while the inside is solidifying. It is truly a great survival technique. But there are at least two very serious negative effects.

First, a socially acceptable facade perpetuates what is socially acceptable. In other words, girls support some of the pressures and limits that pressure and limit them!

Second, they sometimes fall for their own act and stay in the mode. For example, the overpleasing girl can become the overpleasing woman. I know it is folly to expect that all teens would rise up and refuse to wear an unhealthy fashion, like towering heels, for instance. But if enough girls did it, their action would widen the band of what is acceptable in teen fashion. Quantity counts. It takes enough teens doing something against the perceived social acceptability scale to change that perceived social acceptability. When federal mandate boosted the number of girls' sports teams, and the number of girl athletes grew, so did the social acceptability of girls wearing athletic shoes.

As parents and teachers, we want to respect the facade when it serves to protect a girl, as she continues her core building behind it. We also want to create environments in which girls feel safe and affirmed in stepping clear of the facade and showing this core self in action. When the core is out in the open, it is easier to help enhance its growth.

I call this stepping out the hermit crab phenomenon. In my days as a principal, I encouraged each class to adopt a pet, so they could care for it and watch it grow. The sixth-graders decided to get a hermit crab. This crab was so scared about its new environment and all these little hands in its faux-beach terrarium that it never came out of its shell. After some weeks went by, it poked out its little head, then a little more each day. Then one day—voilà!—it was out of its shell, walking around shell-less. The children were so excited, and one little girl reached in and grabbed it! In a panic, that crab wriggled free, darted back into its shell, and never came out again.

Funny as it might seem, I find this so apropos, in the sense that when teens manage to have the strength to put the shell aside and show what they're like without it, so often the world doesn't react in supportive, encouraging ways that nurture this stepping out. That is what we must do as frequently, as consistently, as possible at home and at school. The more a girl feels she is in a safe place to be herself, the more willing she'll be to step away from the facade; each time a little more confidently.

Remember the hairdresser's daughter, the girl who explained her plans for breast reduction surgery? She had found the courage to say what she needed, and at first her friends and peers were critical and laughed at her. Her family support allowed her to be strong enough to continue, and to openly suggest to her friends that there was more to this than what a boy thinks. She talked about the dents in her shoulders from the bra, and the pain and numbness going down her arms. She didn't talk to her friends about what it's like to have boys stare at your chest. If a girl has enough safe space or enough encouragement on the home front, or in some other sector, it allows her to extend her stance with her peers. Maybe not completely, but enough so that she can grow from it. In this instance, her girlfriends were now changed by this experience. When a girl is as pretty as she is, as together and well-liked as she is, and is able to go against the grain, it changes all the people around her at least a little bit, and it helps to widen what is acceptable for all girls.

But girls can't go against the societal grain on everything. It is just too heavy a load, even for an adult. So we can't just say, "Be independent and stand up for what you believe in." We need to have conversations about making choices and deciding which of so many things we are willing to swim upstream to get, to make a point, to be independent.

Sex: The Scariest-Ever Three-Letter Word

For many of us, when we were teenagers, sex was a hidden, sometimes even secondary, agenda in a teenage girl's life. Today, sex is right out front, in their face, so to speak, and exerting its influence in every facet of their lives. With virtually no societal limits on adolescent sexual behavior these days, the question to do it, or not to do it, is immediate, especially for teenage girls.

Every girl, regardless of her own sexual awareness, has to deal with the fact that boys her age are primed by nature (and, now, by culture) to assume girls are, or want to be, completely sexually active. Every girl has to deal with that reality, the sexual culture and its consequences, whether she likes it or not. Sex is, without a doubt, a key crucible event of adolescence. How it is handled shapes and molds a girl's reputation, social niche, view of intimacy, and style of handling relationships in life. From a social psychology, sociologic, or Darwinian perspective, a female's sexual behavior sets the foundation for how her life will evolve.

If that idea makes you uncomfortable, scares you, or pushes some other defensive button in your psyche, you've got a lot of company. The bad news is that as long as those feelings define your thinking, you're not going to be much help to your daughter. The good news is that there is also unprecedented openness in talking about sex. Just tune in to any talk show and that will be confirmed! So the door is open to communicate with your daughter about this topic, to share your views, listen to hers, discuss the pressures, the costs, and the long-term versus the short-term effects.

However, if you invest all your energy in taking a stand against teenage sex, you may undermine your goals. You can make your point that you value abstinence during these teen years without closing the door on discussions of what life is like for her and how she feels and what her moral code is becoming. Investing your energy in creating a relationship with your daughter in which sexuality is a comfortable topic of conversation will ensure your continued participation in her thought processes, and your influence will be much more powerful.

For my generation, "it" happened in college. Now "it" is a fact of life for high schoolers. Whenever I have the chance to talk with groups of high school girls, one of the questions I ask them is, "What percentage of girls in your school do you believe are virgins when they graduate?"

I asked Suzanne, an eleventh-grader, that question.

"Ten percent," she said.

"You're sure?" I said.

"Well," she paused, "it could be less."

Her answer is not unusual. I hear it consistently across the country; the percentage hovers at around 10 percent. Now, obviously, this is not a scientific study, but it is a rather large anecdotal sampling of what teen girls believe to be true. And what girls believe to be true influences their decision-making, attitudes, and behaviors.

The world is a phenomenological place. Everything is in the eyes of the perceiver. If you perceive you have worms on you, you're going to act on it. If you perceive that 90 percent of the girls in your graduating class are not virgins, then that will change your behavior. That perception can lead to reality. The more you go with the flow, the more you act on it. Most troubling, that perception of casual, all-the-way sex as the norm is first generated by the media and by the fashion industry, then it is accepted as fact by boys and girls, and then they act that way, making it a reality. As destructive cycles go, that's as vicious as it gets.

Everything that was part of sexual exploration and adventure in college when we were that age has been expanded and moved down a level to high school. Casual sex, birth control, monogamy, bisexuality; all of it happens in high school now.

All high school girls feel an incredible pressure to deal with sexual issues. All high school girls are struggling with boys who also feel the social pressure to have sex, and the physiological urge to follow through on it. In the tween chapter, we talked about the pressure to have oral sex, which is not considered "real sex" by many tween girls, and by some teen girls, as well. Sometime during the teen years, early or late, depending on such factors as peer group, dating, parental parameters, etc., girls are faced with whether to have sex or not. For some girls, it is a natural progression of their strong feelings for a particular boy. But for many teen girls, it is the extension of the dating scene and the expectations of being with a boy for more than a few dates. In some ways, it is the pressure experienced in middle school to dress alike and talk alike and follow the group, only now ratcheted up several notches into the sexual world.

When girls can talk openly about this topic, they vividly express their physical and emotional dilemma. Teen and mainstream media scream to girls that having sex is fun, expected, and cool. One memorable TV news feature report on the growing hypersexuality in music videos reported that many well-known singers and music groups were hiring people from the X-rated movie industry to star in and/or produce their new music videos. Certain body parts were fuzzed out on the TV screen, but the overall effect was just as clearly sexual. As the norm moves farther and farther out on the sexual continuum, it moves farther from what is maturationally healthy for a teen.

In the brain development section of this chapter, I purposely didn't mention the frontal lobes. The frontal lobes are the seat of judgment. The corpus callosum may kick in big time during the teen years, but the frontal lobes are still in their gangly, not fully matured state. Combine immature frontal lobes with hormones that affect body sensations; hormones and social pressure say yes, and the frontal lobes are not strong enough to resist or wise enough to argue.

So the body is sending yes signals and the culture is sending yes signals. It means that we—parents, teachers, and other caring adults—have to do our best to balance the teeter-totter for teens as they face these decisions. Most schools certainly cover the reproductive facts with a sex education curriculum. Almost all teens know about sexually transmitted diseases, types of birth control, and many other facts of sexual life. But information dissemination is not the same as candid conversation in which girls can talk openly about the sexual pressures and expectations that are consistent parts of their lives.

It's up to us to create a comfort zone for conversation. It's a good time to watch a TV program together like the one about music videos and to talk about how that affects the world. Or to watch MTV together, even if it makes your daughter squirm, so you can share what you think, and ask her what she thinks. The trick is to keep the conversation going and share your values, but also let her know that you understand that her decisions aren't simple. This is also a more positive approach than jumping right in and saying that sex is bad and you should never do it. Girls who feel they have strong support at home and who have had many conversations about life and sex seem to be more resilient when faced with the pressures of their world. The other point that seems to be agreed upon by most professionals in the field is that family rules and expectations do help girls stave off societal pressures.

Measuring Up: The Never-Ending Story Girls Can Rewrite

Remember the comment from Nora, the high school senior whose quote appeared at the opening of Chapter 1?

"It's pretty hard being a girl nowadays. You can't be too smart, too dumb, too pretty, too ugly, too friendly, too coy, too aggressive, too defenseless, too individual, or too programmed. If you're too much of anything, then others envy you, or despise you because you intimidate them or make them jealous. It's like you have to be everything and nothing all at once, without knowing which you need more of."

Nora was a particularly articulate high school senior, but the environment she described—the constant pressure a girl feels to shape her self to meet others' expectations—is what every teen girl lives and breathes. In a sense, the gray has lifted in terms of her seeing the world with decent clarity. However, the gray remains in terms of the path or the fine line that she will walk.

Measure up: It's a message, an order, an expectation, that pounds at girls from the outside and from the inside, from their parents, from their peers, from the media, and from their own inner voice. There is no arena where the voice is absent: SATs, sports, class rankings, friends (who has the most?), boyfriends (who has the coolest?). Competition, real or perceived, permeates the lives of girls today, and it absolutely can distort our own view of girls, our responses to them, and the goals and expectations we communicate to them. Some of this, strangely enough, relates to freedom. There are two aspects of freedom: freedom *to,* and freedom *from.*

Freedom *from,* in this case, is the freedom from obstacles, such as gender bias about girls becoming doctors or bankers or entrepreneurs, or freedom from perceptions that girls cannot be world-class athletes.

Freedom *to,* in this instance, is about the freedom girls have now to do whatever they want. Freedom from leads to freedom to, and that is where girls are right now, historically and individually. Girls are free from most restraints and constraints, and are free to choose and do just about anything.

The underbelly of freedom is increased expectations of what a girl will or should do, now that obstacles are eliminated or greatly diminished, and now that most doors are open. Girls should achieve, compete, succeed. Like freedom, "should" has two edges: logical and moral. The logical *should* is data-based and makes sense. The moral *should* is emotionally and morally based. In concrete terms: If you are about to cross the street and a car is coming quickly, the data tells you that you shouldn't cross. This is a rational should. If, however, you want to stage a protest, and stopping traffic in a dramatic (and dangerous) way is part of it, then stepping out in front of a car would be a moral should.

And so it is with competition and measuring up. The prevailing view is that opportunities are there, and girls should take advantage of them. Some see this as a logical imperative; some see it as a moral imperative. Most people see it as both. The possible paths for girls have increased exponentially since their parents were the same age. Girls are expected to measure up, to do well in the academic scene, the sports scene, the social scene, and whatever other scene is in vogue. In this light, the prevailing view is that the dependent, passive girl should become extinct. A recent TV commercial showing a young woman in a business suit cooking dinner, running the vacuum, and answering her cell phone captured perfectly the tone of contemporary expectations for females, and girls are taking that media image to heart.

Competition, and the need to be able to handle it and play the game, so to speak, seems to just be an accepted wisdom of the day. There is no doubt that competition and measuring up as successfully and as high as possible is the accepted standard. The issue is that some of us are shorter than others! By the very nature of being a species with great diversity, the ability and even the drive or need to compete is very dependent on the individual. So I would change the accepted wisdom of the day that says all girls need to learn how to compete. I would adjust the words to:

> All girls need to learn that a large part of the world has many competitive components.
> All girls need to learn that there will be incredible pressure on them to be competitive.
> All girls need to be equipped to handle a world that is highly competitive.
> But, all girls do not need to be highly competitive, or spend their lives trying to be something they are not.

As the adults in the lives of girls, we need to be brave enough to say that they have the freedom to opt out of some or all of the drive and pressure to compete; that they don't have to measure up in the way that is hierarchical, that literally means "I am better than you." There's a way to do well, to achieve, without it being a comparative and competitive thing. The term *measure up* means comparing yourself and your achievement to others.

I prefer the concept from the sports world of "personal best." By aiming for your personal best, you compete only against yourself, and the standard is improvement. However, for girls, even pushing the concept of personal best too hard is potentially damaging. Satisfaction and peace can never be achieved if you are always striving to be better. And then you are right back to measuring up, either gauging it against your previous achievement or comparing where this personal best fits in relation to others' personal bests.

I've made the case before that girls are predisposed to please, to fit in, to connect with the world. Being better than others—aiming for it, even just thinking it—feels uncomfortable or wrong to some girls. It goes against the grain of their life view. The push to measure up can make some girls feel like failures, even when they have great attributes. Or it can make some girls sick, because they never feel successful in a driven world. On the other hand, there are those girls who are interested and motivated to achieve and win and be the best. The whole range is represented by femaledom. And the whole range needs to be allowed and accepted.

Several of the girls I've known through the years come to mind in representing this continuum. There is no single kind of girl behind a competitive drive.

I was asked to work with Shawna, a brilliant junior who had abysmal grades but had just received perfect scores on her SATs. The gap between her ability and her performance was making her parents and teachers crazy. When I pointed this out to Shawna, her first response to me was, "I care about learning, not letter grades. Grades in most classes reflect nothing but being able to jump through the hoops the teachers set up. Ask me anything about any subject I've taken, and I'll be able to answer it."

After many conversations, it was clear that this deep thinker was really railing against the world's pressure to achieve, visibly and as prescribed by her milieu. She wasn't driven to compete; she had a passion for learning, and the competition and what she considered meaningless work to get grades got in the way of her passion. It took a long time for us to reach the point at which she could see where her passion for learning could lead her in life, and how "playing the grade game," as she put it, would keep those doors open for her—doors she was now slamming resoundingly. But her point was important; she was telling the world that competing, as defined by getting the best grades, was not important to everyone and that her motivation needed to be respected and not just put down.

On the other end of the continuum was Linda. She never went to bed before midnight because she spent so many hours on her homework. She studied diligently for tests and had a straight-A average. Linda also played very competitive tennis. When she got an A-minus or lost a set, Linda didn't cry; she just worked harder and longer. The typical end result would be that she crashed and burned, but not so. Linda had been given the physiological gift of having great energy and a very resilient temperament. She loved working hard, playing hard, and winning. Her mental health was excellent, and she was thriving on her busy and demanding schedule. Often, though, her parents, teachers, and friends worried about her and felt that this kind of "obsession to achieve" (her teacher's words) was unhealthy.

As my mother used to say, "You can't win for losing!" Shawna wasn't competitive or driven enough; Linda was too competitive and too driven. So is health and well-being somewhere in the middle? Should we put Shawna and Linda in a bag and shake it so they blend and even each other out? No! The word *individual* literally means that each person is different and on these continua of competition and drive, girls will stand on every inch of it and not just on one end or the other or in the middle.

Sally is probably smack in the middle of the continuum, midway between Linda and Shawna. In some ways, being in the middle is harder than being on either extreme of the need to measure up. Sally was a decent athlete who, with a lot of work and practice, made the team. Her grades depended on the subject. She loved science and did well in it. She thought her English teacher was great, and she did well there, too. But both French and math seemed insurmountable to her. Her teachers and parents saw that hard work and motivation led her to succeed quite well in many areas, so why not all areas? And Sally, too, felt she should be good in everything, but she also felt herself getting into a catch-22: In order to really measure up, she had to pour on the energy, hours, and hard work *all the time*. It felt as if she had no life after sports, school, and lessons. The days started to feel like a treadmill: Get up, go to school, concentrate all day, go to basketball practice on weekdays (and to her class at the art museum on weekends), do homework, go to bed, get up . . . and the treadmill started all over. The need to measure up and be good at everything was incredibly wearing, and over time, Sally suffered, and her performance did, too.

We hear about the growing incidence of depression in teens. Wouldn't you be depressed if you knew that every day, without exception, you'd be placed on a treadmill, and each day you'd be expected to do better than the day before, or at least never worse?

Perhaps the most difficult part of this for parents is knowing where a girl is on this continuum and knowing whether to tamper with that in any way. As significant adults in her life, we have a responsibility to help her to be healthy and thriving. There are no magical diagnostic tests. But there is always the direct route: ask and discuss.

This is about negotiating the gray, so let's freshen up those skills for use in the adolescent realm:

- Have a discussion about the drive and interest for competition of the world in general. Take your time!
- Talk about individual differences and how they kind of line up on a continuum. You can even draw a continuum.
- Ask honestly and interestedly where she thinks she is on the continuum of drive to succeed or measure up or compete.
- Talk about the pros and cons of where she is on the continuum and how significant others and society seem to feel about her position.
- Discuss whether she needs or wants to change, and whether you should help her to change her position on the continuum (becoming more aggressive, less aggressive, etc.).
- Sometimes it can be elucidating for her to ask others who know her to place her where they think she is on the continuum and to discuss the discrepancies between her own analysis of herself and others' views of her. This takes maturity and courage to do.
- If you dare, and she allows it, describe where you'd like her to be on the continuum and discuss why. Be careful, though, about making your unfinished emotional business your daughter's burden. Beware of the enmeshment trap! Focus on her hopes and dreams, and what she needs to make progress in her own life direction.

These discussions and reflections can begin the continuing conversation and exploration of coping with a world that values and sometimes demands competition. And, just by the nature of the conversations, a girl can begin to see and accept a range of competitiveness in herself and in others and know that there is not just one standard.

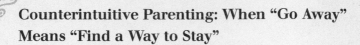

Counterintuitive Parenting: When "Go Away" Means "Find a Way to Stay"

To negotiate the tricky transfer of power, enabling your daughter to grow into a healthy independence, you have to come to terms with the adolescent's need to push and pull away from adults. In the early teens, a girl walks away, figuratively speaking, from her family. In the late teen years, she begins to take some steps away from her friends, too, to find out who she is, all the while clutching them ferociously. If you've ever been torn between holding on and letting go of something or someone—even just the high-dive your first time up—then you have a sense of the internal tug-of-war that goes on all the time in the heart of an older teenage girl.

If you can embrace this change as a healthy sign, instead of a stop sign, you'll be less insulted and more open to new ways to forge connections that respect your daughter's blossoming autonomy. It's natural to feel shut down or sidelined by this normal distancing that takes place as she sets about finding herself, discovering and creating the distinctively individual self she wants to be.

This "leave me alone, but don't leave me alone" tug-of-war happens so frequently with adolescent girls that it is a dizzying experience. Susan had had a fight with her mother about curfew time, which resulted in her canceling a date with a boy rather than tell him she had to be home by midnight. After the cancellation phone call, she slammed her bedroom door and told her parents to just leave her alone, they had ruined her life. Her mother would periodically ask if she wanted to talk, and a resounding "NO!" emanated from her daughter's room. Finally, she quietly opened the door and sat next to Susan, who immediately tried to push her away. But this mother held on, and gradually Susan's pushing turned to holding and sobbing. In the end, Susan told her mother that she actually was afraid to go out with this boy because he was "wild," but that she was old enough and trustworthy enough to stay out later. Instead of arguing about curfews, they ended up talking about how to handle aggressive dates. I doubt this conversation would have happened if Susan's mother had steered clear during this vulnerable crying time. By the next morning, Susan's anger or pride would have prevented her from having this conversation.

One book calls adolescence our "last best shot" at influencing our child's development, suggesting that if we screw up this last shot (and since we are human, we are bound to screw up some way or another!), there are no more chances. I don't believe this is true—I know so many young adults who still look to their parents for wisdom—but I do believe that it is easy to be scared off from an angry teenage girl, and to pass up critical moments in which we could strengthen our relationship with her, if only we understood her need.

Adolescence is not a parent's last best shot. It is merely a continuation of the strudel layering. Admittedly, the texture and flavor of our strudel are fairly well set with layering that's been done up to now, and it can be pretty tricky to add completely new ingredients, or change other aspects of the recipe, but in no way does this mean your layering days are over.

Whatever else anyone tells you, I want you to know that, as a parent, you are never finished. I also want you to know that, despite appearances to the contrary, your adolescent daughter needs, and even wants, your involvement and input, even though you may have to do it as gently as if you were walking on eggs. Although you may feel otherwise, you and your experience and insights are of value to her now and forever.

It was easier when we were teens, because the world wasn't in hyperdrive. My father was an owner in his business, and he made a point to work only until five o'clock, Monday through Friday. My brother and I had after-school activities, but none of them lasted past five o'clock. And my mother may have been doing a myriad of things during the day, but she was cooking dinner by 4:59 P.M. So our family time evolved naturally to be around dinner. We were all there, as were most families together for dinner during those years.

In hindsight, and, I think, unpremeditated by my parents, the core building part was the conversation. During and after dinner, we shared our stories of the day. We listened as my father talked about his plans for his company, or my mother weighed whether she should get a part-time job to help pay for the cabin in Canada that she and my father dreamed about. It wasn't all roses. We also talked about why I got a C in conduct, and why my brother spent so much money on gas when his activities were so close to home (we later found out that he had a crush on a girl who lived a good distance from us, and he spent a lot of time riding past her house). It was normal stuff, but it allowed us to get beyond the facade of our everyday lives and connect with our parents. It subtly layered that experience into our lives, and, for my brother and me, became part of our respective cores. To this day, it bothers me if someone jumps up after dinner to start doing the dishes or to pick up the phone. I still like to sit at the table after dinner and talk.

Back then, there were fewer obstacles to spending time together at meals. One of the hardest challenges in parenting teens today is to have enough time with them and enough conversation that occurs at noncrisis moments. Our lives are so full and active and rushed, that sometimes conversations are limited to the moment. If I could wave my magic wand, I would slow down the life of a teen girl to give her time to think, to be, to be heard, and to hear. That would really help her find her own solid, resistant, and resilient core.

Some families handle this by saying that a certain day or time is sacrosanct for the family, like Sunday morning leisurely breakfasts, or the first two weeks in August for a family vacation. One family I know keeps one of their computers in the central hangout room in the house. It is outfitted with all the "popular" games and a connection to the Internet. In this way, the teen daughters who bring their friends over hang out in the midst of the family territory. It may sound corny, but doing things like inviting your daughter and her friends to help you make cookies or surprising them with your own version of a Big Mac will help you stay in her life and keep her grounded in family life.

In addition, girls who are active are often sturdier emotionally. Participating in sports, volunteering at the food pantry, taking advanced placement courses are all examples. Doing something that feels satisfying or has some challenge to it is the key. I'm not saying that a girl needs to do everything, or needs to be constantly busy, but fertilizing her motivation and interests to be active just enough is good for parents and schools to remember. This concept is so important that I've devoted an entire chapter to it—see Chapter 10, "Girls in Action: The Magic of Doing."

Every teen girl needs a special, trusted adult with whom she can talk, or even just simply be herself. Remember the green blanket story? Probably more than any other time in a girl's life, the teen years are when she needs that green blanket: someone with whom she can talk about her myriad of choices, her huge decisions about sexual issues, her dreams for the future. And, as I've said before, it is important that she have one green blanket, a trusted adult, and not just her best friend.

If you're very lucky, and you've been layering the communication strudel the last many years, it could be you. However, even if you've done everything just right, there is a good possibility that it won't be you during part or all of her teen years. One overriding bit of advice for all parents of a teen: Don't take it personally. But at the same time, don't let go. This is a critical time for holding on with everything you've got to family time, traditions, time together, more time together. In the midst of sports, overnights, academic demands, talking on the phone, and spending hours in chat rooms with friends, hold on to enough time to maintain and even strengthen your connection. To stay connected, you need to spend enough time with her that you continue to know who she is, continue to hear and see the bits of her life that keep you informed.

Pearls for Parents and Pearls for Girls

- Ask, listen, discuss, and decide together on as many issues as possible.
- Knee-jerk reactions kick back! Ask, listen, discuss, and decide together *especially* when you feel a knee-jerk reaction coming on.
- Shift the power. Gradually decrease even the discussion phase of decision-making so that your daughter develops confidence in her ability to think things out effectively on her own. By the time she's ready to leave the nest, the discussions you do have should be mostly reflective, hindsight discussions, after the fact.
- Ask if you can read her health book about sex and social diseases; you want to see what has changed since your school days.
- Ask her to read the part in this chapter about camouflage because you want her opinion on whether this is really an issue with girls her age.
- Use the news. News events, TV, and other popular media offer timely ways to bring up important subjects for general (i.e., indirect, noninvasive, non-threatening) discussions about topics like sex, achievement, goals, and other potential hot spots, so you have a basis for more direct conversation when that time comes.

CHAPTER 5

Mothers and Daughters:
Roots to Grow, Wings to Fly

"What I like most about my mother is that we have a relationship that is so close that it is as if she isn't only my mother, but my best friend, minus the boyfriend-stealing and backstabbing."

—Dina, eighth grade

"The older I get, the more I learn from my mother," says Hope, a friend of mine in her late fifties. Her mother has been dead for a number of years, but Hope's memories of her mother's wisdom, her foibles, the traits people admired about her, as well as her most-unpretty qualities, emerge in everyday moments that inform her in subtle and sometimes surprising ways.

"When I was a girl, it would drive me crazy when she would sit on the sofa and read a book as if there were no one else in the room, as if she were in another world and no one was looking for the folded laundry or waiting for her to make dinner," Hope says. "Now I'm amazed that she was able to pull that off, with a husband and three children who took for granted that she always made the meals and did the housework. I only have two children, and my husband pitches in on the housework, and still I have such a hard time putting myself first, even just for fifteen minutes to read something purely for pleasure. Now when I remember her sitting there so immersed in her book, refusing to be distracted, it's as if she's modeling a way of being for the older woman I am now, showing me that it's important, and she's showing me how it's done. She's teaching me something new that I couldn't have understood when I was young, but I'm ready to learn now."

It's hard to imagine this relationship of infinite inspiration evolving from two females who, like most mothers and daughters, at various times through those growing up years, found each other absolutely confounding, inscrutable, ignorant, insensitive, stubborn, maddening, and disappointing. Did I say bitchy and opinionated?

And this isn't to say that, despite it all, every mother and daughter share a relationship that ultimately feels like love. For some, that is not to be.

What is true for all is that the mother-daughter relationship is a unique environment in which a girl looks at what it means to be a female, with her mother as the first benchmark. What she learns from her, and how this relationship unfolds over time, shapes a girl in ways that aren't always clear early on. I'm always surprised, the older I get, how frequently my mother's words pop out of my mouth as if they were my own words. And, when I stop to think about it, they are, now, my own words. When I was younger, I may have thought of what my mother would have said, but now, sometimes, it has actually become me. The obverse is also true for some adult women. Their relationship with their mothers was so strained or their view of their mother's characteristics or behaviors was so negative, that they spend a lifetime trying to be the opposite. No matter where an adult woman falls on this continuum of becoming like her mother or consciously unlike her mother, the power of the influence of this person and this bond is lifelong.

It is almost impossible to talk with a girl or a woman for very long before some mention of her mother pops into the conversation. In a continuing informal survey that I hand out to girls and their parents in schools, at talks, and in my circle of friends and colleagues, the responses mirror the sometimes tender, sometimes trying condition of the mother-daughter connection.

From daughters:

"The thing I like most about my mom is how she likes to do a lot of the same things as me and I like that she is not that mean. If I could change one thing about my mom, I would change her personality a little, like make her be a little bit more fun, not so serious." (Age nine)

"I like my mother because she is always there and understands what I'm going through. She always encourages me in what I do and think." (Age fourteen)

"What I don't like about my mom is the fact that when my sister and I try to do something nice, as the lazy people we are, she'll try to find something wrong with what we do. It sort of bugs me. Also, sometimes she'll start yelling at us because I guess she's cranky. All I say in my head is, 'Don't sweat the small things.' " (Age eleven)

"If I could change one thing about my mom, it would be her tendency to get anxious at times, which I inherited from her." (Age fifteen)

"If I could change one thing about my mother, it would be that she would drink a little less at night, because sometimes she does not remember what happens after seven o'clock at night," an eighth-grade girl mentions in a write-in survey. "If we get into a fight, she will not remember it the next day. And I can't have friends over that often because it is embarrassing to have people see her like that." (Age fourteen)

"My mother and I have never been close. I always wished I had a mother like everyone else's mother—you know, the kind that loves you—but my mother was always very hateful toward me. Like some evil stepmother out of a fairy tale. When I was younger, I used to pray that she would die and I would get a stepmother who loved me. Then I just moved away." (Age thirty-seven)

"What do I love most about my mom? This one is easy. Her positive outlook on life. Her cup is always half full, if not full to the brim. The door/window is always half open. She's usually able to find something positive in every situation. I love her because she taught this to me, and that's how I survived my divorce." (Age forty-six)

And from mothers (Sorry—I didn't get the ages and wouldn't begin to guess!):

"My daughter is the light of my life."

"Hang on tight—it's a wild ride, but worth it. Your heart will break a thousand times when you see them go through all the hurtful things you went through growing up, share with them all that you have learned, share with them all that is better, all that they can do, and when the time is right, let them go. Wow, who knows where they'll end up, but you will always be their safe place."

"My daughter went off to Outward Bound at the age of fourteen. I gave her a necklace with a star, moon, and heart on it. She would be gone for her birthday, and on the box I wrote a note. I told her to 'reach for the stars and the moon, and remember that my heart will always be with you.' When she called from the Seattle airport at the end of her trip she said, 'Mom'; I said, 'Lindsay'; then we just both cried. She has never taken that necklace off."

"As a mother, I was very conscious of how many activities, expressions, behaviors I literally copied from my mother."

"My daughters? They are my heart."

"It is a steel link—an inexorable connection, which exists despite the most vehement denial. . . ."

"No matter what happens to you in life, you can always go home or call your mother and it will be okay."

"To be honest? I wish I'd stuck to raising parrots."

"Little girls like to cuddle, and hug, and snuggle up close . . . it's a feeling that as a mom lights an internal candle of joy."

"I have three daughters, and we just basically don't like each other, you know?"

"I love my daughter more than my own life, but I don't think she sees that. I don't think she can hear that. She is twenty-three now, and into some very self-destructive behaviors. She blames me for her problems—maybe because I can't just fix them like I could when she was little. To see her hurting herself hurts me deeply. It's beyond words."

"I can only tell you there's nothing like a daughter. . . . I can't pinpoint what makes a daughter-mother relationship so amazing, but I can look in their eyes and know what they're thinking. We finish each other's sentences, complete each other's breaths. My heart aches when they're sad or hurting, and bursts with joy when they're happy—and I know they feel the same way about me. They're my guidance counselors and my best friends."

Images of the mother-daughter relationship remind me of the fragments of colored glass in a kaleidoscope. Each one is different, and together they create a chaotic mix of colors. When you look through the lens of the kaleidoscope, however, the picture that emerges is full of patterns. In schools, in conversations with thousands of parents and girls across the country, and especially in programs designed specifically to bring mothers and daughters together, I've had the opportunity to watch a great many pairs of mothers and daughters interact. Despite all the ways that mothers and daughters are different, and all the ways that mother-daughter pairs are different, certain qualities of connection create patterns in mother-daughter interactions, for better or for worse. The strongest, sturdiest, and most satisfying relationships are those I describe as synergistic. The most difficult, and sometimes seriously troubled, relationships are those in which the connection has been either damaged or broken, creating an experience of disconnection; or, at the other extreme, those in which the connection is overpowering, and permeates most waking moments.

Like most characteristics relating to humans, the texture and type of mother-daughter relationships are really on a sliding scale or continuum. There are not really separate and discrete categories, only variations on the theme of connectedness: too connected, not connected, or an interactive and somewhat balanced connection.

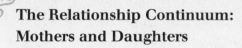 The Relationship Continuum: Mothers and Daughters

Disconnection	Synergy	Enmeshment

Most of us can look at that continuum and honestly say that our girls and we would seem to fit in each of these categories at one time or another—sometimes all in the same day! Whether your relationship seems fluid, or more fixed, if you can find your place on the continuum, then you can have a better understanding of how your relationship *is*. From that *is,* you can go on to deeper thoughts of why, and if there are reasons or times to try to change your place on the continuum. Relationships that can stay as much in the middle as possible are the healthiest, since both partners give and take, in relation to what the other needs or wants.

The Synergistic Mother-Daughter Relationship

The synergistic relationship is that give-and-take and balanced interaction. It can happen naturally when a mother and daughter have the kind of temperaments and personalities that are enough alike that there is an instinctive understanding of each other's patterns of thoughts or emotions. It can also be cultivated when a mother sets the pace and practice early on to listen, to try to understand her daughter, even when it is not easy, and intentionally thinks about her reactions in terms of trying to develop this kind of relationship. Keep in mind that understanding and agreeing are two different things!

The naturally synergistic mother and daughter are easy to spot. Often there are enough physical or psychological characteristics of each member of the pair to facilitate such synergism. I know a mother and daughter who move their lips in the same way when they are puzzled. I find it amusing when the daughter looks at her mother and says, "Oh, no, she's thinking about something," referring to her mother's mouth movements. The daughter is totally oblivious to the fact that *she* did the same thing a moment later. This is also the girl who prefaces many of her conversations with her mother with statements like, "I know what you're going to say, but . . ."

The intentional synergistic mother-daughter relationship is harder to spot, depending on how long it has been going on; how old the daughter is. If the daughter is at least of conversational age, you can usually tell by some of the words used in the conversations between the two.

One day I brought a mother and her eighth-grade daughter together in my office at school to discuss a math situation. The mother started the conversation, saying to her daughter, "I know you don't think I understand that you think math is hard, because you know I'm good at it." She went on to say that she did have some understanding because she had experienced difficulty doing other things. The daughter's comeback was, "Yes, but you're so driven to succeed that I'm sure you were able to get past the difficulty." Her mother's response was, "I know we're different in that way, but if we talk about it, maybe together we can figure out how to tackle this problem." A conversation like this always signals to me that both recognize they are quite different, but both want to stay engaged and understand each other and work together.

Whether natural or intentional, the synergistic relationship is one of the kinds of interconnection that stays, well, connected over time. There's some great song about the power of two, implying that two people connected are geometrically more powerful than one plus one. Teachers know this from life in the classroom, when they watch two students working together on a project. Like the story of the blind men and the elephant: If each person focuses on a slightly different part of the elephant, and if they compare and combine their perceptions, they will both see the whole elephant sooner. Between even the closest mother and daughter, there can be, and often are, disagreements. However, when you continue to interact, and discuss or work through those disagreements, again, the end product is more powerful and complex. It's only when the duo lets go and drifts to the disconnect side of the continuum, or one member becomes so entangled with the other's identity that this power of two loses its geometric effect.

Obstacles to Synergy: When Connection Needs Fine-Tuning

Very few of us find ourselves smack in the middle of that continuum, with the ideal synergistic relationship. If you do, don't get smug: It'll change by tomorrow. Most of us find our challenges somewhere to the left or to the right, arising from three key pieces of the mother-daughter picture: history, identity, and personality.

First, there is the unavoidable generation gap in experience between a woman with a past and a girl completely grounded in the present tense. I call this "coming from a different world." Second is identity, and the way a mother's and daughter's identities naturally commingle in the early years, but this can become too close for comfort. When you are too enmeshed, you have difficulty drawing the distinction between your feelings and those of your daughter, your life priorities and expectations and her own, your reaction to events and hers. A girl who is overly enmeshed often has difficulty separating from her mother for any length of time, can become school-phobic, and prefers spending time doing things with her mother at the cost of spending time with peers. This is certainly natural during the formative years, but should diminish quickly as time in school increases.

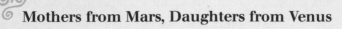

Mothers from Mars, Daughters from Venus

Coming from a different world is one of the underlying themes of this book. It would seem that, as females, we have so much shared physiology and development that this would not be so. But the rapidity of change in the past few decades has made it so. I remember when I was visiting my grandparents and my period had surprisingly begun. I wasn't very experienced yet; this was only a few months into this monthly happening. I knew not to say anything to my grandmother. She would never talk about such intimate issues. My mother wasn't there, but I knew from her not very effective explanation of menarche that at least her generation talked about it a bit. So I felt safe, albeit a bit embarrassed, to ask my aunt Betty (my mom's older sister) for supplies. Aunt Betty silently handed me an old (but clean) T-shirt and a pair of scissors. After sitting in the bathroom pondering this for some time, I realized I was meant to create my own pad!

Today, many mothers and daughters talk openly about personal hygiene supplies and often share them. In moments like this, we can see the positive change in the cultures of different generations of females. We can also see the bit of a lag between generations handling the modern culture. Now that cultural changes are happening at a much faster clip, it isn't just a matter for mothers of changing or adjusting; it's also one of even understanding the milieu and cultures that girls face. It is a fine line for mothers between connecting by sharing stories and feelings about being a girl yourself, and not having your experiences appear so dramatically different that you underscore your daughter's belief that you couldn't possibly understand her life.

As we saw in Chapter 1's story of the bikini swimsuit shopping fiasco, there are times when hearkening back to younger days, when you were her age, only digs that generation gap a little deeper!

This quandary brings squarely to the fore the need for mothers to do both: to share stories like that of the T-shirt and scissors, and then to ask, and listen to, what life is like for your daughter today. It really needs to be a partnership in this era of complexity and lack of clear moral and social parameters.

I was talking to a fifteen-year-old student and her mother in my office one day about parties, and the mother was saying that she'd made an ironclad rule that adults needed to be present at *all* parties her daughter attended. I turned to her daughter, who was trying desperately to be cool and fit in at this new school (which was why both had joined me for this chat), and said, "Well, aren't rave parties *the* place to be, and if you don't go to at least some, there are some social prices to pay?"

Before she could answer, her mother said, "Of course she can go to rave parties!"

Her daughter just looked at me and rolled her eyes, signaling that her mother hadn't a clue what a rave party was, the major definition being that it had to be in a place where there were *no adults* in the vicinity. She hadn't even bothered to ask to go because she knew the rule. Her mother, on the other hand, was seriously worried about her daughter's social fit, since she was not going to all the parties that other girls in her class talked so excitedly about during carpooling. The real issue here was that her mother didn't even know what a rave party was, so she couldn't have a meaningful conversation with her daughter about whether to bend the parents-must-be-present rule in some accommodation to her daughter's present social isolation. Before they could have a productive discussion about the social issues this girl was facing, and whether it was prudent to bend the family rules to attend an unsupervised party, her mother needed to understand the teen party landscape. These are the kinds of conversations that need to happen.

Beyond Empathy:
When Enmeshment Gets Sticky

Deep connection can also lead to issues of enmeshment, control, and anxious parenting. I was struck by so many of the girls' responses to the parenting question in the survey. I had asked them about mothers and fathers. In a very high percentage of cases, the girls talked about their fathers' senses of humor and how that helped them cope with life, and also helped keep the father-daughter relationship healthy. When asked what they would change about their mothers, a high percentage talked about such things as nagging less, worrying less, and a mother's habit of focusing on every little mistake.

One of the hardest things for a mother to do is to resist seeing her own life—her hopes, dreams, fears, and expectations—in her daughter's life. That requires that, even as we forge lasting connections, we establish enough separation and objectivity to see a daughter do things and make decisions, and respect that this is *her* moment, *her* life, and *her* feelings. Or as one girl put it, popping off at her mother: "This is not about you!"

I felt this very tug one day as I listened to a seventh-grade girl who is part of my extended family. She had been suffering lately because of some social issues. One of the few girls she trusted and thought was a friend had suddenly stopped talking to her and had begun to hang with the trendy group. I had this *vivid* flashback of seventh grade. Donna, a member of the popular crowd in my school, saw me talking to a boy she liked. The next day at school she told the other girls not to talk to me. Donna could be quite nasty, and none of the other girls wanted to tangle with her, so they went along with it. I won't ever forget that day, or the forty hours it seemed to last as I went to class by myself, ate lunch by myself, and tried to walk down the hall looking happy when I felt miserable and alone. And that was just one day! Now, forty years later, I wanted to jump in and save this sweetheart of a girl from that hurt. It was a double whammy: I loved her and hated to see and feel her pain, and I was reliving the experience and feeling that sickening pain myself.

In brain science terms, my limbic system was on fire, and yes, some of it was a female thing and some of it was a connection thing and some of it was a memory thing. There is no mystery as to why the mother-daughter relationship is so deep and complex. It really just *is*. This seems to be the case for both biological or adoptive mother-daughter pairs. The connection is strong from day one. It also changes as the years go by.

A new mother wrote to me: "When I am able to pick up Jessica to comfort her tearful cries, I feel an amazing force of strength that I am the one who can make the pain go away. I don't know what her future holds, but I am excited to be alongside her for the journey."

As the years sneak by, most mothers have to make a conscious effort to disengage themselves in obvious, important ways—freeing daughters to explore, discover, make some mistakes, and learn some lessons the hard way. But every mother knows that the bigger job is on the *inside*, freeing a daughter to dream her own dreams, own her own feelings, and express her own self—in short, live her own life.

Enmeshment is such a natural occurrence for many mothers and daughters. Yes, times were different in our growing up years, and maybe even our personalities are different. But there are also so many overlaps. We know what social pain is all about, we know how hard it is to live up to the world's perception of beauty, we know how our monthly cycles affect us. How can we not relate to the developmental ups and downs of the younger version of ourselves? Even the oil-and-water oppositional duos experience enmeshment issues. In some instances, this might even be at the core of the adversity.

I invited one mother to come talk with me about her second-grade daughter's issues with spelling and reading. Her daughter had begun crying hysterically when she missed two words on a spelling test, and sobbed to the teacher that her mother was going to kill her. In our conversation, Mom began crying as she recounted having trouble in school and being teased by the other kids because they thought she was stupid. This very successful architect, who had walked in so poised and confident, was now a wreck, reliving her early school days and living in her daughter's struggles. Her pushy and critical responses to her daughter were really about enmeshment and caring.

Nancy, the mother of a fourth-grade girl, helped her daughter organize a mother-daughter book club for some friends in the neighborhood. The girls loved to get together to read, and the discussions were always lively, full of just the kind of surprising insights that fourth-grade girls can generate. The only snag, Nancy said, was the mothers themselves.

"I thought the challenge would be to keep a book discussion going among the girls, when they can be so self-conscious about speaking up. But they had no problem with the book discussion. The hard part was keeping the mothers from taking over the discussion by correcting the girls, interrupting them, or getting heavy-handed trying to lead the discussion to the moral of the story they wanted to pound in. Some of them just couldn't let their daughters express a thought without jumping in to 'clean it up' or react to it in some way. Once I heard that, and became sensitive to it, I realized how much I do it in everyday conversation in our home, and I started trying harder to just shut up and listen."

Temperament, Personality, and Compatibility

Mothers and daughters are like riders on a bicycle built for two. No matter how different mother and daughter are, as long as they can pedal in a rhythm that works, they'll make forward progress. However, the moment either one falls off the pace, or stops pedaling, the whole contraption feels like one clumsy hunk of scrap metal. One of the things that has been helpful in my work with mothers and daughters has been to identify where they stand in terms of their personalities and relationship on the continuum, so they can get a better idea of how to accommodate their differences and keep their relationship on the road and moving forward.

History, personality, and temperament of the mother and daughter play a large role in how that relationship is characterized from its very beginning, how it evolves, and often how it plays out throughout life. Experience gets layered in along the way, sometimes bridging gaps in the relationship, sometimes creating or deepening them.

Temperament is somewhat genetic, is recognizable almost from birth, and is very resistant to change. This may be due to the fact that it is related to energy level, cognitive style, and sensitivity of the neurological and emotional systems. Simply put, temperaments vary along a positive/negative continuum. Some temperaments and cognitive styles are characterized as critical. This is the classic case of seeing the glass as half empty. The other end of the continuum is the glass-half-full type. When we are tired or sick or worried, we often get pushed to the extreme of the half-empty side. But the best way to analyze personality is on a typical day with a standard task—homework, cooking, shopping, discussing plans for the weekend or an upcoming event.

Jamie was nine years old, in fourth grade, when her mother, Helen, called me one day, concerned because Jamie seemed "more brittle lately" than was typical. Jamie was every teacher's dream—a versatile and enthusiastic learner, good-humored, and very well organized—and no one at school had noticed anything very different in her recent behavior. But at home in the mornings was another story, Helen said. Jamie seemed preoccupied and irritable, and angered quickly if things didn't go just so. This was especially hard on Helen because her older two children's schedules had become more demanding now that they were enrolled in before-school band and chorus classes. If anything, Jamie should be in better spirits, Helen said, because she no longer had to ride the bus, which she had always disliked. Since Helen had to be out anyway, driving the older children to school, she was able to drive Jamie now, too. Helen was mystified and exasperated by Jamie's change in behavior. She wondered if Jamie were having trouble in school, with her teacher, with her friends, with teasing, perhaps? It seemed clear that something was bothering her daughter about school, and Helen was determined to find out what it was.

"It's hard enough to get everybody fed and out of the house in the morning, without Jamie storming around in a snit over every little thing," Helen said.

A conversation I had with Jamie solved the mystery in short order. Several times a week, when Helen drove the children to school, if they were running a little behind schedule, Jamie's brother and sister were dropped off first, so they wouldn't be late. However, this meant that Jamie arrived at school a few minutes late. Jamie's teacher understood, and did not consider this a problem. Helen felt she was doing the best she could, and she always assured Jamie, upon arriving late, that it was okay, and not to worry about it. But Jamie didn't share her mother's pragmatic give-or-take-five-minutes approach to time.

"It makes me mad to be late," Jamie said. "I'm not in kindergarten anymore! It's really embarrassing to walk in when everybody's already sitting down. And it means I never get a turn to take the attendance report down to the office." Further, she said, "It's not fair, because I get ready early so we won't be late, but they still make us late."

Jamie took school seriously, wanted to be on time, and was doing all she could to make it possible to get to school on time. To her, her mother's assurances that "it didn't matter" were not only empty, they were insulting. Once the problem was out on the table, Helen and Jamie could problem-solve together. Helen thought Jamie needed to be more flexible, but Jamie also made a convincing case: A big focus at school was learning to be responsible, and Jamie felt that arriving at school on time was part of that. Why would we want to talk her out of that? In the end, Jamie decided that she'd rather go back to taking the bus routinely, and get to school on time, than take the ride and never know if she would be late to school. Jamie's temperament was such that she needed the structure and stability of the bus routine; it gave her a calm, predictable start to her day, and by being on time, she felt better about herself as a responsible student.

I'm reminded of one of my favorite jokes—the one in which

some researchers studying personality differences in twins gave twin six-year-old sisters the same task, to clean out a barn full to the rafters with old hay and horse manure. The first twin worked for a little while, then, bored, grumpy, and tired, put down her shovel and quit. Her sister kept digging, however, and hours later was still going at it energetically, though she had hardly made a dent in the mountain of muck before her. Finally, the researchers couldn't contain their curiosity any further. "Your sister quit hours ago! Why do you keep working so hard like this, when you could quit, too?" they asked. The little girl, barely pausing, beamed and said eagerly: "With all that muck, there's got to be a pony somewhere!"

Some people are just born seeing possibility where others see problems. As brain research gets clearer, I'm sure we're going to see that part of this is related to how the brain is wired and what perspective our cortex uses in perception of data. So, in the mother-daughter pair, I am convinced, one or both members can have critical, analytical, perspectives. The word *critical,* in and of itself, is not negative; it is how one sees the world. However, in the case of a relationship, a critical perspective of the mother and/or daughter can set up this duo for a great deal of negativity.

Once you can see patterns in your own personality and preferences, and you can see the patterns that define your daughter, you are in a better position to see why your mother-daughter interactions may be smooth or stilted or argumentative, why things are the way they are, and which pieces need some work if you want to create a stronger, more synergistic relationship.

Knock, Knock: Who's There?

Personality style is much more complex than temperament, although they are related. There is a combination of elements that meld together to make up personality, and each can change somewhat with time and experience. Take the extrovert/introvert characteristic, for instance. Are you (or your daughter) an extrovert; someone who typically initiates social contact; is expressive, perhaps gregarious, enthusiastic, and tends to be a participant in the action? Or do you (or your daughter) tend to be more of an introvert; low-key in social situations; perhaps more private or harder to know; preferring one-on-one interactions, rather than groups, reflective and inclined to enjoy solitude?

There are many views of the characteristics that blend together to form a personality. The Meyers-Briggs Personality Inventory provides one of the best-known standard descriptions. After extrovert/introvert, the next characteristic pairing is called "sensing or intuitive": Do you (or your daughter) make sense of things through concrete, realistic information, are you pragmatic and prefer hands-on experience and conventional approaches to learning? Or do you (or your daughter) feel a greater comfort level in the intuitive realm, with thinking about concepts and philosophy and things like meaning in life?

The next category of characteristics are labeled as "thinking or feeling." This is just what it sounds like. The thinking person tries to take a rational approach to seeing or understanding the world, making lists of pros and cons, and so on. A feeling person sees the world through more of an emotional lens; what will make someone happy or what outcome is most comfortable.

And, finally, the Meyers-Briggs Personality Inventory talks about "judging or perceiving." A judging person is systematic, a planner, early starting, scheduled, methodical. A perceiving person is more casual, open-ended, pressure-prompted, spontaneous, or open to serendipity.

These personality differences come into play in a variety of ways, many of them in the simplest interactions. If we are blind to them, they can trip us up. If we are cognizant of them, they may hold insights for us in problem-solving moments. A mother and daughter who are very different on most personality characteristics will have to work harder to understand each other. A mother and daughter who are very much alike on most personality characteristics will have to work hard not to become too enmeshed, either too close or too critical.

A Daughter's Changing Needs

As soon as a baby girl's eyes can focus, she begins her study of her mother, and her education in what it means to be female. From the beginning, and throughout her life, your daughter is watching you, taking cues from you, whether they register in her mind as inspiration or determination to be not-you. What you do, how you look, what you say, what you *are*, has and will have a profound effect on her. Whether she loves or hates her mother, or, like most girls and women, feels some ambiguity about the connection, every girl needs to come to terms with her relationship with her mother before, developmentally speaking, she can become an adult woman.

The issues and emotions that run between mothers and daughters change with age. Certainly the protective instinct and the physical proximity are strongest during the dependent early years. As her age and movement out of the house, to school, with friends, with driving, all progress farther afield, so does the emotional connection become more diverse and varied. It is so hard to talk about a typical pattern because of all of the characteristics we talked about earlier. The only thing that is standard in the mother-daughter relationship is that it will change somewhat with each developmental stage of childhood.

There is also a kind of gradient or unfolding of these tasks over time in how we approach our role as parent. I can't help but see the parallel between mothering and teaching. In the early grades, the task of teachers is to facilitate a student's skill development: learning to spell, learning to read, learning to calculate. By the third grade, it shifts to application: writing for self-expression, reading to learn content, calculating to figure out complex problems. Learning to read changes in a dramatic crucible passage to reading to learn.

The same is true of parenting a daughter. In the first several years, we are in the skill-building phase, taking a more directive approach in helping her accumulate the skills she will need to negotiate life. At some point, she passes through this critical phase, and it is important to let her apply these skills with as little interference as possible. This passage seems to be harder for mothers than fathers because of the enmeshment issue. Her life is still so recognizable, at least parts of it.

At the same time as this gradient for a child is happening, the gradient of a mother's learning is happening also. I have a great friend who is the mother of three daughters. I did not really get to know her until her third daughter was entering school. I commented on how wise she was and how she seemed to handle even the rockiest times with her daughter with incredible calm. She laughed and said that I should have been around to watch how she was with daughters one and two! I laughed and said it must be like beginning teaching, I just prayed that my first- and second-year classes were okay. We agreed that it would be much easier and we would be much more effective if parenting began with the third child and teaching began with the third year!

Mothers as Models: What a Girl Wants, What a Girl Needs

One of my mother's favorite sayings was: "Do as I say, not as I do." She must have gotten that from this secret mother's manual where motherly sayings are passed down from generation to generation. My first memory of her using it with me was when I said something about her smoking, how bad it was for her health, and would she like it if I began to smoke? Now, as I struggle to be clear about the role model effect of mothers, I also struggle with this saying. I used to say to mothers, "It is not what you say, but what you do." I've revised that thinking over the years. It is both what you say *and* what you do, as well as a heavy dose of one more thing: what you *believe*.

I watched my mother smoke and I didn't like what I saw (a cigarette hanging out of my mother's mouth, no matter what she was doing), smelled (her breath and clothes), and heard (her coughing and wheezing). After her classic saying, she also said that she began smoking before health risks were known, and she wished she had not started, and she did not want this for her daughter. And, most important, I'm beginning to believe, is the connection between what she said and what she believed or valued, or what was connected to her wisdom as a mother or as someone who had layered experiences that I could not have had yet. "Don't do it because it is not healthy, it is bad for you." She was very clear about that.

So the effects of a mother on a daughter as the most, or one of the most, significant female role models she will ever have are common sense. How that happens, what aspects permeate to the long-term memory banks and the personality of the daughter, is not quite so easy. It's more like a bowl of spaghetti; the impressions are distinct, single strands in the jumble of them in that bowl. But the full bowl makes an impression of its own. The words of one of the girls in the Laurel/Harvard study are emblazoned in my head. Mattie, a freshman, talked about how smart and good her mother was, but that she saw her mother "disappearing" and losing her strength and individuality. She talked about the mail that came to the house, addressed to "Mrs. Smith" or "Mrs. John Smith," not even "Joan Smith" or "Mrs. Joan Smith" or "Joan Deck," her mother's professional name. She talked about how her mother was a successful attorney, but when they went to a restaurant, her dad always chose the wine. She was saying that she didn't see her mother having as much power or recognition as her father, and that her mother seemed to condone this. It confused and disappointed her.

Remember the kindergarten girl in the cafeteria line who admonished me to avoid the "bad" whole milk and buy skim milk to drink with lunch? By the time she reached middle school, she had developed an eating disorder, much like that of her mother, who still talked about being on a perennial diet. A high school girl who was well known for never drinking alcohol at parties, even though all her friends did, was teased and accused of being too straight. Her mother was an active alcoholic, and as long as this girl could remember, she had helped her mother get into bed at night instead of the other way around.

Mattie is disappointed and feels her mother has "sold out" by giving up her name in marriage; Anna becomes anorexic like her mother; Jane is a confirmed teetotaler with an alcoholic mother as a role model; I've never smoked, but this book is filled with my mother's words, which pour almost automatically out of my mouth. Mothers cannot tell what their daughters will take from them and adopt, or take from them and reject, or just place on a shelf for later viewing and thinking. But that they will all look and feel and be affected for life by what a mother says, does, and believes in: *YES!* And so it makes most sense to say to mothers that all of what you are affects your girl, and it behooves all mothers to be articulate about what they value, what they want for their daughters, and what they see as shortcomings in themselves. With this backdrop of conversation and discussion, what you do can be modified and adjusted in your daughter's thinking, just as I processed my view of my mother's smoking.

Disconnection: When the Fit Is Flawed

Just because a woman becomes a mother, this doesn't change some personalities or serious problems. There are just some instances when a mother is not emotionally healthy, or the emotional fit between mother and daughter is poor.

Jan's mother was an active alcoholic. Jan learned very early not to invite friends home. At her sixth birthday party, her mother passed out on the couch, and Jan had to serve the cake and orchestrate the party around her. That was Jan's last birthday party.

Carol's mother was a screamer and a harsh critic. Even when her temper was under control, it was hard to watch their interaction. You could always tell when Carol's mother was in the vicinity, because Carol's back would become very rigid, and she sat up straight; she seemed to physically brace herself for her mother's presence.

Ella's mother was anorexic, suffering advanced physical deterioration from the effects of that disease, and insisted that her medical complications be the drama at the center of her family's life. Ella took to the stage in middle school, enjoying her role in the school play, and thereafter found a home in the performing arts, where her natural talents bloomed, and where the drama at the center of the cast family life was one of her own choosing.

Short of criminal abuse, there are many ways that some girls suffer painful emotional relationships with a mother who is unable to connect in a healthful way. I rarely get calls from mothers like that; their own emotional issues tend to obstruct their view of their daughter and her pain. I do get calls from other mothers; those whose daughters are friends of girls like Jan and Carol and Ella, and who worry about those girls and wonder what they can do.

In order to survive emotionally, girls must develop their own coping strategies, and often draw strength from other relationships with friends and friends' families, or from therapy while young, and later in life. In almost every case, a caring "other mother" who calls me is already doing the most effective thing she could do: Be there as a compassionate motherly figure, a role model, a listener, and a soft shoulder. And when in doubt, call a professional for additional advice or to report concerns. Remember the green blanket? If a girl can't have one at home, having one at her friend's house really helps.

Measuring Up to Mother

Girls have always felt pressure to measure up to a beloved or admired mother, but more than ever before, today's generation of girls follow a generation of mothers who are high achievers in a public way. It adds another dimension to this complex relationship. In generations past, it was quite common for a girl to be the first girl in the family to achieve publicly, or to advance the level of public achievement beyond that of her mother. Mother didn't go to college, but daughter did; mother didn't graduate from college, but daughter did; mother worked a job, but daughter pursued a career; mother did well, given the constraints on women during that era, but daughter gained greater access to the world of choices. As contemporary women have pushed through those traditional boundaries and gained recognition for their contributions and advancements in all fields, what does it mean to new generations of daughters? How does a mother's outward success affect the inner life of a girl? What's it like for a girl whose mother is highly successful in a profession, or hard-driving, or beloved, or any of those superlatives?

Almost always, it introduces the choice: to measure up, or not to measure up. And that is how it usually goes; one end of the continuum or the other, without much in the middle. A girl will either try incredibly hard to measure up to a high standard or she will look at it and conclude that it is too high, she'll never make it, and might as well not try. It's all in how she responds to the pressure to measure up.

In the best of all worlds for children the term *measuring up* would become obsolete. Healthier terminology would be the classic "doing your best" or "trying your hardest" or "giving it your best shot." It would also include the idea that, at times, faced with so many options and tasks in life, you may not give something that ultimate investment of personal best time and effort because it's not that important to you.

For "superlative" mothers, whether recognition comes through family, community, business, or professional achievement, it is vital to recognize the role model that you are, and the effect that can have on your daughter; acknowledge the high-bar image that you have, and put it on the table. Like the math-whiz mother who acknowledged that it must be difficult for her math-challenged daughter to feel understood and appreciated in their relationship, the first step in achieving that understanding is to address the issue openly and respectfully. Throughout your years together, giving the message that you do not expect or want your daughter to be you, and that you want her to be her own best self, allows your daughter to admire you, and learn a great deal from your life, but not be weighed down by your expectations or her own self-imposed need to measure up to your success.

Mothers agonize so much in their daily decision-making mode—"Should I let her go to the mall alone?" "How much should I bug her about her homework?" These are important questions, but in terms of lifelong impact on your daughter, the more important issues that deserve your time and consideration are thoughts about your behavior, your words, your personal decisions, and your values. These are the mirror of your being, where your daughter will, in different ways through the years, discover herself.

Pearls for Parents and Pearls for Girls

- Share your wisdom and your history. Let your daughter know that you have some wisdom about what it is like as a growing female because you have lived it, and make it real by sharing your history.

- Respect the pioneer in your daughter: Let your daughter know that you recognize that you can't know exactly what life is like for her in each specific situation so you ask or at least listen when she deigns to tell you.

- Establish rules and limits. Use your daughter as a consultant in the process, but also establish that your role as a responsible, loving parent dictates some house rules that may not be as much to her liking. She may grouse about details, but she'll respect your position, and possibly even tell you about it a few decades later.

- Model core values. Take every opportunity to share your core values and moral views with your daughter, even if they only provide fodder for debate. Your voice and your stand as a woman are your most powerful legacies to her.

- Remember the Mother Mantra: I am not my daughter. I don't know it all, but I can learn more if I listen more. I am my daughter's most powerful role model for life as a woman.

- Instead of saying to your daughter "When I was your age," make it a fun tradition to compare notes. Listen, share, and learn!

- When she has just dumped an issue or problem on you, rather than launching into "Why don't you . . ." with a list of problem-solving suggestions, instead start with: "How can I help you . . ."

- Even after a bad connection day, always go to her room and say good night and mean it.

CHAPTER 6

Father and Daughters: Soul Mates, Strangers, and a Delicate Dance

"I know he's not perfect, and there are times when he makes me very angry, but I can't think of anything specific I'd change about him. I don't keep score with him, so when I think of him, I think of him as the whole person, whom I love dearly."

—Kristen, sixteen

I didn't really notice the pattern until October, although this particularly sweet scene had been playing daily since the first day of school. Every morning, Mr. Stringer and his daughter, Em, came trudging up the sidewalk one minute before the morning bell sounded. Their progress was slow because they took such meticulous note of everything along the way: He would point out the new tree planted, the car that looked like theirs parked nearby, the high school girls leaning out the window on the second floor waving to their friends. Nothing escaped their attention. Each day as they passed me, she smiled, put her head down, and held on tightly to her dad's hand as they made their way to the kindergarten room. I knew Em's father was a busy corporate business executive; this man who appeared to have all the time in the world, who dawdled with his daughter each morning because (he told me once) he wanted to ease any anxiety she had about parting for the day, would wait until she was in the building, then, literally, run past me, with his tie flying over his shoulder, in a rush because he was always late for his morning meetings.

This continued day after day, through rain, sun, and snow, until the middle of the year, when they proudly walked up to me, and Em asked if I could wait in the bus circle the next day for a surprise. I did. That morning, Em got off the bus by herself with a huge smile, turned, and waved to her dad, who was across the street, standing by his car. Later that day I stopped to ask Em if riding the bus was working okay for her. She looked at me like I was nuts and said, "I'm fine. I'm hoping my dad will be okay if I don't walk with him in the morning."

A similar sweetness about the relationship between fathers and daughters echoes through comments from many girls and women. Contrary to idealized images or the media caricature of dear old dad, who is, alternately, wise or clueless, the patterns of relationship between girls and their fathers are rich, textured, and varied.

The paucity of scientific research regarding the father-daughter relationship reflects a tradition of cultural silence and a blind eye when it comes to the interior lives of girls and women, especially in regard to this crucible relationship with the first man in their lives. Although newer research initiatives promise greater insights eventually, at the moment, stereotypes of sweet, smart, and/or stoic dads persist, muscled up from time to time by commonsense reports that suggest there is a strong correlation between "successful" women and "involved" fathers.

The definitions of success and involvement are often vague, however. Successful by what or whose standards? I know many outwardly successful homemakers and career women, and celebrated superachiever girls, who are inwardly quite unhappy people, and many others pressured to achieve a certain kind of success by a father whose involvement is, or was, domineering, critical, or abusive, rather than emotionally close or loving. On the other hand, I know many women—CEOs to PTO members—who are, by their own internal measure, successful and satisfied; some of them had affirming fathers, some of them had adoring fathers, some had fathers who died young, and some had fathers who seemed more distant or destructive than anything else. I point this out not to dump on what little research we have but to say that we are just beginning to identify the meaningful questions to ask, and the fuller meaning of answers we get.

In the meantime, we have growing girls, and an increasing number of fathers who are actively trying to be the best fathers ever—well, at least in the life of the pioneering daughter they love. It can be daunting, as well as exciting, for a man to be this key figure in his daughter's life. I often hear from the fathers of daughters when they "can't figure her out." Some call to work at it, others mostly to complain. I also hear frequently from concerned mothers who wonder what they can do to help father and daughter grow closer. And I hear from girls, many of whom treasure their dads, or at least feel they enjoy a good enough relationship. Other girls feel at odds with their fathers, whether by nature or everyday expectations.

In Her Father's Eyes: A Girl's Early View of Herself

From the day she is born, a girl's heart is wide open to her parents, and that includes her father, whether it is her biological or adoptive father, or, in his absence, alternate father figures. From the very beginning, she can learn trust and love from her father, and through the years she remains vulnerable to his influence, whether it carries a message of love, respect, and high expectations, or one of criticism, indifference, limitations, or low expectations.

American suffragist and political visionary Elizabeth Cady Stanton, talking about her own father in 1922, spoke of the deep, hidden hurt of generations of girls when she said: "I never felt more keenly the degradation of my sex. To think that all in me of which my father would have felt a proper pride had I been a man, is deeply mortifying to him because I am a woman."

Social progress toward gender equity has changed this shameful context for the father-daughter relationship, but Stanton's comment makes two important points:

First, societal norms and expectations affect how a father thinks about his daughter and what those feelings communicate to her. In the same way that social mores of his era prompted Stanton's father to be mortified by his daughter's passionate political activism, contemporary opportunities and pressures for girls to be *supergirls* may lead a father to push his own success agenda over his daughter's interests, or be disappointed in his daughter if she isn't valedictorian, star softball pitcher, volunteer of the month, or simply a more traditional girl with predictable (stereotypical) feminine interests.

Second is the truth that a girl feels profoundly about the way her father perceives her—or the way she *believes* her father perceives her, whether their relationship appears close and loving, or not. Imagine a woman of Stanton's intelligence, stature, and accomplishment feeling "degradation" at the core of her identity as a woman because her father clung to his narrow vision of what a woman should be!

Girls today feel immense pressure to measure up to a father's expectations, whether it is on the soccer field, in school, or even in the nature of their hopes and dreams.

"I want to be an archaeologist, but first I have to be a lawyer," said a seventh-grade girl who went on to explain that her father, a successful lawyer himself, considers law school a prerequisite for life. She wasn't complaining (at least not yet); she was resigned. She believed her father to be smart and successful, believed that he wanted the same for her, and assumed that she must satisfy his passion for law before she could turn to her own passion for science.

An older teen recalled the joyful power of the connection with her father: "My dad would fly home from business trips early just to be at my sporting events. I always looked for him in the crowd. Until I saw his face, I was not ready to play. Just knowing he was there made everything all right. Yes, my mom was there, too, but it was extra important to have my dad there. I don't really know why."

This emotional vulnerability is the open channel between a

girl and her father; it is what gives him access, and gives him presence and power in her life, whether he uses it in ways that are affirming or not. The dark side of that father power is that it can be just as powerfully negative as it can be positive. Obvious abuses come to mind: fathers who are physically abusive or sexually abusive. Less obvious, but quite damaging, are fathers who are extremely controlling and limiting, or critical. Clinical observation and studies indicate that girls and women who have experienced highly critical or abusive fathers are very unlikely to have high self-esteem. It can take most of a lifetime for a woman to overcome the emotional scars and handicaps to behavior, achievement, and life-choices resulting from a domineering or critical father.

The Original Love Story

In the beginning, every girl wants to love her father and wants to feel loved by him. When girls talk about their fathers, love often figures into the conversation, defining a girl's experience of her father by its presence or its absence:

"The thing I love most about my father is that he is always willing to help me. If I need help in school, he will help me the best he can by quizzing me for a test or getting a tutor for me to help when he is not around or unavailable. If I need help in tennis, he will play matches with me or set up lessons. My dad is always able to help me in some way. The one thing I would change about my father is if he could stop being so controlling. I would like it if he gave me more freedom." (Eighth-grader)

"What I like about my father is when he makes jokes, because laughter is a great thing for me and goes over everything. If something is bothering me, he'll give me a hug and find a solution to the problem." (Fifth-grader)

"I love my dad, but I also love being with him. What I like most about my dad is his smile. It is very rare to see him smile. It is not because he isn't

happy. He just doesn't get excited easily. When I got my last report card, I was proud of myself for getting straight A's. I could tell my dad was especially happy because he smiled and gave me a big hug. His smile just seemed to light up the room." (Eighth-grader)

"What I like most about my dad is he is so funny and he is a great guy. He is totally in control and cool. He knows what to do in every situation and he is really smart and witty and strong, even though he is seventy-six. He is the kind of guy who people respect but he isn't like 'do what I say' and all that. My dad is really unique and interesting. He is the best dad around. I wouldn't change much about my dad, but I would like him to stay his age, but live a little longer. I like having a dad so old, but I'm worried that when I'm thirty-two he will be almost dead, if not gone already. Otherwise I like my dad just the way he is. He is perfect!!" (Sixth-grader)

"My dad is like one of my best friends, he watches TV with me, he plays sports with me, and he helps me with my homework. If I could change one thing about him, it would be the way he yells sometimes when I do something bad. He yells a little too much. Other than that, he's a great person!" (Sixth-grader)

"The one thing I would change about my dad is for him to stop always pushing me to do things I don't want to do. Like he always forces me to go to tennis practice or play in games even when I make mistakes, and always tells me I am not doing things correctly or not trying hard enough, when I am trying my best! Once I was crying because my dad yelled at me so hard. But my dad is a very good person!" (Fifth-grader)

"What I like most about my father is his great sense of humor and how I can talk to him about most things. He tries his hardest to make my life easier and he is someone I look up to. If I could change one thing about my father, I would change his temper. Sometimes he gets upset about things that are just not worth an argument." (Ninth-grader)

"My father is so fun to be with and he is such a good teacher. He tells me so many different things. I would change that he would be home more often so we could spend more time together." (Ninth-grader)

"I love my dad, but I hate him when he bosses my mom around." (Seventh-grader)

What a Girl Needs, What a Girl Wants

As we've seen, in the school of life, most girls major in relationships. From the very first day of class in Life with Father 101, a daughter generally shows up with all the right school supplies, ready to engage in active learning, taking notes on anything and everything in that father-daughter classroom.

Conversations with girls, women, and fathers, and available research and anecdotal literature about the father-daughter relationship, tell us that at any point in the continuing education classroom for fathers and daughters, three pieces of the curriculum are of particular importance to a girl:

Teeter-Totter Theory: A father can naturally, or intentionally, provide balancing influences to a girl's natural skill base, and to the often skewed how-a-girl-is-supposed-to-be messages she draws from the world around her.

Gender Scrimmage: A father provides his daughter with her formative gender playing field, so to speak—her first learning and practicing ground for understanding and relating to males. Her experience of him, their way of being together, and the way she sees him relate to other women, most notably her mother, will shape her interactions and expectations in relationship with other males, whether those relationships are school- or work-based, or more emotionally intimate ones.

Attendance: A girl shows up for "practice" every day, in her relationship with her father. Where's Dad? To be present in the relationship means to spend time actively engaged and committed. No matter how many excused absences a father claims, at some point he's out of the game, in a daughter's mind, and she suffers the loss.

The Father Study: Nature, Nurture, and Gender Roles

Coming home from work one day about ten years ago, listening to National Public Radio, I heard a report about a study just completed at Harvard. The media had quickly dubbed it "The Father Study." The announcer went on to summarize the core findings: Children who spent the majority of their waking hours with their fathers scored better on measures of achievement and intelligence than those who spent the majority of their waking hours with their mothers. Just after that bombshell was released, further writing in the media gave more details. In trying to determine the reason for these results, the researchers looked carefully at the population of this study to see what the fathers typically did with the children and what the mothers typically did with the children. They found significant differences. In general, fathers *did active things* with their children: playing, building things, and going to events. In general, mothers *talked or read* with or to their children.

Although these are generalizations, the pattern of behavior between mothers and children and fathers and children was fairly distinctive. Brain research supports these findings, though from a different angle. First, studies of the limbic system (emotions central) suggest that females experience connections with others more acutely than males. Then, other brain research suggests that the language centers of most female brains are more developed than the language centers of most male brains. Simply put, females may be genetically predisposed to talk a bit more and also to feel emotional connections a bit more. Combine this with the view that males are somewhat genetically and neurologically predisposed to be active and toward task-oriented behavior, and do not feel emotions quite as frequently or as deeply as females, and we see the biological credence to these gender differences.

Active learning seems to affect the neurological system, and have more beneficial learning effects over time, than passive (listening, watching) learning. For example, playing a game, which ultimately requires the use of strategy, leads a child to be a better thinker than does reading about the game. Fathers often seem to have a natural affinity for doing things with their daughters. Mothers often seem to have a natural affinity for talking with their daughters. Both interactions are very valuable, but layered over time, one enhances thinking and the growth of the dendrites in the neurological system more than the other does.

This positive impact of active learning on daughters' achievement goes beyond the childhood and school years. Generally, the literature reports that a high percentage of professionally successful women point to the influence of their fathers as a key motivational element in their lives. From that point on, the details are less declarative. Girls and women talk about how they did things with their fathers, how their fathers gave them the feeling that they could do anything. School-age girls frequently report that their fathers care about their grades, how well they do in school, if they make the honor roll, and other markers of achievement. It isn't that mothers don't care about these things, but fathers typically appear more outcome-oriented, and communicate more strongly that performance and doing well is critical. Mothers certainly want this for their daughters also, but typically are more process-oriented—they often list happiness and belonging as just as important, or more so, than conventional success and achievement.

I was presenting at grand rounds at a hospital in Boston, and one of the women in the audience came up afterward to talk to me about some of the gender differences I had discussed. She said that she had great memories of her father and all the things they did together. As we talked, one particular incident was clearly detailed in her memory. She talked about making a bookcase with her father in their garage when she was a preteen. Her father had matter-of-factly expected an equal partner in building it, and she had surprised herself by being just that.

This reminded me of a conversation I had had a few months earlier with an Outward Bound instructor in North Carolina. Pandora said that a similar experience with her stepfather had proven to be a crucible moment in her feeling of competence. Her family lived on a farm, and one day, after a walk around the property, her stepdad walked in and announced that there was a breach in the fence that needed repair. He turned to her and said, "Would you take care of that sometime today?"

Pandora had mutely nodded in the affirmative, but on the inside she was a mix of emotions. She felt a bit panicked, because she had never even come close to fixing a fence and didn't have the slightest idea what to do. She also felt incredibly proud that her stepdad just assumed she could handle it. And she felt an incredible surge of I'll-get-this-done-if-it-kills-me come over her. She did figure it out, her stepdad nodded his approval at dinner, and that was that.

There are some important themes in these two stories that are common in many girls' and women's reflections on their fathers' influence in their lives. In both stories, the fathers communicated inferentially, not just high expectations that their daughters were competent and able to get the job done, but an underlying high regard. Everything about the way they approached these girls assumed competence and communicated respect, and the girls got the message.

In fact, from the hundreds of stories I've heard from girls and women alike, it seems that this balance of high expectation *and* high regard, on the part of fathers, is much more powerful than the actual words. Daughters often express initial surprise at this upon reflection, whether it is at the time or forty years later. That says a great deal about the messages girls receive from much of the rest of the world. But more important, it also says how much power and weight the father figure has in balancing out the teeter-totter of life of a daughter. While much of the rest of the world may be giving her limiting sexist messages, her father can balance those messages with one that removes the limits, equalizes gender expectations, and anticipates eventual success.

The traditional patterns that many women describe as characteristic of their girlhood experience with their fathers still resonate today in many, and perhaps most, girls' experience of their fathers. However, social trends are shaking these gender patterns up a bit, so many girls now see out-in-the-world, active, doing mothers, and more openly caring, talkative fathers.

If, as a father, you know you tend to be more goal-oriented and less talkative and emotive than mothers are, then it's up to you to expand your gender role. Holding and talking are the first steps early on. Changing diapers, feeding and bathing, telling bedtime stories, or sitting on the couch watching TV together are all potent layering experiences for a father and daughter. And, if it happens early and often, it changes the nature of the relationship.

I watched a young father say to his wife that he didn't want to hold his infant daughter because he was so big and clumsy that he might hurt her. He assured his wife he would hold her when she got bigger and sturdier. His wise wife just smiled, showed him how to protect the baby's neck, and handed over the little bundle. Once that physical comfort was established, he became very good at holding her and changing her and all of that other critically important bonding stuff that, with continued doing, just becomes part of a father.

Gender Bridges, Gender Gaps: A Father's Unique "Otherworldly" Challenge

One of the most cogent quotes I've run into on fathers comes from American essayist Phyllis McGinley, who wrote: *"The thing to remember about fathers is, they're men."*

This is not a condemnation, mind you—it's just the one true thing we know, and it presents itself as both a gift and a handicap in the father-daughter relationship.

If you are a father, the gift is your opportunity to make your daughter's first relationship with the opposite sex a rich and affirming one, setting a standard for all those to come. Through that relationship, you'll add to the layering process of the three C's for high self-esteem in your daughter, beginning with connectedness. By sharing your perspective and experience as a male, you open that world to her, and add to her competence and confidence in that arena.

A girl also looks to her father as a model in the way he interacts with her mother—whether the two are married or divorced! Girls are especially sensitive to the power and control piece of that relationship: How are financial decisions made, and is power shared or not? On disciplinary issues, whose opinion carries the most weight? Are mutual respect and joint responsibility apparent? A girl is really observing whether this is a balanced relationship or a lopsided one, in terms of power and control. All the subtleties count, too, but ultimately, she is watching this relationship and whether or not it suggests fair play.

There's really no way to predict the long-term effect of a girl's observation and assessment of the mother-father duo. The only clarity is that it is seen, it is processed, and it has a powerful impact. A girl doesn't necessarily go on to marry a fellow just like Dad, but the tone of their relationship will carry lifelong resonance in her choices around interactions with other men. If she has experienced herself as enjoyed, respected, and valued in her father's eyes, in this first male realm, then she is more likely to seek out similar qualities in the relationships she builds with others in the world of men. A girl who has a discordant relationship with her father may deliberately seek out his opposite, or, if she has come to believe that she is unworthy or unlovable in a man's eyes, she may gravitate toward relationships in which that darker echo is repeated.

"I'll tell you why daughters drive fathers nuts," explained one bemused father. "Because most men have never figured *grown* women out, and here is this girl child, and no matter how fun a pal she was when she was little, suddenly one day she becomes one of *'them.'* "

A father communicates a great deal in the way he responds to the gender difference. He can use his daughter's other-ness as an excuse to distance himself from her, leave her to her mother, treat her as a why-can't-a-woman-be-more-like-a-man makeover project, or in other ways criticize her way of knowing and being. Or he can treat it as an invitation to learn, be open about his ignorance, and communicate a desire to understand and appreciate the female experience— most important, *her* female experience.

In speaking of the mother-son relationship in *Raising Cain: Protecting the Emotional Life of Boys,* psychologist/author Michael Thompson referred to the gender gap as the underlying challenge that confronts any mother, since she simply cannot know what it's like to be a boy, or think like a boy. The same holds true for fathers of daughters, but I believe most fathers have an even greater challenge. Mothers, as women, generally bring advanced relationship skills, empathy, and other tools of emotional literacy to the task of parenting a son. Fathers not only have to bridge the "other world" gender gap, but typically come to that task without the best-developed set of emotional tools to work with. Men's struggle with issues of blunted emotional development, intimacy, and expression is well documented, and this raises some logical questions relative to parenting a girl.

If we believe that boys, traditionally and until very recently, were systematically trained away from the complexities of emotional awareness, empathy and self-expression, and taught to be stoic— strong and silent—men, then it is logical to wonder how well equipped this emotionally challenged population of adult males is to engage in a meaningful way in relationship with girls, the most emotionally complex and agile species on earth. If males typically lag behind females on the connectedness curve, and don't practice emotional intimacy or connectedness very easily, or in some cases, very well, how does that affect a girl, who is inclined to judge herself in many important ways on the basis of that very father-daughter connection? If boys and men are socialized from early on to distrust, disrespect, or discount females (and that remains a hallmark of boys' social conversation, even today), can a man rid himself of that misogynist lens to see his daughter in a truer light? In simple terms, from a history of genetic male tendencies and learned behaviors, can men shape their responses to a daughter in a way that supports her optimal growth and well-being?

The Relationship Continuum: Fathers and Daughters

Every father is different in temperament, life experience, expectations of parenting, and parenting style. However, we can look at the quality of the relationship along the way and see markers that suggest a healthy balance or a need for some fine-tuning. We can return to the model of the relationship continuum to see where a father and daughter land:

Disconnection   Synergy   Enmeshment

Just as with mothers and daughters, whether your relationship seems fluid, or more fixed, if you can find your place on the continuum, then you can have a better understanding of how your relationship *is*. From there, you can go on to deeper thoughts of why, and if there are reasons or times to try to change your place on the continuum. Relationships that can stay in some range of middle ground are the healthiest, reflecting give and take by both father and daughter, and in relation to each other.

Synergy in the Father–Daughter Relationship

A good friend of mine who shares what I consider a naturally synergistic connection with his daughter, who is fifteen, describes their relationship this way:

"As my first child, adopted when I was thirty-eight years old, she made my life complete and very happy, although quite complicated. Her energy is very similar to mine—we have always liked to ski and play tennis together. She talks about sports to me, and we watch fashion shows on MTV, and other TV shows. Her mother is much quieter and more serene. It has been a blast having a soccer-playing daughter, a stay-up-at-night and ice-hockey-playing daughter, and a watch-dumb-TV kind of daughter.

"I love her in-your-face humor. She reminds me often that I am not cool, and shouldn't pretend to be. I like the teasing and the joking that we do together. . . . She wrote me an e-mail on Valentine's Day and signed it 'Daddy's Little Girl Jo-Jo.' Now, I know she was being ironic, but it was fun to get. She promises that if I buy her a car, she'll have license plates made that read 'Daddy's Girl.' Her transparent attempts to manipulate me are funny, flirtatious, and occasionally successful. I don't have that kind of relationship with anyone else in my life."

Another father describes how his own childhood experience affects his deliberate commitment to building a loving relationship with his six-year-old daughter:

"I am a father, and I had and have no relationship with my father. He was a brutal man. A child molester of his daughters, physical abuser of his sons, and a criminal—aren't you glad you asked? I have an extremely close relationship with my wife and children (my other child is a fourteen-year-old son). We do a lot of activities together. We draw, play music, read books, play Nintendo, play computer games, ride bikes, and just plain talk.

"I admit I worry more about my daughter than my son because I think that she is more vulnerable in the world. I have always respected women. I work, and I am married to a woman who works and who is independent, and I like that. I will encourage my daughter to develop her skills and have a

career. I want her to be able to take care of herself. I think my daughter is a
great person because she works really hard, always tries her best, likes to help
around the house, and likes to be with her family and friends. She is kind,
interesting, fun to be around, and talented."

Whether naturally or intentionally, the synergistic relationship develops over time, and this layering of communication and connection builds a foundation for continued rapport even when
circumstances might otherwise be awkward.

A friend told me about an exchange between her husband,
Allen, and their daughter, Anna, when she was twelve years old and
just starting her period. My friend overheard the dialogue from
another room, where she was lying on the couch, not feeling well.
Allen was trying to help his daughter figure out how to use some new
technology—a sanitary napkin that had "wings." He stood on the
other side of the closed bathroom door, talking her through what he
thought she should do. Obviously, neither had much experience in
this area, but they were problem-solving together with the same back-
and-forth banter and barks they brought to most challenging
moments. The entire time this bathroom door conversation was
going on, his daughter was intermittently telling him to leave her
alone, even as she continued to ask questions.

It is rare for fathers to even be considered partners in conversations like this, with a young daughter struggling with this intimate
girlhood experience. That Allen was able to do this was clear evidence of his layering of time and communication and nurturing
through all the previous years—synergy in action, and over time. Otherwise, there is no way to begin this kind of connected relationship
during the tween years. And that's a very critical point. Hang in there!
Even when a daughter says "Oh, Dad!" with that tone, don't let it push
you away too far. Sometimes you'll have to give a little ground, but
always come back and always keep talking and always keep doing
things with her. (And, by the way, the wings of a sanitary napkin do
not attach to the legs!)

Temperament, Personality, and Compatibility

Temperament, personality, and compatibility are just as important in the fit between fathers and daughters as they are with mothers and daughters, with the added interface of gender otherness. Some men are conscious of and sensitive to their inner qualities and the patterns of expression and behavior that reflect their temperament and personality. For others, and this includes many men, the exercise in introspection needed to recognize these patterns in themselves, and then in their daughters, is a challenge in itself. As one father said, "What's there to figure out? I'm not that complicated. She's the one I can't understand." For those fathers, there is often an *aha* moment, when they recognize (sometimes for the first time) their own patterns and their own complexity, and see a daughter's personality and temperament more objectively.

Even the least intuitive girls pick up on this undercurrent of compatibility with their father. Most girls can describe their own personality type, and their father's as well.

"My dad is fun to be with, he is sorta like me," a sixth-grade girl says. "We like to do the same things and it sounds weird, but we even like the same music. My dad, he is perfect the way he is."

While similar personality and temperaments may show up as easy compatibility, it's no guarantee, just as different styles don't necessarily doom a pair to conflict.

Denise, a very focused, analytical, inflexible, and high-achieving fifteen-year-old girl, says that she and her father "are nothing alike"—and then goes on to describe, in disparaging terms, a father who is her mirror image. Denise and her father clash over *everything*. He finds her opinionated, stubborn, and uncooperative. She feels entitled to her opinions and is determined to resist what she feels are efforts "to make me into his little clone."

Eileen, sixteen, is very much an extrovert who excels in the performing arts. Her father is an introvert, a quiet man who would rather spend an evening with a book than in an audience, but who never misses one of her plays. "He's my biggest fan. He's great!" she says.

Elizabeth, who is seventeen, in her summing up shows an equanimity I hear from many girls: "I love how my father always says the wrong thing, but because he's my dad, it always makes me feel better. The fact that he's trying to help me lets me know how much he loves me. He gives me advice on subjects that I know he could know nothing about, and even if I don't listen to what he has to say, I know that he is trying to help me."

A father's ability and willingness to negotiate the gray in this regard is critical in drawing a daughter toward a middle ground in the relationship, where her individuality is respected, and compatibility is not defined as compliance. Sometimes the adaptations are fairly simple, as one father noted: "I talk with my daughter way more than I would think of doing with anyone else under ordinary circumstances, because I know that's important to her—that's her learning style."

Enmeshment and Disconnection: Gender Traps and Emotional Betrayals

With open access to education, sports, politics, leadership, and professional achievement, a huge historical barrier has been lifted between fathers and daughters. This opens up tremendous opportunities for sharing interests and activities that weren't available even a generation ago. At the same time, it has upped the stakes. Some fathers invest too much in their daughter's engagement and performance in the wider world. Today, many fathers set the same expectations for their girls as fathers once set stereotypically for their boys. They want them to succeed in sports, go to their college alma mater, be successful in the business and professional world, etc. And although mothers have their enmeshment issues with daughters, the core issue with mothers is often emotional enmeshment. For fathers, it is certainly emotional at some level, but the male predisposition to be goal-oriented often translates this enmeshment into a push for achievement for their daughters.

Fathers and daughters can openly disagree on many things, and they can be complete opposites in terms of personality and temperament, yet they can still enjoy a close and loving relationship. Disconnection between father and daughter indicates just that: an absent, failed, or seriously flawed connection. In some instances, particularly if a girl has been emotionally, sexually, or physically abused, it may be irreconcilable. However, for the most part, degrees of disconnection are less extreme and, like enmeshment, often arise from unexamined gender assumptions and attitudes, which are open to change.

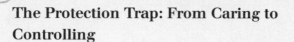

The Protection Trap: From Caring to Controlling

Many fathers feel protective of their daughters. They are very clear on this and communicate their feelings proudly:

> *"I want to protect her and take care of her."*
> *"I want to provide for her."*
> *"I want to make sure she makes it in life."*

These are caring and loving thoughts. However, a father's desire to protect his little girl or make sure that she is strong enough to handle the world can translate into controlling, critical, or driving behavior. Or daughters often perceive it to be that way.

"Whenever I want to do something, no matter what it is, he will always, always, always tell me the five things that can go wrong, and why I shouldn't do it right now," says a high school senior. "He only wants me to do the things *he* thinks are important or 'appropriate' for me."

"My father always made it clear that he was the expert on my life, even though he knew absolutely nothing about what was important to me," says Val, who is fifty-two. "I couldn't wait to leave home, and once I did, we got along best with about two thousand miles between us."

A mother, with a husband and young daughter of her own, concludes:

> *"Fathers tend to be overprotective of their daughters. This may be a function of society. Men are supposed to be the protectors, women are supposed to require the protection of males. The older and more beautiful his daughter becomes, the more protective a father is. Perhaps it is because he knows what can happen as boys and girls enter puberty! I think that if a father is too overprotective, he can force his daughter to react by taking dangerous risks and exercising poor judgment. I think that fathers and daughters can be very close as long as the father's 'leash' on his daughter is not suffocating."*

A girl may find her way around an overprotective or controlling father, either through conflict, rebellion, or geographical distance. If she doesn't, then the sheltered life will eventually impose a more serious consequence in her vulnerability in a society where females are no longer a protected species.

The Goal-Orientation Trap: From Motivation to Domination

Succeeding, accomplishing, and winning are all key words in most fathers' vocabularies. All are potentially very positive motivational messages for a daughter, as is evidenced by the influence of fathers cited by successful women. But also cited, with a little digging, is some sadness, anger, and/or resulting coldness in many of those same women. A father's seemingly minor critical or competitive comments, which may have been meant as constructive and positive, are often heard by a daughter as more negative and excessively critical. Further, when a father is so intent upon motivating or teaching that the moment becomes about his objectives rather than his daughter's experience, his overenmeshment diminishes any positive effect of the lesson he pounds home.

Regan, a high school girl, talked with me about her father's behavior watching her field hockey game. She described how angry her dad was when she came off the field, having passed the ball to her friend to attempt a goal rather than taking the shot herself. Her dad complained that it was just like her, meaning unfortunately typical, to care about her friend more than winning or being an aggressive player, and that she would not be successful in life if she kept making "these emotional choices." Regan was so upset, she couldn't say anything to her dad.

When we talked, she was very clear about the part that bothered her most. She felt her father should have asked why she made the decision to pass the ball, and then they could have talked about it. His immediate judgment about her motivation and feelings made it clear to her that he didn't want to talk about it; he just wanted to tell her what he thought she should do to be successful and a winner in life.

It doesn't take many of these comments to sever communication. And it is hard for a father to tell, because often his daughter cares so much about his opinion that although she may see her own inside story, she also may take the shot next time and change the pattern of her behavior that is related to succeeding *his* way. Or she may just stop listening and become an angry backlash daughter who does things she knows will irritate her father. In either swing along the continuum, their relationship suffers and the layering of those crucible moments between father and daughter works against her best interests.

Absent and Distant Dads

The classic stereotype of the father who goes to work, comes home late, spends little time with his children, does not really know them, and rarely changed a diaper does not enjoy the same societal acceptance it once did, but it is, unfortunately, still the story in many families. Meanwhile, the newer, contemporary version of the absent dad assumes the stance of "an involved parent," but is a chronic no-show when it comes to delivering on that promise.

I see the deep hurt and feeling of betrayal that girls have when fathers don't show an interest in their lives, or when they are unreliable or forgetful in regard to the emotional commitment and vulnerability a girl brings to their relationship. I've seen the girls whose fathers sneak quietly into the auditorium for the last minutes of the choral concert or the school play, technically there, but not there in time for their daughter's moment in the spotlight. Or those who make it, but also make it clear that their busy schedule can barely accommodate the imposition; they're rushed for time, in a hurry to leave, impatient with the expectations placed on their time or attention.

Unless the two have developed special ways of sharing time outside the ordinary, a father's constant absence or tardiness has meaning to a girl. The fifth time he misses the game, or isn't there for the school play, it is a huge hurt that girls don't just "get over." They get sad, they get discouraged, they get self-critical, they get angry, they get icy, but they don't *not* feel about it.

"I wish he were dead," says a nine-year-old girl whose parents are divorcing and who feels a family and personal betrayal in her father's extramarital affairs, his punishing treatment of her mother, and his trail of broken promises for father-daughter time together. "He acts like he's so sad about how everything is working out, but I think he lies a lot."

Another girl, eleven years old, expresses her longing for her too-busy father by wishing that her parents *would* get divorced, like so many of the parents of her friends. "At least they get to go to movies and do stuff with their fathers on weekends—that's more than I get to do! My dad is always too busy or too tired."

Research into the effect of this full range of absent fathers on girls lags woefully behind the divorce rate and work trends that make this fathering style a reality for many girls. If we go with what we know, then it is this:

The layering of gender awareness, interaction, and other experiences that are inherent in an engaged father-daughter relationship are compromised by a father's chronic absence or inattention. To the extent that a father is emotionally absent or distant, for whatever reason, a girl loses the opportunity for a positive layering effect of experiences within that relationship. The emotional distance itself may be layered in, measured not only in the loss of a meaningful and satisfying father-daughter history together, but in an undermining of her ability to relate to other males in her life, or share closeness in emotional intimacy.

"My father wasn't around much," says Lynne, in her forties. "His sacrifice of work allowed us to do and have amazing opportunities. I don't quite understand the balance of accepting the richness of my life to the exclusion of a childhood relationship with him. Resentment and thanks twist on and on into adulthood."

Tilting Toward Sons: Girls as Second-Class Citizens in the Fatherland

I call it the China Syndrome. In China, the ancient tradition of passing the family name and assets from one generation to the next through sons only, combined with the more recent one-child-per-couple political edict, meant that, culturally and historically, the family name and pride were carried by the son. If a family didn't have a male heir, it was problematic. It wasn't that they didn't like girls; they simply couldn't *not* have a boy. The consequences were devastating to girls, of course, leading to the abandonment or infanticide of baby girls.

In our contemporary American lives, and especially in the arena of the father-daughter relationship, the China Syndrome plays out when a father, whether consciously or not, invests more heavily in his relationship with his son than with his daughter. His daughter is assigned second-class status, and she knows it.

Mia was in eighth grade when she talked with me about her brother's favored status with their father. Her brother, in middle school, was talented in basketball, and their father wanted to do everything he could to promote and develop his son's interest. The family was well off, and each year the father-son pair took a week off to travel the country during basketball season, attending the best pro and college games. Their father made no such effort to spend alone-time with her. Eventually, her mother decided to balance things out by using that week to create some special mother-daughter time. Although Mia appreciated the time with her mother, she also experienced it as a compensation prize of sorts. She knew that in her father's eyes, and in the family, she would always be in second place.

"It's not that my father doesn't love me," she said, "but it's just not the same."

When Dads Die: The Untold Legacy of Loss

The father-daughter relationship is critical for so many important layers of a girl's life experience. Freud wrote in terms of sexual innuendoes of this relationship, but whether you are a Freudian or not, the father-daughter relationship is clearly a girl's learning and practicing ground for understanding and relating to other males. The literature on daughters whose fathers have died or left their lives in some way before adolescence points to the long- and short-term deficits girls face in understanding and relating to males. This topic is close to home for me, since my father died when I was fourteen, a terrible age for a girl to lose her father, right in the middle of beginning to relate in a different way to males. I can tell you that it removes one of the training grounds for seeing how a male responds to your words and actions. The contrast of how a mother and father respond differently is also very elucidating for a girl, even if it isn't quite at the conscious level. As much as I loved my brother, and certainly grew familiar with the distinctly male sound and energy that he and his friends brought into our home, it was not, by any standard, a mature male presence, sounding board, or training ground of the kind that a father can provide for his daughter.

The loss of her father fills a girl's reservoir of pain, and generalizes somewhat to tentativeness for intimacy with males. I distinctly remember waiting a long time before I would allow a young man to get emotionally close to me. Dating and caring at the surface level was not a problem; we females are good at playing the game! It's the road to sharing your heart and soul that can be detoured by the death of a father. So it is only logical, as well as somewhat documented by anecdotal reporting and widely theorized by psychologists and psychiatrists, that not having a father figure in the home leaves a void in the layering effect that that relationship can provide. For that reason, I always encourage single mothers to look for caring, trustworthy male role models—an uncle, a neighbor, or close friend—to be around enough for a girl to absorb some knowledge and wisdom about this other half of the species.

Remember the story of Pandora and the farm fence she mended? It was her stepfather who created the can-do climate for her in their relationship. Her story underscores the point that, whether the father figure is a girl's biological father, adoptive father, stepfather, an uncle, a grandfather, a teacher, or a family friend, a good man like this can be a very dramatic and powerfully positive influence in a girl's life. Although we have no research to explain it, it is clear that there is something different and unique about the impact of a father on a daughter that cannot be replicated by a mother. This is not to suggest that single mothers are inadequate, but rather that there is a benefit in drawing from the extended circle of family and close friends to bring an affirming male presence into a daughter's realm. The crucible event of losing a father, or the absence of a father through divorce or emotional distance, cannot be erased, but can be positively balanced by normal, caring relationships with other "fatherly" men.

Mothers in the Middle: Interface or Obstacle?

Related to all of this is how a mother gets involved, or doesn't, in the relationship issues of a father and daughter. If a father tends to be disconnected, should she try to drag him toward synergy? If he is too enmeshed, should she try to help him see it and stop? My first response is that each parent has the responsibility that comes with that title, to work to make a child's environment the healthiest it can be. So, unequivocally the answer is that a mother should try to make her daughter's environment the healthiest it can be, and a healthy father-daughter relationship is a key component of that environment.

Is it a mother's role to make unsolicited suggestions? Sure, sometimes. You know something about girls and being a daughter, and you know something about fathers, your husband, and men. You're all on the same side; it's okay to share intelligence. But don't be the expert. Just ask yourself: If things were reversed and my husband felt that my relationship with my daughter needed some "adjusting," how would I respond, and what would be the best way for him to approach me on this?

Beyond that, a mother has to carefully choose her terms of engagement in efforts to repair or strengthen the father-daughter relationship. In most situations, it's better to leave the two of them to make their own way, even if it requires some struggle—that's where the learning comes for each one. It's just too easy for relationship-skilled mothers to become full-time interpreters, go-betweens, buffers, and you-name-it. But if you're a mother-in-the-middle on a regular basis, then you lessen the need for father and daughter to communicate and cooperate, and the effect is to actually undermine the partnership you meant to assist.

One mother tells me that she has discovered that she is most successful at encouraging communication between her daughter and her husband when she resists doing it for them. Although she helps with translations from time to time, she carefully avoids interpreting one to the other, and her most often-used and useful response to both of them is: "It sounds like you might need to talk with (her, him) and let (her, him) know what you know and how you feel about it. I'm confident you two can work it out."

If a father and daughter's patterns of interaction are digging them deeper into unproductive ruts, then short-term counseling together may be a helpful way to bring about better understanding and improve communication skills.

Changing Boundaries: Hormones, Hugs, and Other Body Basics

Every year I've run workshops for fathers only. One of them is called simply "The Hormone Talk." This is for fathers of girls about to embark on the stage of development usually marked by menarche. It is often a time for girls of more volatile emotions and sensitivity to the world in general, and to the subset known as fathers in particular.

One father talked about a concern of his right away:

"I'm not sure she cares about me as much now that she is getting bigger. She must not see herself as my little girl anymore, and I guess I have to get used to that. Before, I used to give her big bear hugs, and now she kind of cringes when I do that."

Another shared how "everything changed" when, in the course of just a few months, it seemed, "she changed from having a girl's body to having a woman's body and no sense about the need to wear modest clothes."

Several fathers said that as their girls became more shapely teens, they felt awkward about showing ordinary physical expressions of affection that once had been second nature.

Most fathers experience this timeless awkward shift in the father-daughter dance.

I was visiting friends who have a tween daughter. The very loving father was sitting next to his daughter on the couch and was absentmindedly rubbing her back as he talked. She wiggled and said, "Dad!" and then got up to go into the other room to read. Her father looked after her with a hurt and puzzled expression. It could have been that she was self-conscious of her newly acquired bra, or that she had begun to view touches by males, even her father, in a different way, now that she had a maturing body. Both are very representative responses and thoughts of girls of this age.

Since this is not a conversation you will ever hear between a father and daughter, it's important to point out a few body basics that eliminate the confusion and illuminate a girl's changing need for physical connection to a loving dad.

About those hugs: When girls are budding—just beginning to develop breasts—their chests are sensitive, their self-consciousness is total, and their sensitivity to male-female contact is on high alert, so hugs can be uncomfortable at every possible level. For girls with bear-hugging dads, this presents a problem. Many girls hunch their shoulders to reduce contact. Others turn away, or add a put-down to the moment, to send a clear hands-off message.

All of this speaks very clearly to the importance of early caring and connection between father and daughter. That way, when the pulling-away phase begins, the two have a foundation of emotional closeness that will bridge the gap until she's ready for hugs again, which often occurs just in time for high school graduation.

Whatever the girl issue of the day—whether it is about hair, complexion, makeup, posture, clothing, weight, appearance, fingernails, toenails, mood swings, menstruation, cramps, physical development, body hair, shaving, dating, sex, or sexuality (have I left out anything?)—any father with an inquiring mind about his daughter's meaning or well-being is always well advised to use indirect communication strategy: Get a preliminary briefing from a trustworthy woman, preferably her mother. Direct communication is usually the professionally recommended course of action, but not always with a hormonal girl and a father, because this can be a sensitive time for both.

Why isn't direct communication a good idea here? During the

physical development phase for girls, direct communication can often propel a girl away from her father if it is not handled well. A father who makes a teasing comment about his daughter's chest—or "boobs"—is doomed to a period of cold weather from his daughter. Sometimes even a well-meaning question about whether she has cramps can send her storming into another room. This is a hard enough time for a girl to handle and think about herself without having to deal with others, in this case her father, who bring up body issues directly.

Especially in regard to appearance, everything we know about the negative effects a father's comments can have on a girl's body image and self-esteem comes down to this: If you can't say something nice, don't say anything at all. Ed, a father in his early thirties, turned mealtimes into a command performance for his two daughters from the time they were little. He would monitor closely what they ate, and how much, and if they asked for seconds, he would remind them, sometimes in a joking tone, that "you don't want to get fat," or he would point out if he felt they were "putting on a little too much weight." Neither girl was even remotely overweight. By the time his older daughter was in her early teens, her weight wasn't an issue anymore: She was anorexic and had to be hospitalized. His younger daughter became very self-conscious about her appearance and worried constantly about pleasing her father in every possible way; meanwhile, she turned to sneaking food at home, and preferring to extend play dates with friends so she could eat at their homes.

Humor and Hugs Decoded

A word about humor: Careful! Fathers often use humor to deal with uncomfortable situations, and men, typically, find body humor quite amusing in a way that may exasperate a woman but *mortifies* a girl. Even the daughter who has been delighted by "Daddy's dumb jokes" all her life will not find anything amusing about lighthearted comments about her body or her self. Actually, there is never a good time to tease a girl about her appearance, unless it is Halloween.

Ultimately, direct communication and spending time together should continue to be an integral part of the father-daughter partnership. During this age when she is sizing up males and deciding what she values in that part of the species, the salience of a father is very crucial. The bear-hugging father had begun to pull away from his daughter physically, because he thought that was what she wanted. That also led to a general feeling of distance from both their perceptions. She still needed the physical connection, but with slight adjustments to signal to her that he respected her movement into young womanhood. In this case, I told the father how critical it was to continue the hugging and the importance of that bond both literally and figuratively. But then we also talked about how to do more of the "tent hug" that doesn't crush a girl's chest and gives her a little space for her sensitive body and psyche. Perhaps that's a clear metaphor for the relationship between a father and a daughter as she gets older: Give her a little more space, but don't let go!

Staying Connected: Time Is of the Essence

There are certainly an increasing number of exceptions, but whether we like it or not, it is fathers who typically spend the most time outside the home and outside the sphere of influence of their daughters. Lack of time with mothers and families is increasing, but still, mothers, on an average, spend significantly more time with children. And *time*—quantity and quality—is the most important ingredient in the layering of this precious strudel, more important than any other parenting contribution to child development. You just can't have quality of time with your daughter unless you've put in the quantity of time to be really connected to her.

Nicky Marone, in his book *How to Father a Successful Daughter,* uses the word *salience.* Salience refers to a father spending enough time with his daughter, and vice versa, so that they really know each other and the relationship becomes prominent. Sometimes you just have to "hang" together; you just have to spend enough time in the same place to pick up on the nuances of each other.

This came poignantly to mind at my school one day during screening for admission into our early childhood center. A father had brought his daughter in for his Saturday morning appointment. While she was playing with other children, I asked him to fill out a questionnaire about his daughter that asked about developmental milestones such as when she spoke her first word, what she did during her waking hours, what special talents she had, and so on. He looked at the questionnaire and then looked at me like I was a loon. "I can't answer these questions. I'm not there enough to know the answers." Without apology, yet with great understanding and respect for the burden fathers can face in their work lives, let me say that *this is a problem*.

Making choices and sacrifices to be together and to do things together as a family and as a father-daughter duo is a necessary part of being a responsible and effective father. There is no substitute for spending enough time together. The fathers whose comments on earlier pages described thriving relationships with their daughters are busy, hardworking men who take pains to arrange time to devote to family and to being alone with each of their children.

My dad never knew it, but one of the most cherished memories of our relationship was when he took my brother and me to his business on Saturdays. He'd go in to check on something or to complete a small project, and we'd beg to go with him. When we got there, he'd open the office supply cabinet and tell us we could pick out one thing for ourselves. Those days meant more than big birthday presents or butter pecan ice cream cones at the little neighborhood ice cream shack.

"The ideal father," says Karen, a high school senior, "is understanding, with a sense of humor, around when you need him, but not too nosy, a shoulder to cry on, openly loves my mom, a good role model, and always pushes you to do your best, but not too hard, lets you be your own person, and loves you for who you are, unconditionally. What I love most about my father is that I know that he'll love me forever, no matter what, and I love his hilarious sense of humor. If I could change one thing, it would be that he'd be around more often. Other than that, he understands what I want him to, and other girl stuff wasn't really meant for a dad to understand."

Pearls for Parents and Pearls for Girls

- Develop rituals and language with your daughter that signify a special relationship. Keep them up through childhood and don't be put off by those stages when girls claim that their fathers don't understand them. As one dad says, "Hell, there are times when they think their mothers don't understand them, either!"
- Listen. Assume there is more to what you are hearing than what you hear, and assume you don't always get it, even when you think you do.
- Show an interest in her life, participate, and do things together, even when they are ordinary things.
- Find ways to let your daughter know you like her and love her.
- Establish rules and limits that you and your wife/spouse/partner adhere to in a similar fashion.
- Be there. Spend as much time with your daughter as possible during all stages of her life. Your influence is immeasurable.
- Replace many of your "you look pretty" or "you look nice" comments with others, such as, "I loved the artwork that I saw on the refrigerator last night," or "That's a neat way to wear a baseball hat with your ponytail through the hole in the back."
- At least once a month say, "We haven't spent enough time together lately, what would you like to do sometime this week?"
- Ask, "Are there any school or other activities you'd like me to be at this month? I want to make sure it is in my calendar if possible."

CHAPTER 7

The Galapagos Islands of Girls' Social Development

> *"The most challenging thing about school is probably making friends in the very beginning. If you make them right away, you're in; if it takes you a while, you're out."*
>
> —Annie, thirteen

My day started with a commotion on the playground, which I could see from my office window. One girl was crying, two were trying to comfort her, some were looking confusedly around, but most were on the other side of the playground in a huge throng surrounding a core of girls who were talking about the crying girl in very angry tones.

"She did it on purpose!" wailed a girl holding her fingers.

Another girl said, "Yeah, she's just mean!"

"Oh, no, here comes Dr. Deak, and she'll make us all apologize and tell us we all have to be friends, and I don't *want* to be friends with *her!*"

Next was an appointment with a parent who was concerned about her daughter's lack of steel. I think she must have just seen the movie *Steel Magnolias*. "Georgia just lets her friends decide what she is going to do on weekends. She never has any thoughts of her own or takes a stand on *anything*. I think she's chosen the wrong friends because they are all so pushy and demanding. It's turning her into a wimp!"

I went to the lunchroom and joined the middle school teachers, away from the girls. "What are we going to do about this issue?" were the first words I heard as I put my tray on the table. "No matter how much we tell them that they need to do their homework alone, we find them in the hall each morning helping one another! We've got to come up with a plan that works, instead of warning them all of the time."

I smiled, said I had forgotten something, took my tray, and went out to sit with high school girls. At one particular table, they seemed to be having an interesting conversation, so I sat down. They were too involved to break their conversational stride.

"Well, what are you wearing for Exchange Day?" one girl was saying.

Exchange Day was the day that boys from a neighboring boys' school visited the girls' schools, and our girls visited the boys' school. Two girls began discussing the pros and cons of spaghetti-strap tops, even though it was still a bit cool in May. Two other girls chimed in that it would be better to wear bright-colored spring sweaters. Another said she was sure that boys liked girls in jeans and T-shirts. Two other girls, clearly not as socially sophisticated, just sat there obviously uncomfortable because they had nothing to add, or, I had a feeling, if they did add something, it would be the wrong something, and the other girls would just look at them as if they were from Mars.

On my way down the hall after lunch, a teacher flagged me down and asked if I could stop to talk with her about one of her students. She was a first-grade teacher. "I want to help Jenny with her decision-making. She's a friend with one girl one week, and another the next week. And it's been like this all year. She doesn't seem to know how to make choices and stick with those choices."

Back at my office, Marjorie, a fifth-grader, was waiting for me.

"Something's wrong with me, Dr. Deak." She looked fine to me, and I knew her to be smart and kind and an overall good kid.

"*Everyone* in our class has a best friend but me. And all they do is talk to each other all of the time, at school and on the phone at night. I don't have a best friend!"

I asked if she was being ignored or isolated or friendless. She said no, many girls sat with her at lunch or called her in the evening or talked to her during the school day. "But there is no one special for me, and there is supposed to be."

All right, I confess, not all of these things happened in one day. But every day, a number of these themes played out in one form or another. I feel like Darwin's twin sister, having been privileged to be encamped on this island of girls, a witness to, and to some extent a partner in, each girl's struggle for survival in this sometimes brutal, sometimes balmy, social climate. Survival of the fittest was the defining process here, too, in these Galapagos Islands of human female social development. The fittest, in this case, however, were not necessarily the biggest or fastest or smartest, as measured by grades. They were those girls who were best able to forge connections, generate relationships, expand their social skill set, and remain resilient when storms battered their social landscape, or shook the solid ground of their most intimate friendships. Everything we know about healthy adult life points back to these years of social development as a powerful predictor of success.

By all professional accounts, most of us are social animals. But this connection between people isn't just a matter of the heart. Willard Hartup, one of the most well-known researchers in the field of peer relationships, summarizes the critical effects of early social interaction by saying:

> "*Indeed, the single best childhood predictor of adult adaptation is not IQ, not school grades, and not classroom behavior, but rather the adequacy with which the child gets along with other children.*"

Simply put, how well we interact with others is a key determinant in our later success and happiness in life. How well we interact with others also determines the course of many of our friendships and relationships, both in the short and the long run.

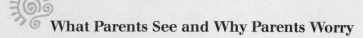

What Parents See and Why Parents Worry

Just as it is the giant Galapagos tortoises that attract the attention of visitors to those islands, friendship tends to be the universal focal point, the most visible, audible feature, in girls' social landscape. Most parents have a clear feeling about the importance of friendships in the lives of their children, both on a daily basis and as a predictor of later competence. It is probably why parents worry so much if things don't go smoothly in this realm. It also makes us uncomfortable to see our child, or our student, lonely or struggling with social issues, especially when a friendship is at stake.

As an administrator or school psychologist in many schools, more of my conferences with concerned parents were about social issues than about academic or disciplinary issues. But then, I worked in girls' schools a great deal of the time! What most parents and girls were relieved to find out was that their friendship issues were not a sign of social failure, but a glimpse of social development in progress.

The Galapagos tortoises are only one of many species of animal life on the islands; together they create a wildlife community, an environment in which each member may thrive, and each contributes to the balance that sustains them all. In the social landscape, friendship is only one facet of social development, and although it is certainly a key facet, our girls fare better, and we do, too, if we understand friendship as part of the larger learning process and purpose of social development.

Friends "R" Us: Relationship Intensity Is a "Girl Thing"

When I speak to parent and teacher audiences around the world, I am often asked to present "the girls' side of the story," while another expert speaks to the issues in boy terms. On many occasions, my partner in this program of friendly gender rivalry is Michael Thompson, the psychologist and coauthor of *Raising Cain* and several highly respected books on boys' emotional life and the social life of children. Michael and I have an ongoing debate on the topic of friendship and gender. He is adamant that friendships are as important to boys as they are to girls. In recent years, incidents of school shootings and recognition of the anger boys feel—and sometimes act upon—because they feel like outcasts certainly attest to this argument.

I see it differently—but then, I've worked predominantly with girls for a long time! I look at the patterns, the way most girls engage in relationships with the fervor and intensity that most boys save for sports or computer gaming. I look at all of the biological and sociological evidence, which we've explored in earlier chapters, pointing to the undeniably high need for connections on the part of females. I think of the literature, including Carol Gilligan's *In a Different Voice* and Mary Pipher's *Reviving Ophelia,* which clearly underscores the unique intensity and impact of friendships for girls.

While the gender debate is provocative and important, my point here is not to argue whether friendship is more important in the lives of females or males. The agreed upon point seems to be that friendships are very important for both genders. But they also seem to follow different patterns of development and play out differently by gender. If you watch girls in play and boys in play, these different gender patterns are very clear.

In general:

• Girls talk more with each other; boys do more with each other
• Girls handle conflict less directly than boys
• Girls seem to display more emotion in their relationships
• Boys seem to display more physicality in their relationships

This is just a brief listing to make the point that girls' and boys' social development and friendships look different and are different in many ways. As we explore social development in this chapter, our feet will be planted firmly in the girl world. Unless it is critical to the point being made, the male side of the story will not be as delineated.

Field Guide to Stages of Social Development in the Girl World

Like most other human characteristics, friendships and social interaction follow somewhat of a pattern of development. In the area of social development, these stages are somewhat sequential. Each one builds upon the one before, and each one has a purpose in the overall growth and developing wisdom of each girl. Remember the scene from a typical day at my girls' school, described earlier? It might seem like chaos, with continuing eruptions of conflict or confusion. But when you look at what's happening in light of what's *supposed* to happen, at what the unfolding of social stages and social wisdom is all about, these vignettes become easier to understand, easier to accept, and easier to figure out how to respond to, as an adult.

It is important for all of us to see the whole path, regardless of where our girl may be on it at the moment. By doing that, we can see how much she learned from previous stages, and discern if there is some remedial work to do, or if she is more sophisticated than her age would suggest (which can be the source of social miscues, or misfit issues). With that perspective, we can begin to understand why a stage that is driving us crazy is nonetheless a critical milestone in social development, and be in a better position to support girls' social and emotional growth through that process.

Stages of Social Development

This chart summarizes the stages of social development of girls. It is based on my observations and the responses of hundreds of girls over decades of professional work:

Stage	Ages
Self-Awareness	Birth–2
Parallel Play	2–3
Interactive Play	3–6
Transitory Friendships	6–8
Friendship Clusters	8–10
Best Friends	10–12
Cliques	12–14
Interest-Based Friendship Groups	14 and older
(Almost) Universal Acceptance	High school seniors

Some people just seem to be born with social ease—the comfort level that allows them to feel relaxed and competent, for instance, at a lawn party. Others of us are uncomfortable at the thought of chatting with many people about light topics. This lawn party ease is certainly a part of social competence. In the same way, some girls have a natural social ease; they go through these stages and the learning involved rather automatically. Some girls have a much harder time. Some girls get stuck in one of the stages. Some girls don't follow any pattern at all. But most girls go through these stages one by one, and need to do that. Sometimes they learn the lessons intuitively, sometimes they need a bit of direct instruction or coaching.

Let's return to the chapter's opening scene and take a closer look at my conversation with Marjorie, the fifth-grader who didn't have a best friend. She was basically saying that from her observation, it was normal to want and have a best friend in fifth grade. She wasn't unhappy because she was unliked or friendless. She was worried because she wasn't following the pattern and she felt that something must be wrong with her. As soon as I explained my theory of Generalists (which we'll turn to shortly), she knew she wasn't weird. Although she would have liked the comfort and safety that having a best friend brings, she was also comfortable knowing that her path was only slightly different from the norm—and in that way was, itself, quite normal—for this stage of her life.

Consider Jenny, the fickle first-grader whose teacher wanted to help her be more focused and committed in her friendship habits. Jenny's floating friendship style actually reflected the typical social development stage for her age. Being fluid and getting to know all types of people is an important early step in life, and leads to wiser choices later. This well-meaning teacher wanted Jenny to make and stick with wise choices before she even really understood what all of her choices were. This is the Baskin-Robbins concept of social learning (which we'll also explore more fully, shortly). You can't just look at the flavor selection and know what you like—you have to try them!

Each stage of social development has a clear development task or purpose that layers over time with the next learning phase and stage of social development. This will become clear as we go through each of the stages. And remember, regardless of your daughter's present age, it is elucidating to see what came before and what will come after, and why. One footnote: There is some slip and slide between stages and some periods of regression or acceleration, depending on the girl and her environment. So don't expect every girl to follow the time line exactly.

Stage 1: Self-Awareness (Birth to Two Years Old)

Watch an infant look at her fingers as if they were foreign objects, not really aware that they are a part of her body. This is where it all begins. Soon she's pulling her dad's ear and seeing that it doesn't feel the same as pulling her own ear. Eventually she'll yank on her brother's ear, knowing full well whose ear it is, and who is going to yelp in pain. All of this illustrates the purpose of this starting stage so clearly: What am I all about and where is that line between self and others? Although this task will continue throughout life, it is the very elementary version of separating self from others that is the developmental milestone of this first stage.

I was talking with a mother who sat with her four-month-old daughter in her lap as her five-year-old son played a few feet away. He stopped over, en route to his toys, and leaned over the baby to make a face. His baby sister smiled and stuck her finger in his eye! It took Mom quite a bit of talking to explain to her son why the baby did this, that it was not meant to deliberately hurt him, and that babies don't know that another body feels anything. He looked at his mother in amazement and said, "Boy, she's got a lot to learn!"

Stage 2: Parallel Play (Two to Three Years Old)

Once a girl knows her physical self and a bit about what this self can do and feel, she is usually put in proximity with her peers. This is where adults in the lives of children begin to act on good intentions and make mistakes.

The first classic mistake is to attempt to shepherd a child too quickly through this parallel-play stage and on to the next stage, which looks to the adult eye to be the positive model of cooperative play. For example, I've heard parents or teachers instruct a two-year-old to "play nice," and then scold her at the first sign of conflict with another child.

During a visit to a nursery school one day, I watched as a volunteer parent admonished two little girls who were having a tug-of-war over a stuffed animal: "If you girls can't play nice, I'm going to take the animal away and you'll just have to sit there and watch the other children play!"

When we hurry a girl through this, or any stage, we reduce the learning that can and should occur in that stage. The purpose of parallel play is just that: to be in parallel activity—not collaborative interaction. This parallel existence is how a child begins to move away from a total self-focus to watching and beginning to understand others. In the nursery school example, given the girls' ages, it would have been better to have had two stuffed animals. Then the girls could have played alongside each other, each watching how the other played, learning something about stuffed animals and other little girls, for starters. (One word of advice: Parallel play will go more smoothly if the stuffed animals are *exactly* alike!)

Two-year-olds will often play with the same materials in the same room, but not talk or interact much. In fact, it is important *not* to try to get children this age to purposely share. This is not the time to put two children together with one favorite toy. This stage is designed to see that there are others in the world somewhat like you, that they like to play and talk, too, and that you are not the center of the universe. With this foundation, a girl can move gradually into the next stage.

Stage 3: Interactive Play (Three to Six Years Old)

In the literature, this is often called *cooperative play*. While that is the end goal of this stage, or the development objective, the real work of this period is in interacting together to gradually build the skills that lead to cooperative play. These are the means to the end goal. Now is the time to allow, or even purposefully set up, a situation of limited resources. Limited resources, in this context, does not mean inadequate. It simply means not having the same number of objects or toys as children who want to use them.

Putting several three-year-olds—we'll call them Mary, Terri, Sherry, and Joan—together at a table with paper and a set of Magic Markers is a good example. (And yes, you *can* try this at home!) It is only by experience that Mary learns, for instance, that if she reaches for the red marker and Terri wants the same one, Terri will hit her. On the other hand, if she and Sherry want the same marker, Sherry will smile and let her have the marker. Joan, on the other hand, will cry and wait for the teacher to come over and fix things. I could go on, but you can see that over the days and weeks and months of this kind of interaction, a girl begins to gain a reservoir of wisdom of what other human beings are all about and then can begin to act on that wisdom. If Mary wants a red marker, and Terri is using it, she may decide to bypass potential conflict with Terri and finish coloring her green spaces first. If Sherry has the red marker, then Mary might simply ask for it, anticipating success. On the other hand, Mary may have the temperament, or be in the mood, to want to see Joan cry, or to find out if Terri is always a hitter when confronted.

Adults do have an important role in this high conflict stage. If a child is spinning her wheels and doesn't seem to be gradually improving in her wisdom, a little mediation is in order.

Here's how that looked one day at school, as two preschool girls and their teacher stood in the hall outside their classroom. One girl was steaming angry, the other was in tears, and the teacher was in the middle.

"Jo, I'd like you to tell Ellie why you pushed her off the tire swing," the teacher said.

"Because she wouldn't give me a turn!"

"Ellie, would you tell Jo why you wouldn't give her a turn?"

"Because she was on the tire swing all the time yesterday and it was my turn!"

"Jo, did you tell her that you wanted a turn?"

"No."

"Ellie, did you tell her why you wouldn't get off?"

"I didn't have a chance, she pushed me and hurt me!"

You can see how this conversation progressed, using the classic "use your words" recipe, which neither girl had been doing much that school year. Had this been the first episode, and had they begun to argue and fight about it, letting them go would have been a good idea. As much as possible, it is important for adults to let these little episodes of conflict and learning happen without interfering with the developmental task at hand. If an adult controls the situation, or if the conflict is too great, then learning at this stage is much diminished. But if learning to handle conflict is not happening well over time, then guidance—not punishment—helps a girl become competent and confident as she moves into the next stage.

Observational and Interactive Learning

During the formative years, covering several stages of social development, a girl's access to learning social lessons grows richer through a range of improving observational and interactive skills. Most girls are better at reading other people's emotional cues than boys are. Ample research has shown that generally females can see and read facial expressions and body language much more adeptly than males. So, by and large, girls learn a great deal by observational and interactive learning. However, there are some children, albeit fewer girls than boys, who just don't have this perceptive ability. They seem to be born with a blind spot when it comes to understanding social cues and the nuances of the responses of others.

These children often need direct teaching, kind of like shining a spotlight on the details that most other children can see in regular lighting. For instance, going back to our three-year-old girls around the art table, if Terri not only continues to hit but begins to hit harder or more when she doesn't get her way, it's time for a parent or teacher to intervene in a guiding, not punishing, way. This is an absolutely key point in the development of socially effective children. Many adults move into the censure or punishment mode during a child's learning phase, and the lesson is reduced to one about adult power and punishment.

In Terri's case, instead of telling Terri she is bad or removing her or the marker from the situation, it is much more effective to bring Terri and Mary together and mediate the interaction so Terri can experience the details of effective interaction and begin to employ them. This is the classic "use your words" conversation, which might better be called a "learn your words" conversation, because in these conversations a girl learns to use her voice, express her feelings, listen to others, and look for solutions. Mary, at the art table, learns to say to Terri, "It hurts when you hit me and it makes me mad and I don't want to play with girls that hit." Terri gets her turn to express her need and her feelings: "But I don't want to give you the red marker. I need it!" The parent or teacher might point out that there is only one red marker left, and invite ideas for figuring out how both girls can use the red marker for their drawings.

Some girls just need to see and hear the details and be led down the garden path. Other girls could be president of the garden club without much training! In either case, you can see why this is such a critical phase of social development. The goal is, as with every stage, that a girl accumulate enough wisdom to move on to the next phase, even though interactive learning will be a lifetime's work.

Stage 4: Transitory Friendships (Six to Eight Years Old)

This is the beginning of the Baskin-Robbins years. The developmental task during these years is to taste all the flavors of friendship. How can you know which flavors really make your taste buds sing (or scream) if you haven't tasted them all? It's important to allow and encourage girls to be somewhat fluid (some would say fickle) in their choices of friends, rather than hitching exclusively to one particular friend or small group.

Again, adults sometimes act in ways that are counterproductive to the purpose of this stage. We often encourage a girl to narrow her play date interests to children we like, or children of our friends. Or we take the indirect public-relations approach, putting a positive spin on the playmate of our choice, saying something like, "Isn't Marsha a nice girl?" At this age it is still a good idea to invite everyone in a class to a party, and you should encourage your daughter to do things with many different girls.

The first-grade teacher who worried that Jenny was "fickle" and indecisive about friendship was missing the purpose of this stage and underestimating the value of Jenny's social explorations. This stage really is the practice ground for seeing how you interact and affiliate with every type of person. It helps a girl know what she likes and dislikes, and what she values in human beings. Pushing it to the

limit, it is part of the sorting process of interactive choices for life. You
can see how it leads so logically to the next stage.

Stage 5: Friendship Clusters (Eight to Ten Years Old)

Once a girl has tasted all the flavors, it may be the flavors with
nuts that just hit her taste buds better than the others. So she narrows
down the flavors she wants to be around most frequently to pistachio,
maple walnut, butter pecan, and almond mocha. This narrowing of
flavors or types of people is the next phase in the layering of social wisdom. It's not that she doesn't like the other flavors or appreciate their
differences; it's just that her natural preference is for the nut flavors.

Trina was a very lively girl who invited everyone in her class
to her birthday parties in first and second grade. In third grade she
told her mother she wanted to have a sleepover party with five girls.
Her mother was concerned that this was the start of clique behavior,
something to be discouraged.

Meanwhile, Brady was in tears because she was not invited to
Trina's party, and she considered Trina a friend of hers. After all, they
sat next to each other in class and sometimes got together on a Saturday when Brady's parents had to work.

Trina and Brady were smack in the middle of the clustering
stage. Often, friendship or relationship choices are not logical at the
beginning, or based on accumulated evidence or characteristics. It is
somewhat more magical than that. If you ask a girl why certain girls
are in her friendship cluster, or why she wants to spend more time
with some girls than with others, she may try to put it into words, but
ultimately it is reduced to: "I just like them better."

This stage should not be confused with the clique stage, which
will rear its head soon. Friendship clusters are more fluid than cliques,
more accepting, less impermeable. The cluster doesn't freak if bubble
gum ice cream comes up to them during their trek through the mall.
The developmental task is to reduce the number of friends to a likable
group that is small enough to get to know better, rather than all the fla-

vors in the universe. This allows a girl to go below the surface of inter-actions and begin to know the content and character of another person; it is the beginning of real friendship, real relationships.

Stage 6: Best Friends—BF's (Ten to Twelve Years Old)

Now she knows she likes the nutty flavor ice creams, but of all the possibilities, it is clear that nothing can compare to butter pecan. Maple walnut comes close, but it just isn't butter pecan. A girl still engages with her friendship cluster (maybe even including bubble gum from the mall day), but it is butter pecan that she spends hours talking with and being with. She spends all day at school with butter pecan, and gets home and immediately gets on the phone or e-mails her, too. Interestingly, this 24/7 kind of friendship is also practice time for choosing a mate or partner later in life. Since it is too early to have such a deep relationship with the opposite gender, this same-gender intensive relationship helps a girl learn how to interact at the intimate level with another human being.

For most girls, there is such a need, such a longing for a best friend that many girls feel there is something wrong with them if they don't have one. The potential for conflict and pain is at an all-time high at this age, whether a girl has a "BF" or not. If she does have a BF, the deep connection can lead to deep pain when things aren't going smoothly. If she doesn't have a BF, she can feel incredibly lonely and alone, or just incredibly different. Some girls, a bit of a minority, don't have this same need for intimacy at this point in life. They are what I call the Generalists.

Generalists (G's for short) are just built temperamentally to appreciate all flavors and continue to keep their social net wide open. They also serve a very important function in the social realm during this stage as well as the next stage.

After having this Baskin-Robbins discussion with a group of fifth-grade girls, one of them came to see me. She said that I had made her feel a lot better about not having the best friend that she wanted.

She said that she was maple walnut and her choice of best friend wanted butter pecan. We talked about the fact that she could not change this girl's taste buds. She had tried everything to be this girl's choice for best friend—she had been nice, had helped with her home-work, had listened to many of her boring stories, had put up with her little brother, and more. It was this new understanding of the taste bud theory that had relieved some of the sting of rejection. She ended by saying, "There's someone out there who will love maple walnut!" (And there was.)

Another girl passed me in the hall and then returned to ask me if I knew she was a G. I said that I did, and that I was always impressed with how she associated with everyone. She said that she used to just feel really weird that she wasn't like most girls and that she liked to be with everyone and wasn't very selective. Now she felt almost proud to be a G, someone, I had explained, that was the "glue" of the class (because when a girl can't find her butter pecan, or her butter pecan moved to Chicago, she can always find a friend in a G).

Stage 7: Cliques (Twelve to Fourteen Years Old)

Amoebas. As I walked down the corridor that housed the sev-enth- and eighth-grade classrooms, that's what I saw scurrying around the halls. This entity that looked like an amorphous mass was also intimately connected; almost one teeming organism. The nucleus of the amoeba closest to me was composed of two very short girls that the rest of the amoeba were trying to walk next to and talk with, sometimes walking sideways like crabs to stay in their visual purview. One of the nucleus duo dropped her notebook, and several of the fringe amoeba bent quickly to scoop up the papers. Even if these girls hadn't been in such geographic proximity, I would have known that they were a clique by how they dressed, walked, and, "like, you know," used the same expressions. Not very far behind them was a group of girls that wasn't quite connected, but seemed like one of those organisms you see under a microscope that try to enter the cell wall of the amoeba. They got close, but never quite permeated that boundary.

Maybe it's because, in our culture and society, moving into mating and marriage no longer happens during the tween years as it had been for many centuries. Now a huge time span elapses from best friends to choosing of a mate. What defines the interim? That is the classic definition of adolescence: increasing independence. This is the age at which children begin to figuratively stiff-arm adults along the trail to adulthood themselves. Adults are no longer fonts of knowledge, but rather strange human beings who are just out of touch with reality. At the same time, there are huge body changes and increasing stresses and societal expectations of adolescents. What a time to let go of your adult anchors! So, to replace this stability, as discussed in the tweens and teens chapters, they enter the cocoon of cliques. Surrounding oneself with those who look alike, talk alike, and act alike makes the world feel safer and allows this movement away from the influence of significant adults to be more comfortable.

By definition then, cliques need to be powerful and impermeable to be the most protective they can be of the insecure organisms that make up the clique. In fact, most experts agree that the more impermeable and wielding of power a clique is, the more insecure the members are. Unfortunately, this type of coalition is often perceived as the most popular and coveted group. Girls who are not part of the popular clique often feel less popular, more tentative, and at risk in the social scene. Even though they may be more mature by adult standards, they feel less secure in the company of the clique. The end result is that cliques wield incredible power and influence, much of which is generated by fear. Those girls in the clique often do hurtful things that they would never do if alone, because of their fear of being ousted by the other clique members.

I heard one powerful clique leader make a snide remark about her Latin teacher. I knew one of the members of the clique who loved Latin and loved this particular teacher, but instead of saying that, she just nodded her head in agreement and smiled. That is a mild version of the pressure clique members face. You see a similar fear and sub-mission of the majority of the class when a small group of girls in a particular clique wield their negative power. In one eighth-grade class, the power clique made it clear that they "owned" the premier hangout space in the hall and no one else had better sit there, even when it was vacant. I watched all of the other members of the class, some of whom were quite capable and strong as individuals, abide by this unwritten dictum.

Girls not part of the clique either imitate the norms of the clique (protective coloration), or try to be somewhat invisible and fly beneath the radar of the clique. It is extremely rare for an individual girl to go against clique norms in seventh and eighth grade.

This is part of what makes this time period so hard for adults to watch, and why, out of thousands of women I've polled, only three said they would be willing to go through seventh and eighth grade again! Let me remind all of us of the positive task of this social stage: The clique cocoon helps stabilize its occupants until they are strong enough and independent enough to stand outside of the group, or somewhat alone. The task of the adults in the sphere of influence of cliques is, first, to accept this important function, and second, to draw the line when a clique's influence moves from unpleasant to down-right unhealthy.

The director of an independent middle school called me one day with a mystery to solve. This was a school that, as a part of the admissions process, routinely invited prospective students to come spend a day at the school. In this eighth grade, very few girls who vis-ited ever decided to come to the school. Upon investigation, it became clear that the power clique was making sure the female applicants had a bad visit day, so that there would be no new girls to challenge their turf. Meanwhile, girls not in this clique could have benefited from having new members added to their available social group, but they dared not be overtly friendly to the visiting girls.

It takes courage for a parent or a school to tangle with the power of a clique because we often don't have much control. That is one reason why it is often more practical and effective to deal with the issues of individuals unless it is really a continuing and extremely negative situation. In this case, the school really drew a distinctive line in the sand. They talked to all the girls in the class, told them what was happening, and that the negative impact on the school was serious. They explained that each applicant who did not choose to come to the school would be interviewed, and that anyone who had interfered with a positive visit to the school would be put on probation, etc.

Parents have even less ability to interfere or intervene with clique behavior. Most often, as I said before, talking to your daughter and discussing how to handle situations is the best modus operandi. Or just listening, if your daughter is the target of clique meanness, or imposing consequences if your daughter is part of clique meanness, are viable avenues. Sometimes, total removal from the influence of a clique is the only alternative in very serious situations, such as influence in terms of drugs or alcohol. (Stay tuned for Marta's story in Chapter 9, "Parents Under Pressure.")

This extreme version of clique power really underscores the extreme possibilities of clique influence. But most often the influences of a clique are less life-threatening and more cosmetic, like talking or looking alike. In these cases, I often counsel parents not to go to the mat over these issues. In other words, if your daughter just has to wear the same fashion shoe everyone else is, it's not worth it to use this as the arena to make the independence speech. On the other hand, if your daughter wants to join her clique in slicing a teacher's tires, then it's time to say, "Think for yourself and don't follow the group!"

Stage 8: Interest-Based Friend Groups
(Fourteen to Forever!)

Just as you're about to pull your hair out about the influence of cliques, a girl moves into this next stage in the early or middle high school years. She doesn't need the cocoon of the clique, and in fact, finds it somewhat suffocating. Now she begins to affiliate with peers who are interested in the same kinds of things she's interested in. And, more than ever before, her friends can be girls or boys. If, for instance, a girl is into theater and the arts, she begins to affiliate with the theater crew. Or if she's an avid athlete, her group is often composed of other jocks. This is not exclusive, and there is some interest crossover. However, from this age on into adulthood, the major choice of affiliations and friendships has to do with commonality of interests or passions or philosophy.

What is the developmental task of this stage? I'm not sure. Since it occupies most of adult life, perhaps it offers the benefits of clusters and cliques without the downside: acceptance, activity, and social creativity, without insecurity, narrowness, and meanness. Whatever it is, it is just a fact of social living. Something needs to be the glue of relationships. In the case of mates, it is love and/or sex and then, possibly, family. In terms of other relationships, it is a matter of bloodlines (relatives) or shared interests (friends).

Stage 9: (Almost) Universal Acceptance

One of the most special qualities of senior year in high school is that it is a time when the lines of cliques and even interest-based friendships are blurred or disappear, and these older adolescents find themselves in almost universal acceptance of all types of human beings. Do you remember the magic of senior year? They're about to be leaving their families, their schools, their teachers, and their friends. That pending separation causes seniors to spend most of that year appreciating, accepting, or positively tolerating most human beings in their geographic vicinity. Now girls who never talked with other girls or boys in their class are seniors *together*. They can afford to be generous, too; even those underclass girls and boys are not so bad. Teachers and parents temporarily regain their status. It is a very emotional and holistic time.

Although adults often rediscover this stage at an advanced age—and for similar reasons, as we see a different end in sight—the universal acceptance glow in late adolescence typically fades, and interest-based friendship resumes its dominant role, as everyone begins to focus on their individual work or college or other post–high school endeavors. Interestingly, though, I'm hearing more these days from young and older women who are finding great satisfaction in circles of diverse others drawn together not by traditional work or play interests, but by this core value of universal acceptance and the opportunities it presents for life growth.

Friendship Patterns: A Matter of Sophistication, Serendipity

I'm often asked to identify the biggest mistakes we adults make in teaching girls about friendship, or in responding to a daughter's distress over friendship. Most parents have their own collection of four-star mistakes, times they said or did something to make things better and only made them worse—or simply looked foolish and overreactive in the light of the next day.

At a deeper level, the biggest mistake going is the common misunderstanding of the correlation between personal qualities and popularity. Parents and teachers often mistakenly believe that there is a high positive correlation between these two things. We all tell girls to be nice and kind and respectful of others, and they will be happy and have friends. Yet we all know many girls who fit this description who feel that they don't have friends, or whom no one calls with invitations to do things.

Social development and friendship are very much related, but they are also different enough that the discrimination needs to be clear. Social development is the long-term process that, over time, yields increased social interaction skills and wisdom. Having effective social skills is the best predictor of overall success in life, and it would make logical sense to assume that someone with good social skills would be popular and make a good friend. Well, yes and no. Until girls are strong enough to handle serious conflict and social pressure, and stand up for what they morally believe in, power is a better predictor of who will be popular and who will have many friends.

During most of the social development stages, what I would term *social sophistication* seems to have the most weight. Although hard to define, it is easy to see. These are the girls who just seem to know the latest fashion, or else, what they wear becomes the in thing at their school. These are the girls who have some chutzpah, and will not hesitate to use their words to keep their followers in line and let other girls know to back off. These are the girls who have charisma and are fun to be with. These are the girls who set the pace and rules in a social environment. While there are many things a school can do to moderate this force, it is very difficult. Schools, understandably so, feel their focus should be on academics, and often do not tangle with the social web. Parents have no effective means of dealing with the social scene on their own.

These social sophisticates are the proverbial leaders of the pack. Outside of that leadership circle and the power group, however, acceptance in groups, and the friendships that emerge, are more serendipitous and are *not* necessarily related to the positive characteristics that we adults would like children to have. For example, the leaders of the most powerful group choose or allow membership in their group first. Then the other girls begin to affiliate with the remaining girls, searching for connections and forming other groups or duos. It really is a social pecking order, so to speak. If you ask any girl to rank the popularity of the subgroups in her class or school, she can do that.

Where does this leave a parent who wants to help her daughter negotiate the gray of this social realm? Well, I'm not saying that we should stop encouraging girls to be respectful of others. And the golden rule will always be golden. But we have to stop telling girls that if they would just be nice and kind, they will have friends, because it is not true. If a girl is perceived as loyal, trustworthy, and respectful of others, she may or may not have a lot of friends throughout the years leading to high school, or even into high school. However, she probably will be recognized as a natural leader by other students, will find that girls and boys come to her to talk or for help with homework, and that people like her.

Julie, a seventh-grader, talked with me from time to time about not having any friends. Yet when her class had an election to choose representatives to meet with teachers about the school climate, she was amazed to be one of the two chosen. None of the celebrated popular kids were chosen for this task. In this case, it was clear the students wanted someone who was a classic representative: someone they could trust, someone who would take the task seriously, someone who understood what would be good for the kids in their grade level.

Social pain misses no one; it just happens for different kinds of girls at different times. The mean and popular girls of middle school have very reduced friendship groups by high school and beyond. Often, many of the girls who feel friendless in earlier grades have good friends in high school. As adults in the lives of girls, it is much more effective if we help girls see that sometimes what they do or say will not net them friends in a complex social scene. Once they understand the nature of the hierarchy of social groups and many of the choices dictated by power or by nonlogical ice cream flavor choice, it takes some of the sting out of it. A girl can then stop thinking that something is wrong with her. The lonely girl feels lonely, but the truth is, she's got lots of company; *most* girls feel socially neglected during a good portion of their school years.

One of the most positive things parents can do to keep their daughters socially healthy and continuing to develop good social interaction skills, as well as friendship options, is to provide opportunity and access to groups of kids outside of the school scene. School social environments become very hierarchical and very static social webs. Other group affiliations, including camps, church or synagogue, a neighborhood sports team, or Saturday art classes at the museum, are far less socially complicated and far more open.

A mother came in to see me after her daughter had had a great camp experience, had made friends easily, and was very happy. This was in stark contrast to her feelings about social fit at school. She talked about how this had been a life-changing experience for her daughter, that her daughter felt healthy and okay now, and that she, the mother, dreaded the beginning of school when all of the old social scene stuff would wash over her again. We talked about how important it would be to continue out-of-school interaction experiences for her daughter to keep her new view of herself alive and well.

From Balm to Battleground: When Friendship Hurts

The second biggest mistake we good-intentioned adults make is that we intervene and interfere with conflict situations too early and too often. Most of us are programmed to protect children and to take care of them. So when we see a girl in social pain, it is a caring reflex to try to fix, or at least help, the situation. Ah, here's the rub: *Conflict is good!* Disagreements and dealing with harsh words and the hurtful behavior of others is what allows a girl to figure out how to respond, and to negotiate interactional waters. The saying "No pain, no gain" is apropos here. If we step in too soon to stop the behavior or interaction, or to punish or to fix, the girl becomes less effective and less able to handle conflict, and more reliant on others. If she can't deal with it, she's likely to want to avoid it, and a girl who routinely avoids conflict begins to build her life around compliance instead. Overpleasing, as we'll see in Chapter 8, holds greater risks for a girl's health and safety than any normal conflict.

The key goes back to that darn fine line again. How much social pain, lasting how long, do you allow to happen? And the usual answer is: that depends! However, the basic guideline is the duration and depth of the pain. If it is an argument over a toy, let it play out and watch how it goes. If your daughter comes home crying almost every day and this has been going on for a month, it is time to step in. The challenge is in figuring out how to step in and make it a positive growth experience for your daughter. In most cases, social pain is an undercurrent of school life, but the current moves around and so does the pain. Because a parent's control or sphere of influence is very limited, it's important for you to have a key contact at school each year of your daughter's school career. Whether that is her adviser, homeroom teacher, or guidance counselor, you should have a person who can help figure out how best to proceed. Without that inside information, parents can only act as sounding boards and absorbing sponges.

In most social conflict situations, it is important to watch and wait a bit. If you have the kind of daughter who immediately seeks assistance, your job is to send her back with words like: "I think you two can figure out how to handle this." If your daughter is the pleaser and constantly gives up in a conflict situation, your response is not to intervene at the moment, but to have conversations with her about how to handle situations like that the next time around. These are basically sound principles of conflict management, which is what all girls need to develop. It is also just another version of the Teeter-Totter Theory of parenting. Our job as adults is to help balance the teeter-totter. If she is an avoider, we gently turn her around and push her back into the fray with some viable verbal arsenal. If she is a pleaser, we practice how she should stand her ground without put-downs; if she is a bulldozer, we teach her to count to ten (or in the parlance of conflict management, verbal mediation) before lashing out.

When Bad Friends Are Good

The most classic parent faux pas in this social sea is trying to influence friendship choices. It's a caring parent who wants a child to interact with other children of good character. In that way, we all hope the social learning will progress down a nice smooth path. But remember Baskin-Robbins? If girls don't experience all the flavors early, they will not be good discriminators of human beings later in life. I believe that bad friends are good, in the same way that conflict is good. It's better to learn how to manage them than to spend your life trying to avoid them. But, just as with conflict, there are some parameters to bad friends. If I could choose the best time to make bad choices that would result in social wisdom, it would be before high school. In most cases, the consequences are fairly minor. If you make bad choices later in life, it can result in much more serious consequences like drinking, drugs, pregnancy, and poor partners in commitment.

Just as with conflict, having a friend who talks you into cutting class or who talks behind your back or who does any of those myriad things we find offensive as adults, does two important things. First, it almost forces a girl to figure out what to do in these situations and that adds to her bank of coping skills. Second, it provides valuable information about types of human beings, which will add to her wisdom in making affiliation choices later. And pain or conflict seems to imbed into the long-term memory banks far better than parental words of advice.

Linda's seven-year-old daughter, Haley, was friends with a number of girls her age who lived within easy walking distance from their home. The girls often played at Haley's house, and Linda was privy to their conversations and conflicts. One of the girls, Sonya, wasn't "my type," as Linda put it. Sonya bragged about her toys, her trips, her parents' jobs, and just about anything else that came up in conversation within this group. It also became apparent that any time a game wasn't going her way, she would find a way to end it, usually by creating a conflict that put other girls at odds until the game dissolved in argument. Finally one evening, after watching Haley's dismay as one of Sonya's diversionary tactics had spoiled the afternoon, Linda suggested to Haley that she simply not invite Sonya over any more.

"No, Mom, it's okay," Haley said. "The rest of us decided already, the next time she does it, we're just going to tell her that we're not going to stop playing—she's the one that's got to stop making trouble!"

"But you know, you don't *have* to invite her over at all," Linda said. "Maybe she needs to learn that her inconsiderate behavior has consequences she doesn't like."

But Haley had a different strategy. "Mom, she doesn't have any other friends, and it would be mean to just leave her out. From now on, when she does stuff like that, we're just going to tell her to stop it or go home. She can choose."

In the weeks (and I can tell you now, *years*) that followed, conflicts with Sonya came and went, and although the girls didn't remain the cohesive group they were when younger, whenever the neighborhood girls did get together, they always included Sonya, even when she was a pill. And whenever her behavior crossed the line, they set her straight. Over the years, Sonya struggled with a number of difficult issues, but the continued interaction with these girls proved to be a valuable learning ground—for all of them.

In a daughter's field of friendship, parents struggle through feast and famine, and monsoon seasons in between. In the end, our girls will pick their own friends, learn their own lessons, grow their own wisdom. If we're lucky, they'll share it with us, sometimes with startling clarity.

"I just made up with my mother after a long, bitter fight, basically because I gave my friends more weight in a decision than she had," says Elizabeth, who is seventeen. "That's not exactly what it was about, but pretty much anything that teenagers and their parents fight about involves that theme, and the basic question: 'Are friends more important than family?' Well, it always seems that way, I guess, but I think that the only reason that we teenagers rely so much on what our friends say is because we are testing what our parents taught us, to make sure it was right."

Pearls for Parents and Pearls for Girls:

- Share the Baskin-Robbins ice cream description of the social scene, or let her read it for herself. If the moment invites some playful conversation, ask her if she knows a butter pecan or a bubble gum. Ask her what flavor *she* is.

- If she is experiencing some routine social pain, let her see the light at the end of the tunnel by letting her know about the next stage.

- Open your house to her friends as frequently as you can.

- Practice being a listener instead of a fixer.

- Let her friendship choices be hers.

CHAPTER 8

Aiming to Please: Moving Beyond the "Tyranny of Niceness"

"The worst thing about being a girl is, you have to always be thinking about how you look and whether people like you. You have to be nice all the time, or people say you're mean, and it's hard to be nice to everybody all the time. The thing I wish I could change about myself is, I would like to be nicer."

—Laura, fifteen

At first I thought it was just that Pat was such a strong leader of the group that Cindy went along with everything she said because it was easier than arguing. But then I saw her at lunch. Another girl had forgotten her napkin and Cindy jumped up and said, "I'll get it!" Maybe she was just taught to be helpful, I thought. We had the best-loved dessert that day: giant chocolate chip cookies, limit one. Jan said that she really wanted another cookie because she hated all of the rest of the lunch. Cindy said, "You can have mine, I don't really like them." On previous giant cookie days, I had watched her relish each bite. Hmm. Then came the episode that branded her as an overpleaser. Karen had come to lunch late and wanted to sit at this table, but there was no space. Cindy didn't say anything because she really wanted to stay with this group, but the giveaway was that everyone, without any prompting, looked to Cindy when no one offered to give up a seat.

Cindy just smiled and said, "Sure," although no one had asked her to do anything. Sounds like first grade? No, it was *tenth* grade!

Carol Gilligan was the first to coin the phrase "tyranny of niceness" to describe the way our culture stunts girls' emotional growth by training them to be pleasers, shaping their behavior, their expectations, and even their life dreams to accommodate or please others. Throughout history and well into the 1950s, girls were raised to be nice this way, to be compliant, and to devote their talents cheerfully as directed at home. The sixties and seventies were liberating in many ways, but the underlying expectation remained that girls could be liberated *and* nice; they could pursue higher education and careers and even free love, but if they wanted to get anywhere, they'd better be nice about it. In the eighties and nineties, girls saw the world of careers and competition open wider. They heard the social mantra to be true to themselves and they used their voices to speak up in the world, but their role models were women stretched to the breaking point trying to please *everybody*, at the office *and* at home.

In this early part of the new millennium, will we continue to send the message that to be valued, girls must please others first and most? Or can we raise girls in a new middle ground that nurtures healthy self-esteem, self-expression, and pleasure in caring about others without an accompanying drive to please them at all costs?

What's So Bad About Wanting to Be Good?

Most of us would rather be liked than not liked. It's normal to seek the approval of those you respect. So what's so bad about wanting to be liked? Don't you want your daughter to care about other people? Of course you do! Don't we feel happier as human beings when we care about others? Of course we do! Wouldn't the world be a better place if *everyone* tried a little harder to be pleasing? Of course it would! But the people who do it most predictably to excess are girls, and the problem is that when a girl invests too much of her emotional energy in pleasing others, it's a sign that she feels she *has* to do so to gain approval. Being herself isn't good enough. A girl who feels the need to please will sacrifice a lot of herself—her feelings, her intuition, her judgment, her ambitions, and her dreams—to keep others happy.

Self-esteem is an important piece in a girl's emotional life. In the pleaser's life, it is a twisted piece. We build self-esteem by doing things that make us feel confident, competent, or emotionally connected in fairly equal measures. The girl who is fairly confident and competent, but not very connected to others, will not feel as great a sense of self-esteem. However, with pleasers, the connection piece is distorted: Pleasers spend so much time pleasing others (staying connected with them) that their competence and confidence is stunted.

It might appear that pleasers must feel quite good about themselves, raking in the compliments on their behavior, their helpfulness, their selflessness. The opposite is true. Their self-esteem is often very low, and it is a vicious cycle: The more they try to please, and negate their other needs in order to do so, the worse they feel. Their self-esteem takes a steady drubbing when they routinely put other peoples' feelings and desires ahead of their own, marginalizing themselves in their effort to stay connected. Pleasing is no substitute for the full array of experiences and feelings that build genuine self-esteem.

How can you differentiate a girl who is struggling to please from one who is simply being cooperative or collaborative? Avoiding conflict is one of the key signs. A kindergartner who always lets someone cut in line in front of her at school, an eight-year-old who always lets her brother pick which program to watch on TV, a tween whose refrain to her friends is: "I don't care, whatever you want to do." In fact, variations on these pleaser themes are a signal throughout life that someone may need help in breaking free from the tyranny of niceness. "It doesn't matter to me." "Whatever you want is fine." "You choose . . ."

There are certainly times when these responses are appropriate because the choice is something that is genuinely a low priority, and a girl really doesn't care and has no reason to. We just need to look at the frequency and consistency of such responses.

Many girls aren't even conscious that they do it, but when they do see the behavior for what it is, they'll explain that they do it because it's "just easier" or that it "feels better." If you ever in your parenting life gave your toddler a cookie to buy a few minutes of peace, or picked up your teenager's laundry from the floor yourself because it was easier than nagging; if you have ever said yes when you really wanted to say no, then you know the feeling.

Pleasing behavior feels easier because it eliminates conflict and enables a relationship to move along more smoothly. That feels better because conflict generates negative feelings, and agreement produces positive ones. The payoff for a pleaser, then, is first that it makes her life easier and it produces positive feelings. Second, she feels better because when we please someone, we generally feel that the result is that she or he likes or loves us more. And being loved is very high on the female hierarchy of life goals.

Talking about pleasing as a problem may come as a surprise if you've never thought of it as one. Most people don't. In all my years as an educator and psychologist, pleasing behavior is not something parents and teachers have been concerned about very often. After all, girls like this are so nice, so compliant. Girls who strive to please aren't often identified as girls with a problem because their behavior is so rarely problematic to anyone else. But once you understand the reasons for the behavior—that it is a reflection of a girl's low self-esteem and her fear of losing connection—then you begin to see the potential for problems down the road, and this is really what it's all about. The trouble with pleasing is where it leads. Let me share two stories with you.

During my time as an in-school interviewer with the Harvard University study of girls, most surprising for me was how seriously the girls took this research and answered our interview questions with brutal frankness and honesty. I had known these girls as their school psychologist and principal for almost ten years, yet I learned new things about them and from them in these interviews. The interview that was the epitome of the overpleasing girl was from Kim, a savvy and sophisticated seventeen-year-old senior.

The interview question asked each girl to think of a time when she had faced a moral dilemma and describe what she did about it. Kim had a hard time coming up with an example, but then picked one she said "was kind of a moral dilemma because I was faced with deciding whether to do something that was wrong or not." She went on to talk about how she and her friends spent most weekends partying, going to friends' houses, drinking beer, having a good time. One Saturday night, the boy she was dating had had too much to drink at the party. As he staggered to the car, she knew he shouldn't drive. But she didn't have her license, and everyone else was drinking. She knew she shouldn't go with him, but she just couldn't bring herself to say anything. She got in the car, and away they drove, careening off the road several times, but eventually making it home.

When I asked Kim why she did this, she said that she hadn't wanted to upset him. "Even at the risk of losing your own life, you were willing to get in the car so he wouldn't be upset?" I asked. "Yes," she answered, without hesitation. "Would you do the same thing again?" I asked. Another yes.

More recently I attended a training camp for women who were to ride bicycles across the United States. Among these interesting and strong women was Candace, the first woman to cross the United States with a hand-pedaled bicycle. I had read her biographical sheet before coming to the camp, so I knew her physical handicap was due to an accident. We ended up spending enough time together that I felt comfortable asking her if she would tell me her story, and she did.

She was a card dealer in Lake Tahoe at the time. As she said, "long fingernails, short skirts, and lots of makeup!" Her boyfriend and his buddy came to pick her up one early morning—3:00 or 4:00 A.M.—to go for a ride in the hills north of Lake Tahoe. As she started to get in the little sporty car, she noticed that he had been drinking heavily, and could barely talk or keep his eyes focused. She told him that she would drive and he could just rest. He said no, he wanted to drive and he was just fine. His buddy added in a taunting voice, "If you're so scared, just sit in the back—and put on your seat belt— we're going for a wild ride!" Candace stayed where she was, up front, and didn't put on the seat belt. She didn't want to seem the prude, didn't want to be a spoilsport, didn't want to ruin their fun. As they were rounding one of the big curves in the hills, her boyfriend lost control and the car rolled over. In the force of the impact, she hit her spine on the door and it snapped. The two guys suffered only scratches. In adjusting to her new life as a paraplegic, she jokes now, she eventually had to lose the long nails and high heels—they dragged on the ground from the seat of her new set of wheels, her wheelchair.

Candace is very active now in handicapped athletic events, and rounds out her career as a speaker at high schools, where she shares what she knows about seat belts and safety, and the hidden dangers of being a girl who aims to please. I think of Candace and I think of Kim, the seventeen-year-old from my school who risked her life to please her boyfriend's drunken whim and would do it again to avoid displeasing him. It is very hard to miss the staggering implication of Kim's response: Being a pleaser is so deeply ingrained and deeply felt that it is more important than a risk to one's life. Certainly a component is that no one ever truly believes that she will be in an accident or critically injured. However, in both cases, these two females felt enough fear to be highly uncomfortable, but still felt that displeasing those they cared about was a worse feeling than fear. This is very powerful and, literally, deadly stuff.

Even when the risks don't appear to be life-threatening, they do impose lifelong consequences. I see pleasing as an issue of short-term benefits versus long-term damage. In the short run, pleasing works. There is less conflict. Things go more smoothly. Others respond more positively. However, it is also a very insidious emotional programming that leads to patterns of behavior that are very hard to change; patterns that become ingrained and eventually become almost automatic, without a lot of thought.

A very bright, scholarly colleague recalled the day she recognized the pleaser in herself, after years of striving to earn respect from the male-dominated university faculty in her department. "I would go to committee meeting after committee meeting and politely share my ideas, but they were routinely ignored until one of the 'good old boys' would put it forth as his own, and then it was considered a stroke of brilliance," she said. "I wasn't so concerned about not being recognized, and it made me feel good to think that what was really my idea was, in fact, valued by this group. But without that recognition, I was passed over for opportunities to participate in shaping the important work that followed. One day it hit me that I was always trying to say things in an unthreatening way so I'd be accepted and 'fit in.' But nobody was threatened by me at all. I just wanted so badly to fit in and be liked. And I thought, why am I doing this? No one is going to find the cure to cancer by 'being nice.' That's when I stopped worrying about whether I seemed too bold or too confident for their taste. I began speaking up, showing some ownership of my ideas and taking some risks. Some of the good old boys were slow to acknowledge me, but my own experience of speaking my mind made a tremendous difference to me, and eventually I became a more acknowledged and valued member of the group."

A friend struggling through a divorce shared her hard-earned clarity on her life as a pleaser: "I've been the dutiful girl for as long as I can remember, but it's just been lately that I see the truth, which is that I've been a doormat for everyone in my family—not only for my husband, but for my own brother and sister, and even my parents. I always thought of myself as a good sport—helpful and all that—but the truth is that I never said no because I felt I couldn't. I was afraid of my father's temper, I didn't want to disappoint my mother, didn't want to set myself up for criticism by my husband or my in-laws, hurt other people's feelings, or come across as selfish. As scary as this divorce is, it's such a relief to finally stop feeling obligated to please all these people. I feel like I'm coming out of the Dark Ages."

These are both strong, smart women who were well into

their forties before they even recognized the pleasing behavior that had held them hostage for decades. These two women, and most other mothers that I have talked with, don't want their daughters to spend so much of their time and energy shaping their choices and their lives to please others. Adult women, with hindsight, can see all that they couldn't see when the need-to-please lens colored their vision: all the ways they adjusted their dreams and expectations to please a teacher, a parent, a friend, a boyfriend, a husband, a boss. They can see it in their parenting, too, waking up after too many years of overserving their families to keep everyone happy and keep conflict to a minimum. "Not for my daughter" seems to be the universal wish.

Many, many women are living stories like these. We want to change the story line for girls today. To do so, we can take the time-honored advice to recognize those things we cannot change and change the things we can. What part of this behavior is nature, what part is nurture, and what can we do to create a more healthy balance of those influences in a girl's life?

The Nature of Pleasing

I'd like to trash that tired old nursery ditty that tells us that girls are made of "sugar and spice and everything nice," but there is a grain of truth in it.

Females are genetically and emotionally programmed to nurture and take care of other humans. That is what having a uterus does. In all species, not just the human species, the female has to be genetically programmed to *want* to take care of her young to ensure survival of the species. In our species, that want translates into caring deeply about other humans. Although we typically form our strongest emotional attachment to our own children, the female caring gene sets girls and women up to care, and the layering effect of those caring experiences reinforces that caring behavior. Simply speaking, females are programmed to care about attachments, relationships, and other human beings. The current brain research is also providing supporting evidence for this. Remember the emotional nugget of the brain, the amygdala? A new term is being coined for the professionals who are looking at the neurological evidence delineating "her brain and his brain": neurological Darwinism.

Strictly speaking, the cortex is the only part of the brain needed for a strictly rational task. But in females, brain scans indicate that the emotional part of the brain seems to be part of almost all tasks, even factual ones. So, for example, if you ask people what is the square root of four, most male brains are activated in several areas of the cortex. Most female brains are activated in several areas of the cortex *and* the limbic system, the emotional center of the brain. She is not only trying to calculate the answer, but also worrying that if she gets it wrong, the teacher will be upset; or if she gets it right, her boyfriend will think she is a nerd!

But all humans, *including females,* are programmed to strive to survive. This part of the genetic blueprint leads to behavior we associate with being independent, being a problem solver, a doer. So both males and females have a natural capacity for both behaviors: to care and nurture, and to be strong and independent. In computer-age terms, Darwin might say that the female of the species is born with an upgrade for caring and nurturing; the male includes enhanced connections for strength and independence. It makes sense. Ideally, then, if we could effectively nurture boys and girls differently to achieve balance in each gender, we would end up with boys who are strong and caring, and girls who are caring and strong! However, this is not what our society traditionally has done. Instead, through the powerful social influences of community, family, school, and the media, we have reinforced the patterns of gender stereotypes and wired each one to be even more so.

So in all humans there is a built-in teeter-totter, in this case reflecting the weight we give to self or to others in our attention, our thinking, and our behavior. When that weight distribution is fairly balanced—we respect our needs and wants, but also take into consideration those of others—then life feels balanced, and we take turns on the up-and-down. As we place more weight in our thinking on one side or the other, that heavier side controls the balance and action of the teeter-totter. Throughout life, as we learn how to balance give-and-take in relationships, it is normal for the weight of our thinking to shift somewhat. Other factors also affect the balance.

Our view of what is happening in the world in relation to our self shifts constantly, influenced by gender, age, interests, environment, events, and other circumstances. It's not fickle, but flexible. However, if one side stays more heavily weighted for too long, the back-and-forth mechanism of the teeter-totter action rusts in place, leaving one side stranded in the air. Then to get the balance back takes a great deal more energy and special tools. Overpleasing is like that; the weight on the "other" side grows too heavy for too long, and a girl gets stuck in place, stranded.

The Nurture of Pleasing

Strudel Theory tells us that how the world responds to you over time becomes part of the layering of experiences that, along with what nature gave you, make you the way you are, whether it is bold, hesitant, confident, or anxious. For girls, the training for pleasing and being nice starts early. "Be nice." "Be good." "Be polite." "Be quiet." The instructions are clear from parents, schools, the world. For example, researchers studied how adults talked to very young children. Comments to young boys included: "Isn't he a big guy!" and "What a good runner you are!" For girls, examples included: "Isn't she sweet?" "Isn't she cute!" "What a nice little girl!" Teachers of young children continue the layering. "Your daughter is a great teacher's helper, I can always count on her!" "Your son built some great bridges in the block corner!"

In the final days of school one year, I overheard two seventh-grade girls comparing the notes that students and teachers had written in their yearbooks. Both of the girls were very hardworking, intelligent, committed students who made excellent grades. The first girl glowed as she read aloud her teacher's compliment on the quality of the work she had done that year. The second girl sighed and rolled her eyes in resignation as she read her teacher's comment: "To a really *nice* girl!"

This is how the healthy female tendency to care becomes distorted. In simple terms, most girls get too much training in pleasing from the world, adding to the ample gift of caring bestowed on them by nature. The end result is that the two ingredients combine almost geometrically to create too much of a pleaser.

Boys hear it, too, but not in the same volume, consistency, and context. In fact, if boys are too nice, too polite, too quiet, they are considered "sissies." For girls, for most of their formative and adolescent years, there doesn't seem to be any upper limit. Girls can't be "too nice" or "too good." Too quiet can raise some questions, but too loud or aggressive raises more. And then, as a girl gets older, there is another societal tune that begins to play with more volume as age increases, saying that girls should also be strong, independent, and stand up for their own opinions. But, as Nora said earlier in this book, a girl can't be "too much of anything," or nobody will like her.

When we talk about child development or moral development, it's safe to say that the stage in which children want to please their parents is a critical one on the road to becoming an effective member of society. Both girls and boys need to feel reinforced by their parents when they behave appropriately. And when a child is young, parents are the focal point of her life; wanting to please them is natural. It is all a matter of how much and for what. As I said earlier, we need to deliberately set out to balance the effects of nature and nurture to equalize the gender continuum.

When we create wholesome opportunities for a girl to grow more competent, confident, and connected, strengthening her self-esteem, we balance the layers of nature with strengthening layers of nurture.

Carpe Diem: Seize the Moment to Teach Striving and Thriving Behaviors

It was a typical high school dance. The girls stood on one side of the gym and the boys stood on the other for most of the night. This was my third dance-chaperoning experience this year. Some things never change. The next day, as a bunch of girls were entering my class, one of the juniors was talking about how "chicken" the boys were at the dance. "They always wait until the last half hour to get up enough courage to ask anyone to dance."

I ventured into the conversation with: "Why do you wait that long?" All heads turned and looked at me. Terry opened her mouth to say something, got a thoughtful look on her face, and just shrugged her shoulders. Next month, next dance. Terry and two friends walk over to a cluster of boys just as the dance is beginning. They all put their heads together forming a huddle. When the next song started, the six of them headed to the dance floor, dancing more in a throng than as couples. Within ten minutes, the dance floor was filled. The next day, everyone in the room talked about how that had been the best dance "EVER!"

This was a crucible moment, a moment that might seem insignificant in the scheme of happenings that day or week or month or year. But, layered over time, that kind of response, encouraging girls to handle a situation and having them find out that they can, forges them into more competent, confident girls who create their connections in healthy ways.

"Use Your Words!"–Rescripting Our Responses

If we want our girls to resist the allure of the easy pleaser behavior, we need to give them the words to understand the problem and find new responses of their own. Give clear and direct messages to your daughter about her need to please others and her need to please herself. For instance: "I want you to care about others, but I also want you to think about what is best for you. Making decisions is about weighing both. It is hard to know which is most important with each decision, but you need to think of both always. And if you ever want to talk about anything, I'm here."

Don't denigrate either the desire to please yourself or the desire to please others. In balance, they are the building blocks of a healthy emotional life. In addition, following the theme of crucible moments, be conscious of the way you respond to your daughter in everyday interactions involving conflict and cooperation. She needs to learn skills for conflict resolution, which is not the same as conflict avoidance or compliance. Conflict resolution means recognizing your own needs as well as those of others and negotiating the gray between the two; or not compromising, as in matters of personal safety or integrity. Be on the lookout for how the rest of the world responds to your daughter. Encourage her to speak for herself, but be willing to model how it's done by stepping up with her, as her advocate in talking to teachers, and other family members, about this issue.

Girls struggle with this issue every day—and so do parents. If we want them to think for themselves at important moments, if we want our girls to "use the sense God gave them" and make better decisions, we have to give them the opportunity to practice. We have to create a lab for that at home and school. It won't always be a comfortable place for us. When we teach children to think for themselves, we are bound to get irritated at times with the results.

This happens so often at schools where the stated core philosophy espouses independent thinking and initiative, but the reality isn't always greeted with open arms. In one school that had a long tradition of wearing uniforms, the middle school teachers were aghast at the student movement to abolish them. As the girls began taking steps to formalize their proposal and to bring it to the administration, many teachers were informally discouraging them and saying things like: "Uniforms help discipline" or "Uniforms are a deep tradition of this school and we're not going to change," or worse, "You're just going to get in trouble if you keep going with this." Whether or not uniforms are a good idea in a school is not really the issue at this point. The fact that middle school girls had the courage to challenge a long-standing tradition and go through the confrontational and direct steps to do that was amazingly positive. Some teachers did respond by saying things like: "If you think you have a good argument for your position, go for it." Or "I'm glad to see that you care about your school and your environment enough to do this." Taking sides or saying the idea is good or bad doesn't help girls to keep on the path to striving and thriving. However, encouraging them to question and not just agree with all that the world hands them is very healthy.

A father of one of my middle-schoolers came to see me one day so irate he could hardly speak. "How dare you teach my daughter to talk back to me?" he sputtered. I asked him to explain this a little more to me. He said that he was tired when he came home from work and just wanted some peace and quiet. So he told his daughter to stop watching TV and to go upstairs and do her homework. Expecting the usual "Okay, Dad," he was astonished—and unhappily so—when she replied that she would rather do her homework after dinner. He repeated his order, at which point he was sure of her compliance. But instead, she said she didn't think that was a good idea because she had had such a long hard day at school and needed a break. At this point her father reverted to the classic "Do what you're told!" and when confronted with the stereotypical response of "Why?" gave her the automatic: "Because I said so." At which point, she stomped upstairs and he stomped to the phone to make an appointment to talk to me about this unseemly and atypical response of his daughter.

I asked him what bothered him the most. He said, "Two things. First, she has always done what I've told her to do, and second, I've taught my children to obey me, and now the school is undermining my authority."

I asked if his daughter had used a respectful voice and if there was any validity to what she was saying. He glared at me and said that wasn't the point; she was supposed to obey him, period. I could tell this was going to be a long conference, and decided to go back and lead him more deliberately through the thought process on this issue.

"Do you remember when you came to apply to this school with your daughter? You were so proud of her, you said she was smart and good and could do anything. You said you wanted her to be in a place that would help her to do whatever she wanted to do in life."

He agreed, but said that didn't include disobeying her father.

I explained that questioning your father is not the same as disobeying him. In fact, the way I see it, questioning someone you respect and love deeply is very hard for a girl to do. If you can question your own father, legitimately, you are well on the road to being able to "do whatever you want in life." I explained that that was why, at school, we encouraged the girls to question all of us. The hard part is us. It is very hard for the adults in the lives of children to have their directions challenged. It means we either have to have good reasons, or be ready to acknowledge that we don't. It is far easier to have a compliant child, whether you are a parent, a teacher, or a child molester. The last word seemed to reach him. He left with a begrudging "I'll tell her I just wanted some peace and quiet."

I think that this dad is a very brave and wise man on the road to raising a brave and wise daughter. It takes some emotional fortitude for a father to move beyond "Because I said so" to sharing his human need for rest and relaxation after a long day. By engaging his daughter in dialogue, he facilitates her questioning and encourages her to understand human beings.

This particular father's reaction might seem extreme, but I understand it. He had moved his family to the United States from another country where the patriarchal expectation of children was absolute obedience—especially from girls. That said, however, the truth is that a version of this same obedience theme plays out in all kinds of families. Pleaser training is rooted in the very language and fabric of our culture and in most cultures in the world, even today.

Training Away from Pleaser Behavior: Three Do's, Three Don'ts

Here are three straightforward do's and three simple don'ts you can use at home to create an environment in which your daughter can be herself without being a pleaser.

Three Do's
Love, with no strings attached

First, love your daughter for who she is, no strings attached. "I love you" should not be said or attached to pleasing behavior or to performance. I like to share the wisdom of Dr. Carl Rogers, a psychologist in the 1960s and 1970s who received acclaim for his theory and practice of "unconditional positive regard." By this he meant that every person needs to have someone who will love her totally, regardless of her flaws and foibles. Every girl needs rock-solid, unconditional respect and caring. Don't confuse this with positive reinforcement for a job well done. A parent's caring and love should not be handed out like candy when your daughter brings home an A from school or a boyfriend who doesn't have a safety pin in his nose. Instead, this is an overall feeling and bond of trust that is set during nonperformance and nonjudgmental times.

Here are three traditional lines that act as emotional blackmail, followed by three that communicate more clearly in the same situations:

1. "You're a bad girl."
2. "I'm disappointed in you."
3. "Wait until your father hears what you've done."

We've all said these things, but for girls they can really be emotional blackmail. Instead, see how these rescripted lines address the issues:

1. "When you hit your little sister, it could hurt her, and I can't allow you to do that."
2. "I'd like to talk to you about why it's important for you to do your homework and not to lie to your teacher when she asks you about it."
3. "Let's talk about how you're going to share with your father what happened today."

The change in wording is critical. The first three hit at your love and relationship. They crack the foundation that is critical for the relationship that guiding and teaching (other words for parenting) must have. They weaken a girl; they make her a pleaser to emotional blackmail.

The last three are examples of how clear and specific feedback can allow a girl to make mistakes or misjudgments, yet still feel that she is loved and supported—and guided, as well. This feels safe, and at the same time sets the standards for discipline and learning.

Allow and accept a range of behavior

This is a hard one. I'm not saying you need to accept outrageous or rude behavior, but we need to be careful not to be too narrow in setting expectations and boundaries for them. Much of the world is trying to shape young females to be compliant. As parents and teachers, we need to create places where a girl can take some risks, make mistakes, and practice some challenging behaviors.

A sixth-grader I know came home one day and told her mother that her music teacher might be calling after school because of something she had said in class, implying that her teacher was not happy with her. I think all parents have an instinctive negative response to a comment like this. Putting that reaction on hold is important. The sixth-grader went on to explain what had happened. The teacher had returned a test that her students had taken and then proceeded to read the grades, from A to F, and the associated names of the students receiving the grades. This girl raised her hand and told the teacher she didn't think she should do this in the future, and why!

Mother and daughter had a productive discussion, first about why she felt so impelled to say this to the teacher, and then about choices in how she might have done it. Should she have said it in public, or talked to the teacher afterward? After weighing all of the aspects of this discussion, the girl decided to go to the teacher the next day. First she apologized for putting the teacher on the spot in front of the other students. But then she had an interesting discussion with the teacher about why she felt this teaching technique was not appropriate.

Let's look at three more common phrases we can trade in for more effective ones.

1. "Talking back to adults is bad."
2. "Be nice."
3. "Never talk to strangers."

All of the above we have either heard as children or said as adults. Again, for girls, our language needs to be adjusted with modifiers so that sensitive girls don't incorporate these adages across the board and thus diminish their repertoire of skills and behaviors. For example:

1. "Sue, pretend I'm your music teacher and say just what you said to her so I can help you figure out what happened."
2. "It's important to respect others and to be kind, but it is also important for you to stand up for important principles, even if someone thinks you are not being nice."
3. "There are some times when talking to strangers is not a good idea. There are also times when talking to a stranger is needed or the right thing to do."

Well, I'm sure you're getting the gist of all of this. The world has so much gray, not very much black and white. Helping your daughter understand and negotiate the gray areas is what will help her be strong and successful.

It's how you play the game

The third *do* is to reinforce the value of winning *and* of losing, succeeding and failing. If you respond positively only to straight A's or to making a goal at the soccer game, you can and probably will push your daughter down the pleaser road. The idea that "It's not whether you win or lose, but how you play the game" isn't just about good sportsmanship; it's about life! When it comes to asserting themselves, girls need to be reinforced to step onto the field, to try, to risk, to fail, and try again, but to stay in the game. Females are so sensitive to others, so connected to the people they love, that those significant others need to be careful to reinforce strength as well as caring.

1. "You need to be on the honor roll."
2. "I want you to be the best skater in your age range."
3. "You know the old saying—'A girl can't be too thin or too rich.' "

There will always be someone smarter, more skilled, prettier. These kinds of comments are very discouraging. It's not healthy for a girl to think that she *must* be a winner or the best at something to win your approval. If you set the bar too high too often for a girl, she will quit trying.

1. "I'll read each teacher's comments first, before I read the grades, because I want to know if you've worked hard."
2. "I want you to learn to be the best skater you can be."
3. "There is a healthy weight for your body, and as your parent, I'll help you be healthy."

Three Don'ts

Don't see your child as an extension of you, or as a possession

"I want my daughter to get better grades." Sometimes, sentences that start with "I want" related to your child really mean just that: what you want as a parent. Sometimes that is absolutely altruistic, but sometimes it is just a reflection of what is important to you, which is very difficult to see and face as a parent. The world is quite a competitive place, and it is easy to get caught up in appearances and what others think. Parents care not only what the world thinks of their daughter, but also how their daughter reflects on them as parents. It is only human to feel this way. It is also critical to be able to see when what you want for your child is not necessarily what is best for your child.

Advanced algebra offered in eighth grade is a perfect example of this.

Sharon's mother demanded that her daughter be placed in this class, even though the girl's grades and performance up to this time suggested that math was not really gelling for her yet. After all, her mother reasoned, *she* had taken all advanced classes in school and her daughter could, too. Sometimes just listening to your words as a parent helps you to see where the locus of need is.

Don't set the motivation trap

Using your connection with a child—your love—to premeditatedly reinforce pleasing behavior can be very insidious in the long run. Teachers can fall into this pattern so easily because good and quiet students make it easier to handle large groups. In my school, growing up, we had conduct grades on our report cards. Conduct grades reflected whether we were quiet, obedient, and unquestioning. Conduct grades didn't reflect whether we got into arguments on the playground because someone was taunting another student and we had the courage to do something about it.

As always, it is a matter of balance. The salient point here is that girls, especially, respond to the powerful motivation of pleasing others, especially people whose opinion they care about. How parents, teachers, and others use that connection and what they reinforce has long-lasting effects.

Sometimes as a parent we rely on a quick fix, like plunking a child in front of a video on a day when we need to get some things done. That kind of short-term abeyance of our overall philosophy of what is good for our child doesn't have a serious long-term effect. But even quick fixes using the motivation trap move girls along the path of overpleasing.

Don't let your pendulum swing too far

Removing clear limits and guidelines and allowing too wide a range of behavior will promote not just a girl's voice but also constant screaming, whining, and ordering people about. As is true with most of the psychological, educational, and parenting wisdom, balance is the key. Being an effective parent is like being a tightrope walker on the fine line of setting the boundaries and opportunities for a child.

Some of the most common comments, loaded with good intentions but misguided, are:

1. "You can do anything you want to do."
2. "Be true to yourself!"
3. "Always look nice."

When the messages that girls hear most frequently are more balanced, the girls are more apt to find a balance: independent yet respectful of others, risk-takers but not foolishly risky, aware of society's expectations but also an individual.

1. "You're capable of doing so much, and I think it is healthy for you to have really high goals for yourself."
2. "It's important to have clear values and know what is important to you."

3. "Your appearance is the first thing that people use to make judgments about you, so there are some prices to be paid if your appearance doesn't match the situation."

Our society and most others throughout the world continue to place particular pressure on girls and women to defer to authority: to dress, speak, walk, think, and dream that which is pleasing to others. We may not be able to change the world for our girls, but in our own homes and schools and in our relationships with girls, we can change their world to one in which they can thrive as nurturing, caring, strong, independent thinkers and advocates for their own best interests.

Pearls for Parents and Pearls for Girls:

- Be a role model of balance on the pleasing continuum.
- Limit your use of the word *nice* and be more specific. For instance, instead of "Be nice," say "Please offer your friend a turn . . ."
- Encourage your daughter to ask questions, even of adults.
- Look for strong female roles (good luck!) in movies and TV shows, and talk about why you like to see girls and women portrayed as active, intelligent characters.
- Invite your older tween or teen daughter to read this chapter, and tell you about any ways she feels pressure to please. Don't respond defensively or critically; listen and learn.
- At tuck-in time, make it a routine to ask: "Tell me one thing you did today that you were proud of."

CHAPTER 9

Parents Under Pressure: How to Think Straight When Worry Sets In

"It seemed cool at the time."

—Angie, fifteen

"How do I worry? Let me count the ways . . ."

—Mother of three girls

One of my earliest memories is from when I was about two years old, sitting on my mother's lap while she was busy drinking coffee and playing cards with her circle of other young mothers in the neighborhood. This crew got together almost every day to have coffee, go for a walk, or play cards, but mostly to talk. My memory of those get-togethers isn't that good, but I know from my mother's later accounts that much of the talk was about us, the children. It was this sharing of stories of developmental changes, of worries and advice, that, I understand now, was so needed and special. The tribal wisdom "It takes a village to raise a child" has been so overused by politicians lobbying for money and programs that it may be difficult to hear in it the more intimate human truth for parents and teachers, but here it is: When we pool our wisdom, our children benefit; we fare better when we can share the burden of our worries or concerns, use some objective feedback to see issues more clearly, and draw from others' experiences to guide our own responses.

For most parents today, the village is missing. Or, if it is there, it is sometimes as much a part of the problem as it is a piece of the solution. When so many adults are underwriting conspicuous consumption; encouraging early coed activities that facilitate early sexual activity; fueling excessive competitiveness among children in sports, academics, and extracurricular interests; abandoning limits, rules, and consequences for their children; and turning away from the truth about drinking and drug use in their community—or in their own homes—where is the caring village? Faced with a crisis, or under mounting pressure or concerns, parents often feel isolated and unsure.

Four women I know get together every Monday morning for coffee. They are mothers with a combined total of six girls between the ages of ten and eighteen and three boys covering roughly the same age range. Unlike the mothers of my parents' day, they don't live within walking distance of one another, and their children attend different schools and Sunday schools. One is Catholic, one is Protestant, one is Jewish, and one maintains an interfaith family and spiritual outlook. And yet they met through serendipitous encounters of one kind or another, and they have become their own self-selected village. They share core values about life and parenting, and they trust one another to be honest, trustworthy, caring, and supportive. When they get together every Monday morning, the conversation weaves steadily through the triumphs and trials of the week, with deeper and more deliberate attention paid to new or ongoing concerns about their children.

In one morning's conversation, for instance, on girl topics alone, the mothers discussed recent incidents with their daughters, or within their daughters' circle of friends, that prompted justified concern about cutting (self-mutilation), depression, suicidal behavior, anorexia, experimentation with drugs, social cruelty, menstruation at age ten, and some emerging "fast crowd" influences. These are active, intelligent, seasoned women, and well-read, thoughtful, involved mothers, and yet they are challenged by the scope, complexity, and seriousness of issues that confront their girls today. Even as veterans of the 1960s, they feel ill-equipped to respond to the more potent, and potentially lethal, risks in the contemporary world of girls. By discussing the problems candidly within their circle of four, they are able to share insights, information, and inspiration. They feel fortified, and much smarter by the end of coffee than they did when they started! Best of all, they say, they are able to bring perspective, and an extra measure of calm and clarity, to subsequent discussions with their daughters.

What would your reaction be if you discovered, on your own or from someone else, that your daughter was lying to you? That she was shoplifting or stealing money from your purse? That she was secretly vomiting after meals? Skipping classes? Cutting herself? Talking about suicide in e-mails to friends? Using alcohol or drugs? What would your reaction be if her grades began to slide, if her friends stopped calling, or if her mood seemed to grow markedly downcast or angry?

Even the most seasoned and wise parents can feel temporarily helpless, disoriented, panicked, or at least unsure about how best to proceed when trouble hits. The accumulated parenting skills and wisdom they have used to handle years of daily childhood challenges seem to evaporate. There is an axiom in the therapy world that when we are angry, upset, or in any extreme emotional state, we're instantly dumbed down and should avoid making any important decisions or trying to think through complex issues. When we "lose it," in a moment of anger or fear, what we lose is our ability to respond with clarity of thought to a complex issue.

Brain science tells us that the amygdala—the center of emotions—when highly active, can slightly cloud the thinking process, and high emotion can propel us to ignore thought and to act very quickly. That's a built-in feature of the human brain—for parents and children alike. If a human feels fear, for instance, upon seeing a grizzly bear, it is not the time to think a great deal about bear life, it is the time to run! Thinking is not designed to be at its best during times of high emotion. So although emotion is designed to motivate you to do something, and you should attend to that message, wisdom says: Step carefully as you go.

I often use this as a way to explain to girls why it's best, when angry or upset, to calm yourself before responding with the first words or actions that come to mind. In the chaos of the moment we're not thinking at our best. It's true for parents under pressure, too. In a crisis, which is any situation that feels like one to either a parent or a girl, our parenting instincts and intelligence are dumbed down in a cycle of counterproductive emotions.

What I see most in my conversations with parents under pressure is *fear* that they will handle the situation wrong, and they'll make matters worse instead of better. They also fear that the situation could have a long-term effect on their daughter's self-esteem or her options in life. With no clear guidelines for most issues, confusion and uncertainty are heightened, as even professionals in the field disagree about different aspects of the problem as well as the best response to it. The expert in the middle—the girl herself—may or may not be able or willing to contribute much to clarifying the issue. Anxiety is nature's kick in the rear, the feeling that is supposed to propel us into action. However, without any clear-cut way out of this threatening place, anxiety triggers more fear, and we're trapped in a frantic cycle, a spiral of mounting fear, confusion, uncertainty, and anxiety.

Although some concerns build over time, this full panic process can unfold, as any parent knows, in the space of about 1.5 seconds. Like a pilot who hits unexpected turbulence, it takes some conscious reckoning to defuse the fear response, get a grip on the controls, and move toward that calmer air space—all in that first full second.

From a girl's perspective, this same seemingly horrific situation may be just as disconcerting, or not really a big deal. That is why it's always important to compare your perceptions with your daughter's view.

I was having coffee with a friend who is the mother of a middle school girl. When her daughter came into the room to get a snack,

Mom said, "Dr. Deak has a lot of experience with teachers—do you want to talk to her about the problem you're having with your math teacher?"

The daughter's response was a smile and a: "No, it's not really a problem." Incredulous, her mother said, "But last night you cried and said you didn't want to go back to school and face her!"

The response: "Well, yeah, but I found out this morning from Mary that she says things like that to most of her students, so I don't see why you're making such a big deal out of it!" And off she stomped, leaving her mother just a little perplexed, confused, and exasperated.

On the other hand, what a parent perceives as no big deal, a girl may feel marks the end of her life, literally. That's why I often wear a simple sterling necklace with a diamond chip to remind me that the world is a phenomenological place—what we believe shapes how we think and what we do; if a girl feels like her world is ending, it doesn't matter what her parents think. Craig, a longtime friend of mine, called about his younger sister, who was a senior in high school. Tricia had been moping around the house for several weeks; the boyfriend she had planned to marry had just told her that he loved someone else. When she talked, she'd give "my life is over" types of responses to her parents. Her mother listened and commiserated, and as the days went by, offered, as any of us might, assurances that time heals everything, and there would be someone else for her, intended to soothe her daughter. Gradually Tricia stopped talking about her pain. Her family began to breathe a bit easier. When Craig called, Tricia was in the hospital recovering from an overdose of sleeping pills. She had asked to see me when she was released the next week; she didn't relate to the professional who was assigned to her at the hospital. More on this story later, but the point is that her family believed this was just one of life's predictable lessons from which she would learn and grow. By the way, the necklace was the present Craig gave to me later when his sister smiled and went out to the movies for the first time!

Sometimes a serious issue is front and center; it is clear that a girl is in trouble, and parents and daughter agree it is serious. Eating disorders at some point fall into this category. Girls will admit they are focused on wanting to be thin and lose weight. Early on, when the erratic or picky eating is correlated with seeing a daughter's clothes get looser and looser, parents begin to worry more.

This was the case with Chrissie and her parents. The more she cut back on eating in front of them, the more they pushed her to eat. She agreed that she wasn't eating enough and promised that she would eat more at school, more at the next meal, more later, don't worry. This kind of false agreement on her part is part of the syndrome. In my conversations with girls like this, they talk about playing the game with observant parents, understanding their worry, even agreeing with it, but they don't *really* feel that they have a problem, because they believe they can stop dieting whenever they want. However, the motivation to be thinner hasn't diminished.

So Chrissie would eat nothing all day at school, and would eat a bit at supper to keep her parents' worry in check. She later admitted that it also kept her worry in check when they felt appeased. But as the weight loss continued, their nagging and cajoling increased in frequency and duration. That's when the seemingly easy way out began: eating dinner then throwing up afterward. No hassle from her parents.

Wanted: Psychic Wisdom, Long-Range Perspective

The conundrum for parents is the tension between early intervention and allowing development and process time to work. On the one hand, you can think of it like tending to a cavity in a tooth. If you intervene early, you can stop the spread of decay; if you wait too long, you may lose the whole tooth. In difficult situations for your daughter, if you intervene early, many issues are easier to remedy and you lessen the risk that trouble will escalate. On the other hand, when adults intervene early and often in a child's struggling moments, the child is trained toward a path of dependence and ineffectiveness. This is an especially significant issue for girls, and parents of girls, because in so many ways, our media, our families, and our society continue to echo the traditional damsel-in-distress response that assumes girls are helpless and need to be rescued at the first sign of difficulty.

Most of my sessions with parents have been about interrupting their cycle of worry or helplessness, and shifting to a more productive response process. Whether the issue falls into the serious categories (sex, alcohol or drugs, eating disorders, and depression), or the situational categories (social conflict, sibling fighting, routine peer pressure), or daily trials (what is not too risqué to wear to school, how late a curfew is appropriate), in certain fundamental ways, the parenting strategy is the same: to see the situation clearly, engage carefully, and leave room for a girl to do her own learning and problem-solving, as much as possible. Obviously an eating disorder or a friendship woe or choice of wardrobe are different issues, in scope and depth, but all represent important growing experiences that both parents and girls face, alone or together. All of these issues and conflicts, and how they are addressed by girls and their parents, not only form the repertoire of behaviors of a girl, but they also form the attitude toward self, the world, and personal judgment, that a girl will use throughout her life.

No matter how a girl may resist help, no child wants to believe that she is so confused or so bad or so in trouble that she is beyond help. When girls are under pressure, or when we're worried about them, for whatever reason, the way we respond has meaning and becomes an important part of the learning experience, and the potential effectiveness of any strategy.

Beyond Chaos: Finding Perspective Under Pressure

Every parent has stories of times when inexperience or mistaken impressions have spurred them to action they later discovered was unnecessary or overblown, sometimes laughably so. Every parent also has stories of times when a problem cured itself—meaning their daughter figured it out on her own, or simply outgrew it. However, as girls grow older, and the landscape grows more complex and, in many ways, more risky, it becomes more difficult to sit back and let matters play out.

For those of us who live or work with girls, optimism and concern are the air we breathe: optimism, in the steady, grounded feeling that comes of feeling that our girls are creative, capable individuals with wide-open access to a world of opportunity; concern, in the background noise we hear in their vulnerability, and the harsher realities of female life in contemporary times. Then one day a question signals a more immediate threat: If your twelve-year-old daughter has skipped breakfast three mornings in a row and seems recently preoccupied with her weight and appearance, is she in the early stages of an eating disorder? If you smell marijuana on your teen daughter's clothes, does she have a drug problem? If her grades have become a source of serious tension for her, or between you and her, is she having school problems?

What may seem like a serious issue of depression may be a temporary reaction to the daily trials of academic pressure or friendships. With an invitation to a party, or an A on an exam, it is stunning how fast the so-called clinical depression dissipates. On the other hand, what might seem to be fatigue from not enough sleep may really be symptomatic of an underlying depression or drug or alcohol use. Nothing is simple or linear in young peoples' lives these days, and this is particularly so with girls, whether you feel you are dealing with a serious or a not-so-serious issue. A girl's reaction, attitude, mood, and involvement can move at a dizzying pace on that continuum from one day to the next.

As one frustrated mother put it: "There are times when you can't tell an onion from a piece of toast."

I'd like to say that observation or available research offers a definitive way to decode the red-flag behaviors we see in girls' everyday lives. It would make things so much easier if we had a wait-and-see time line and action guide for each issue, something like this:

> *Picky Eating: Age 2—Wait and see two days, then call grandmother*
> *Age 10—Wait and see two weeks, then call pediatrician*
> *Age 16—Wait and see three weeks, then call psychologist*

Instead, we have ambiguity, and the need to negotiate the gray, first in our own minds, and our own understanding of the situation, and then with our girls, in whatever way serves them best.

The first step, then, is to respect our instincts and experience. The mother of a twelve-year-old girl called me one day and began our conversation by apologizing for calling at all. She didn't want to seem "like one of those obsessive mothers," she said, but she was concerned about her daughter. She explained that her daughter seemed increasingly withdrawn and listless, and the mother was worried that she might be suffering from depression. The mother then went on, "even though it's probably nothing," and detailed a list of life events in the recent past, which, one by one, didn't seem problematic, but in succession, and with her knowledge of her daughter's personality and history, just had her worried. Those events and that history included two moves over the previous five years, which had required a total of three new school transitions for her daughter; her daughter's best friend's move to another state two years earlier; at about that same time, her husband's bout with cancer, now in remission; the death of a beloved grandfather about a year later; and most recently, an injury that ended ice-skating as her favorite pastime and only significant physical activity; finally, the determination that she had a slight vision impairment requiring that she wear glasses. Somewhere about midpoint in all that, her cat had run away, and, oh yes, she had begun getting her period.

Whether her daughter was clinically depressed or not, she clearly had been dealing with a succession of events that, especially in the life of a girl that age, were difficult and could be depressing. This mother had good reason to be concerned, and no reason to apologize!

When worry sets in and doesn't go away, it is usually a signal that something merits further attention. The cortex is a wonderful rational thinking machine, but worried feelings are located in the lower brain, and that wonderful little amygdala is at work again. A parent shouldn't ignore persistent amygdala niggling. Those parenting signals and intuitive feelings are built into the system for a reason, even though they are not always supportable by data (because, if they were, the cortex would be taking over!). My best advice is to always act on niggling worry. Even if there is nothing serious going on, it will help your mental health. The additional benefit, of course, is that it is likely to help your daughter, too.

The Intervention Questions: To Do or Not to Do? How Much and How?

When I worked in a large public school, we had so many referrals of students for counseling services that we were simply unable to handle all of them. Under pressure to prioritize by severity of need to whatever degree we could, we began work on some cases, and relegated other case files to the windowsill, literally, hoping to get to them later. By midyear we decided to evaluate the difference in the progress of the children who had been referred, but received no intervention (the windowsill group), and those in the direct intervention group. Although it wasn't a scientific study, it was clear that many of the "windowsill" students had improved with no direct counseling intervention, and some in both groups failed to show appreciable improvement, with or without counseling. Sometimes children naturally outgrow problems, and sometimes they need help to grow out of them.

Stacy: Mired in Gloom

Lynne, a usually calm, thoughtful mother, called me one day to say that her seventh-grade daughter, Stacy, came home from school every day and cried. She was the type of girl who was a bit quiet and always had one or two good friends. This past summer, one friend moved and the other chose to go to another school. So Stacy went into her seventh-grade year friendless. That year continued with the crying, sadness, feeling alone. Stacy's lack of joy affected her interest in outside activities as well as the atmosphere at home for the entire family. Eighth grade wasn't much better. Her parents tried counseling, but with no success. Antidepressants were prescribed but had little positive effect. In ninth grade Stacy became friends with two new girls. They did everything together. She started to smile and laugh again. She had the energy to go out for sports and a boy had noticed her great smile and had invited her to go to a movie. Life was good! Stacy's depressive mood lifted, and it never came back in any significant way. Clearly, she had suffered through a tough time, a depressing time, but none of the interventions on their own succeeded in a breakthrough. It was finding a satisfying connection to other girls that proved to be the turning point for Stacy.

Marta: On the Fast Track to Trouble

For several years, I had known another family with whom I was involved in periodic conversations as their children's principal because the parents had separated and divorced and were working hard to keep this as smooth a process as possible for the children. But it wasn't going very smoothly for Marta. She was the emotional and sensitive one. At first she was really angry and wouldn't communicate with either parent with any civil conversation. This lack of civility soon turned to silence. And then as she entered high school, her collection of friends changed from the pals she'd had since grade school. Her mother felt this change and it began to worry her. Marta didn't show as much anger; she just kept getting more distant. She stayed out of the house as late as possible, spent all her waking hours with this group of friends or in her room with the door shut, and shared nothing with her family.

Cheryl, her mother, called me. She needed a sounding board

and I knew her daughter and her family well. Cheryl couldn't give specific data, but she had this feeling that the situation was becoming more serious. Marta's room had always been her private space, and her mother now had thoughts about going in and just looking around. She had always considered Marta's room as private, and was surprised at herself for feeling the need and actually wanting to look through Marta's room. As we talked, she ultimately guiltily confessed that she had gone through Marta's stuff and found beer in her closet and in her drawers. She began to talk about how Marta was staying out with her friends more and more and that she had heard rumors that these girls had a drinking problem and often missed school.

I encouraged Cheryl to call the school and go in to talk to Marta's adviser, the school counselor, or a teacher who knew her well. She did that and called back, panicked. The counselor had told her that Marta's grades had eroded seriously, that she had been absent and tardy several times in the last two months, and that he had been about to call her to see if something was wrong at home. In her panic, Cheryl came home, removed all the beer and the telephone from Marta's room, and waited for her to come home from school. She confronted Marta as she came in the door, spewing out all of her concerns, what the counselor had said, what she found, and ended by grounding Marta—including from seeing or communicating with her friends after school—until further notice.

By this time, Marta had formed a very dependent bond with her friends and with drinking. It was simple: When she was with them or slightly high, she felt good. So her mother's clamping down only prompted Marta to move her actions underground. She drank with her friends in the rest room at school or sneaked out of the house when her mother wasn't home. Then two events happened in quick succession. Marta came home drunk from school and, in an angry blowup with her mother, she smashed the wall with her fist and broke several bones in her hand. When they got home from the hospital, there was a phone call from the school principal, saying that

Marta had been suspended because she had been caught with beer in her locker.

At this point, Cheryl decided to circle the wagons. She called Marta's father—her ex-husband—and his wife to join her for a conference with Marta's teachers and counselor. It became clear at that meeting that Marta's group of friends had a profound influence on all of its members. This wasn't only an issue of drinking, it was also an issue of Marta's needing to belong and having finally connected with a group that made her feel needed and wanted. Marta had been lonely and adrift since her parents had separated, and she hadn't had any close friends through the middle school years. Almost at any cost, she was going to stay with her friends, whatever was necessary to do that. Since Cheryl worked at a job some distance away, there were many opportunities for Marta to break her curfew.

The final decision by the adults in the family was to remove Marta from the influence of this peer group. Her mother agreed to have Marta move in with her father, who lived across town, where she would be attending another school. Her father went in to talk to the counselor at the new school, to ask for help and support in introducing Marta to some girls that she could connect with. Luckily this counselor knew how to work behind the scenes and arranged for Marta to be invited to join the school newspaper staff, where she met and became friends with several girls who liked school and were fun to be with.

With Stacy, progressive stepped-up interventions seemed to have little or no effect. Two years is a long time for a girl to struggle with loneliness and depression, and Stacy's parents struggled all that time, too, desperate to do something to help their daughter. In the end, it seemed that simple friendship—something that has to develop naturally—was the curative remedy. However, no one can know what part the process played—what part of Stacy's recovery might have been due to the combined effects of age, developmental growth, hormones, antidepressants, her particular temperament, and her experience of feeling that her parents loved her and cared enough to keep trying. Might Stacy have recovered to the same extent had there been no interventions at all? The truth is we can't know.

With Marta, had there been no intervention, I doubt she would have fared so well. Should Marta's mother have searched her daughter's room? Is it okay for a parent to do this? Questions like this are too complex to be answered with a yes or a no. The answer always seems to start with "It depends . . ." In general, it shows some respect and trust for children to feel privacy and a sense of self-space. So routine rifling of a child's room just for curiosity is not an effective parenting mode. But if there have been continuing issues and worries that an objective bystander would consider "just cause," then going into your child's room and looking around can be needed and helpful. As with all decisions that we agonize over in our attempt to be wise adults, we need to be able to articulate why we do what we do. Our children need not agree with it, but deep down they do have a sense of fairness that will prevail when the storm is over in a week or a year, or more.

Given what Marta's mother learned, the data suggested the need for abrupt intervention. On the other hand, this radical change could have propelled her into a deeper negative reaction in her new home and school setting. There was no way for her parents to be sure at the time that this would lead to better days.

So if the answers can be so different, girl to girl, what can we learn from their experiences?

Point one: Communicate conscientious parenting, concern, and caring. Do not remain silent or appear to be indifferent to any situation that causes you or her to worry. Silence and indifference *are* a response; they carry meaning. Express your caring, even if, in the beginning, it is merely to say: "You seem a little (quiet, tired, sad, edgy, angry). If there's anything you want to talk to me about, I'm here."

Point two: Do your homework, then do what you feel is right, and then be prepared to do something different if things don't improve. As the adults in the lives of children, we are trying to make sure that they grow healthily and don't stray too far into dangerous waters. In difficult times, we have to do what we have to do. We look at the situation, gather data and wisdom, look at our options, and make a choice we think is a good one at the time. When it doesn't seem to be working well, we try to pick up the pieces and move in a different direction. That's all any of us can do. This process of observation and information gathering is another version of negotiating the gray, as outlined in Chapter 1. When the situation is more challenging, however, and concerns build, it helps to have a sense of how to step up your attention in a reasonable, responsible way.

Lessons from the Lake

A friend of mine who lives near Lake Michigan described the way she used to keep a watchful eye on her six-year-old daughter as she played along the shoreline in the waves as they broke and rolled upon the beach. Her daughter was a novice swimmer, and liked to swim just a little way out to practice her strokes, but mother and daughter had agreed to some basic safety rules that included not going in any deeper than chest high. As long as her daughter played in the very shallow water, this mother felt comfortable sitting on her beach towel. But as her daughter moved a little farther out, where the lake bottom was uneven and subject to undercurrents, the mother would casually stroll closer, basically maintaining the same distance from her daughter, but increasing her watchfulness. The mother's rationale was that she wanted to stay far enough away so her daughter could enjoy her freedom and learn to ride the waves, but close enough to be handy should her daughter run into trouble and need some help.

Similar "lessons from the lake" apply to parenting under pressure.

Walking the Beach

Life has its awkward, uncomfortable, difficult moments, and a girl needs to experience her share of them if she's going to figure out strategies for working through them. Negative emotions are natural, normal, will happen frequently, and are often what I'd call appropriate affect. If she got a D on her science quiz, it is okay to be upset; it is healthy. She may be distressed, but she doesn't need rescuing. We have a tendency to want children to not experience negative feelings, which is quite understandable. Adults have an instinctive reaction to come to the aid of someone hurting, especially someone young, and especially their own young one. The greater the perceived or real pain, the more we feel compelled to step in to help, fix, or remove the source of the pain. So we might say that at the first stirrings of concern, there is wisdom in moving a bit closer to keep an eye on things, and taking the time to observe and think about the situation, even talk with her about it, without running in to intervene.

While you're keeping a closer eye on her situation, it's a good time to make yourself more available. Try to hang out and spend a bit more time together so you can get some hints about how upset she is and what might be going on. Talk with your spouse, partner, or whomever you consider your closest consultant, who may validate your concerns or offer a different perspective. This process can go on for some time, but it ends either when things improve or when your mild worry develops an edge of urgency. Then it's time for action.

Wading In

Acting on your worry does not necessarily mean jumping in with both feet and demanding to know what is going on, or trying to immediately fix or change the situation. In fact, it is almost always more effective to do just the opposite. The more worried you are, or the more it seems that this could be a serious situation, the more important it is for you to wade into the process, rather than jump in for the dramatic rescue. Discussing the issue with your daughter, within your family, and with a couple of trusted adult friends grounds your perspective in a helpful way.

How do you approach your daughter with your concerns?

Some girls are very much like hermit crabs, and need to feel safe to venture out of the shell. Saying how much you care, that you're a bit worried, and asking if you can talk about it, may draw them out. Other girls are more direct and will respond to your simple, concerned "What's up?" The point of this step is to engage in some type of direct conversation with her so you can better size up what's happening, and if there is an issue, what it is and what to do next.

Wading in Deeper

As with all phases, if your worry continues, regardless of what your daughter says, wade in a bit more. Going back to Marta's story of drinking with friends, she originally gave her mother the basic "Leave me alone, I'm fine" message, which did not help Cheryl at all. She turned to outside consultation; in this case, her ex-husband and a few other friends who knew Marta well. When that only confirmed her worry, she waded in more and talked to the school counselor. At this juncture, many parents would have chosen the counseling route. Marta's parents skipped this intervention step because they felt a broken hand was evidence of this being a situation that had moved to a physical safety issue and they wanted to have an immediate change of venue. However, getting professional advice, either for yourself as a parent in terms of how to handle a serious concern, or for your daughter directly, is a key step by the time you have reached this level of worry.

Calling the Lifeguard

If your daughter's situation continues to be of concern, whether it is because her behavior or distress is extreme from the outset, or because she has shown no improvement, or seems to be growing worse, then it's time to call for outside help. Back to Tricia and the attempted suicide. It would have been great if her family had called on professional help as she seemed to be drifting into deep water over the breakup with her boyfriend, but they didn't know how deep the water was at the time. It was only after the pills that they knew she, and they, needed a more direct, professional intervention.

With Chrissie, the anorexic-turned-bulimic, the depth of the problem was much more visible. They saw her losing weight at a steady pace. As the days went by, they also saw other things that began to make them worry more:

- Avoidance of places where there is food: Chrissie used to do her homework in the kitchen, but now did it in her bedroom.
- Drinking large quantities of water. Diet Coke used to be her thing, now a water bottle was her pal.
- Toothpaste or mouthwash breath: Chrissie was doing this whenever she went to the bathroom. Just like an alcoholic tries to cover up the alcohol smell, the eating-disordered girl covers up the vomit smell.

Her parents couldn't stand their worry, the tension, and Chrissie's pale face and listlessness anymore. They began to ask for advice from friends, the school counselor, and a friend who is a social worker. They knew from Chrissie's behavior pattern that she had crossed the line between experimenting with anorexic behavior and becoming an anorexic and bulimic, and she needed professional help.

It was only after the entire family began a counseling program that they really understood the line that Chrissie had crossed. Once a person has not eaten much at all for a sustained period, and she has lost a significant amount of muscle mass, the chemistry of the brain is affected, and perception is distorted. In this case, Chrissie had reached that level, and could no longer see her situation accurately. Her parents' intervention with professional help was essential.

When It's Time to Call, Whom to Call

My mother's words, as always, come to mind. "Better safe than sorry." Or, in my field, "When in doubt, refer out!" But to whom?

A school counselor? A psychologist? A social worker? A psychiatrist? A pediatrician? In Tricia's case, she had been assigned to a psychiatrist at the hospital, and might logically have followed up with a psychiatrist or psychologist once she was home again, but it wasn't my professional title that brought her to me. She trusted her brother, and her brother knew and trusted me. She felt that connection. Luckily she also felt the connection to me. *And with girls, connection with the person with whom she is working is the most critical variable.*

Ask people you trust for references. Find someone who has had as much experience as possible with the issue you are facing, has sterling evaluations by clients, and whom you interview to see if you think there would be a good fit between this person and this girl you love. No single professional is effective in dealing with all issues or all girls.

Keep in mind, too, that each type of professional brings a different perspective to the diagnosis and treatment plan:

Pediatrician: the study of childhood diseases
Social worker: issues especially related to social and cultural
    factors
Psychologist: human behavior and feelings
Psychiatrist: medicine in relation to behavior and feelings

Each category of professional then operates either as a generalist or a specialist in a particular field. For instance, some social workers specialize in abused children, some psychologists in the area of learning disabilities, some psychiatrists in the area of panic disorders, some pediatricians in the area of attention disorders. There are some issues that are very specialized and need very specialized care. Learning disabilities and eating disorders fall into this category.

One of the key issues with girls is that they need to like and respect the person they are working with, and it is not just a matter of expertise and talent. When you are talking about girls, there needs to be a bond, a connection, a caring, and with a person who is wise and talented on top of all that. That is a tall order. So cast your net wide for referrals, take the time to interview them, and follow up with both the therapist and your daughter to see if the match is a fit.

Change can take time, and it is important to give any professional intervention enough time to work. If your daughter says she doesn't like the counselor or therapist, or that their work together is not helpful, it may be difficult to tell whether this is a valid perception you should listen to or not. Obviously there can be some resistance or reluctance on your daughter's part to change, or she wouldn't be in this situation. That is also true of changing venues, like Marta's changing schools. Things were very rocky at the beginning, Marta didn't want things to work, but her parents held tight and set a time line that was not negotiable: She had to stay there for the remainder of the school year, which was six months. Almost in spite of herself, Marta started to enjoy what she was doing at school, and very slowly she fought everyone less. The same is true for seeing a professional. Talk with this outside consultant to determine up front how long a trial period should be and let your daughter know she will be staying the course, just like any other ground rules you have for giving things a chance, or following through on commitments.

Under Pressure to Measure Up at School

Serious issues of health and safety claim the spotlight when it comes to discussions of parenting concerns, but probably the most prevalent source of chronic worry and tension among parents and their girls today is school performance.

Ask any seasoned educator, and she will hold her head in agony when you bring up the topic of grades and test scores, as will most parents. In our culture and at this time in our society, these measurements are just a fact of life, but they bring with them a host of peaks and pitfalls for all involved.

The Smiths called for an appointment to see me because they were in a panic about their middle school daughter's academic performance. I was perplexed because I knew that Noreen was a good, conscientious student, and I had just read her name on the honor roll list. This school gave standardized achievement tests every year and sent those results to the parents. The Smiths came in with scores in hand. The report showed that Noreen was above average in everything; her scores varied between 60 and 90 percent. The Smiths were upset because these scores did not match Noreen's grade point average, and what did that mean, and what did that mean for future test scores, and would this interfere with taking advanced courses in high school (she was now in seventh grade), and could this possibly reveal a learning disability?

Noreen was upset, too, they said, and she was worried about how her teachers would perceive her ability and capability as a student. Mr. Smith was the owner of a large and powerful corporation. Mrs. Smith was the president of several community organizations. I knew that Noreen respected her parents and saw them as high achievers, and wanted that for herself and for them. She cared very much about measuring up to their standards. My belief was that the difference in her test scores and her school grades was due to her motivation and hard work. She was bright, but not a genius. However, she was getting the 100 percent at school from a combination of ability and hard work.

As we talked, it was clear that the Smiths were very loving, and never put overt pressure on Noreen to achieve. They didn't need to; the whole family, including her older brother, were models of high achievement. When I asked the Smiths why they cared about these test scores, they basically said that they didn't want any obstacles in Noreen's path of success. And if something could be done right now to remove those, they wanted to do that. Under that sterling parental sense of responsibility, however, was the fear that Noreen might not be able to achieve and, they also admitted, it would be devastating to them and to Noreen if she couldn't be in advanced classes in the future (and all of what that meant).

When pressed again to tell me what success meant to them, and why that was important, they, like most parents, got down to the bottom line: "We want Noreen to be happy." But her dad added, "And to be happy in this world, you have to do well."

So here we were, two caring parents, a girl who was giving her best at school and doing very well, and some preliminary evidence that she would have to work very hard to stay at the top of the academic stack, because she wasn't brilliant in everything. The Smiths had come in hoping to hear that there was some course Noreen could take to improve her test scores, or that there was some splinter learning issue that tutoring could ameliorate. But instead, it was the thorny, and common, issue of measuring up to standards that did not take into consideration the vast difference of individuals.

This turned into many conversations with the Smiths and with Noreen. We reviewed her record and recognized the incredible way she had worked and achieved for so many years. We moved to discussions of personal best, and how, sometimes, it is hard to not focus on being the best in the class. Some of the discussions centered on how to take standardized tests, some techniques that help improve scores somewhat. But we also spent a great deal of time talking about Noreen's and her family's goals for the future, and how to best move toward those with the talents and skills she had.

In the end, Noreen continued to work just as hard, and she continued to have good grades, but I think that she and her parents had a new appreciation for what that really meant. And when things like a B or a 70 percent on a standardized test came up, it bothered all of them far less.

Teaching and Learning Lessons for Life

At some time or another, we all make an error in judgment, or take a wrong step, and find ourselves in deep water. Your daughter will do it, and you will, too, as a parent. Making mistakes, taking missteps, doing incredibly unintelligent and sometimes even dangerous things, are all part of negotiating life and figuring out your strengths and weaknesses, for children *and* parents. There are no perfect answers, but if there is such a thing as perfect parents, it is those parents who care enough to weather the tough times: pay attention, listen to their child, follow up on concerns, and include their child in that learning process.

Finally, the influence of parents was covered separately for mothers and fathers in previous chapters. It is also a relevant concept here. As a parent, when you respond to pressure or problems, you are not only acting for yourself, but you are providing a dress rehearsal for your daughter; a hands-on learning experience, actually, that will shape the way she thinks and acts under pressure, and inform her judgment. Remember, any challenge your daughter encounters offers an opportunity for learning—for you and your daughter alike!

Pearls for Parents and Pearls for Girls

- Listen to your instincts.
- Don't be a rescuer. You can't fix or be all that your child needs when she is in trouble. Know your limitations and seek support and assistance when the worry begins.
- Stay connected. Consult with your daughter about your worries, and tap your network of trusted adults for a reality check of your emotions and judgments.
- Encourage the growth that comes through hard work, struggle, and even mistakes. Let her fall, and let her deal with the natural consequences as much as you can stand it.
- When you're saying no and being unpopular with your daughter, add: "It would be easier for me to cave in and say yes, but I love you enough to do what is really hard for me to do."
- When not in the middle of a crisis, tell her that she can always talk to you about anything, and that it would mean a great deal to you if she did.
- Always go to her room to say good night, especially if you've had a rough day together.

CHAPTER 10

Girls in Action: The Magic of Doing

"I will never forget that feeling of being strong, the feeling you get knowing you completed what your task was and you gained so much from it. It's worth a million dollars!"

—Emily, fourteen

Years ago, when I was working in a high school, I was asked to see a girl whose absenteeism was setting all kinds of records. Cecelia came slouching in to see me on a day when she managed to come to school. Actually, she was sent to me. I asked her what the school's consequences were for skipping school on a continuing basis. She laughed and said, "They suspend you!" It was a truant's dream come true!

Just as I was preparing myself to launch into a very long session, in walks a little boy named Joey. Joey had been trying to see me because he was doing terribly in school. His parents had just separated and he was truly a lost soul. *Aha!* I told the two that I needed to make a quick trip to the bathroom, and I asked Cecelia if she would just help Joey with his math for a few minutes while I was gone. Well, I knew they needed me gone a little longer than that. I came back a half hour later to see them both with their heads bent close together over a piece of paper.

On his way out, Joey gave Cecelia a dazzling smile and said, "Will you be here tomorrow?" I couldn't have scripted it better!

Cecelia, though, the jaded teen, yawned and said, "Maybe, maybe not."

Joey got a hurt puppy look and left. The bell rang and Cecelia got up and sauntered out without saying anything. The next day she wasn't in school. But when she appeared again (with a little help from the truancy team), she discovered that Joey had taped a drawing of his on her locker. That sealed it, and the story did end happily for each partner in this tutor-tutee twosome.

In her work with Joey, Cecelia discovered what I call "the magic of doing," the most important layering experience a girl can have to develop strong self-esteem. Remember the three C's of self-esteem: competence, confidence, and connectedness. Cecelia, drawn back to school by this serendipitous connection with Joey, was able to experience her own competence—in math and in her ability to help someone struggling in school—and build her confidence in herself as a valuable and valued person there.

Doing attends to all three Cs, in different ways, with results that are transformational in a girl's life. In emotional fitness terms, *doing* allows us to work on those three different emotional muscle sets, which often are unevenly developed in girls. In math-chemistry terms, the magic of doing takes one plus one plus one, and bubbles it into a perfect ten!

The Myth of Empowerment

We each have a list of things or words that just push our buttons: make us red in the face and determined to set the record straight. One of mine is the word *empower*. When you plug in an electric blender, you empower it to make milk shakes; when you fill up a gas tank, engage the key in the ignition, and press on the accelerator, you empower a car to move. I suppose the term could be used in a few ways to refer to human conditions: insulin injections empower the body to consistently break down sugars, or, to use an example closer to me, hormone replacement therapy might empower my short-term memory to work better!

I'm not such a stickler about word choices all the time, but there is a lot of talk about empowering girls, and the word itself leads to a lot of misunderstanding and ineffective ways of thinking about what we can do to see that girls become healthy and thriving human beings. The key word here is "become." "Become" really connotes a process, something that happens over time and is related to development or the growth of the organism. We can't empower girls. There is no magic plug or fuel or injection or pill. The increasing power or confidence or competence of a girl certainly is related to what happens in her life, including the things we, and others, do and say; more specifically, though, it emerges from how she reacts to the world, and how she experiences herself as an active agent in the world. We can't *make* her competent. We can't *give* her confidence. We can't *forge* connectedness between her and others.

We *can* create environments that support and encourage girls, and we can intentionally layer in opportunities for a girl to actively engage in doing for themselves. Often, when a parent or teacher comes to me with a "problem girl," for whom "nothing seems to work," a focused dose of action therapy—doing—puts a girl in touch with her own resources, which is always a significant first step in the right direction. Action therapy doesn't have to include therapy in the traditional sense at all, although it may. The critical piece is the action—the doing—and a commitment to helping a girl connect up with the opportunities, or create them, for self-discovery through active involvement.

The Power Shortage of Self-Esteem in Girls

Although there are no rigidly controlled scientific studies to prove it, most professionals in the field and thoughtful observers of humans would agree that self-esteem is the key core ingredient for a thriving girl. However, beginning with the 1991 landmark study titled *Shortchanging Girls, Shortchanging America,* by the American Association of University Women, there have been numerous studies collecting data that show that girls' self-esteem, in general, is lower than boys' self-esteem at all ages. Further analysis indicates that girls' self-esteem drops precipitously from about age ten through adolescence.

There hasn't been much work done beyond the teen years, but my private-practice work and discussions with so many adult women prompts me to estimate that for many women, catching up to the level of lively self-esteem they enjoyed before age ten often takes several decades. In my generation, there is abundant anecdotal reporting that many women do not hit their full stride again until age forty-something. That's a long time—three decades—for females not to be operating with a full core of self-esteem.

No wonder we want so urgently to empower this generation of girls! We know about the three-decade power outage that lies ahead for so many of them. I envision a special charging unit, like the one used to charge the battery of cars, that we could plug all girls into during the night while they slept and voilà, a fully charged self-esteem female unit ready for the world each day! As silly as it sounds, we've seen the equivalent fantasies at work in education and in our own best, but misguided, efforts at times.

"Feel Good About Yourself" Is Not Good Enough

In the 1980s there was a big push in schools for what was labeled *affective education*. Stripping these programs down to their essence, they were designed to make children feel good about themselves. In general, they were based on the premise that if children love themselves and feel loved, they will have great self-esteem. Although popular, the programs did not have the promised effect. Self, analysis of self, and appreciation of self are often the core of successful education programs. However, the evidence is quite clear that these programs are not effective. Focusing on self does not increase self-esteem, but it can increase selfishness. Connecting with another human being, feeling a part of a group or community, giving, caring are all examples of connectedness. It is by focusing outward rather than inward that self is enhanced. In fact, as we, as a culture and society, increase in materialism, and focus so much on the needs of self, there is beginning evidence that we are facilitating selfishness—not self-esteem—in our children. I'm not saying that you should stop all of the things you do and say to make a girl feel loved—that is critical to her well-being. It is not enough, however, to enhance her self-esteem.

So what does it? What is the alternative to that magic charging machine that empowers girls? When I ask this question of audiences, someone invariably suggests that it is looks or beauty. My response: Marilyn Monroe. The cinema sex queen of the 1940s and 1950s lived a life that was spiked with deep disappointments, divorces, and drugs before she died "in her sleep" shortly after she turned thirty-six. Beauty wasn't enough.

There are so many incredibly beautiful women who have such terrible self-esteem. In fact, for some females, being very attractive can even have an adverse effect on self-esteem. I've talked to so many teenage girls who echo the assumption that their popularity with boys, and therefore popularity in general, is due to their looks. Over time, this can lead a girl to question her worth as a person, or believe that appearance is all the world cares about. This also happens to girls at the other end of the continuum, the ones who perceive that the world thinks they are not attractive. Have you ever known a girl who declined a chance to do something she wanted to do because she was upset about her looks? Do any of us *not* know a girl who has done that? (Every woman knows one, and most likely was one once.)

So if attractiveness does not ensure self-esteem, then our culture's push for girls to be as beautiful as possible is problematic. Girls believe that if only they were thinner or prettier or had a bigger chest, they would be happier. I'm not saying that there isn't some correlation between how we look and how we feel about ourselves. We all know that a bad hair day can have a dramatic effect on our confidence and comfort level. Physical attributes can affect our overall self-concept, especially when we are younger and we are trying to blend into the camouflage of our peer group. It isn't enough to ensure self-esteem.

Brains and bucks don't do it, either.

Money and self-esteem? Earning it is one thing; receiving it is another. For many girls today, one or both parents worked hard to gain financial security and affluence and they, rightly so, feel pretty good about it. The earning and getting there helped enhance their parents' feelings of achievement and self-esteem, but being surrounded by material things often leaves the children of those strivers unimpressed, feeling entitled or empty. Money only complicates issues of self-esteem, especially in the girl world, where it buys fashionable facades, but is less often invested in experiences that are core-building.

Intelligence and self-esteem? Surely being smart would do the trick? Not necessarily, especially if you're a girl. In previous generations of women, a big part of the problem was that a woman's ability was often much higher than the opportunities open to her. Today, with doors open and the social acceptability of smart girls at an all-time high, intelligence has much more positive weight to it as a tool. But that's not true everywhere a girl goes, and not in every girl's family, school, church, or community; not in every girl's mind. If intelligence were reflected directly in our level of self-esteem, then every female with a high IQ would have incredible self-esteem, and every female who had a moderate IQ would have okay self-esteem, and every female who had a low IQ would have low self-esteem—and that is not the case. Intelligence can have a double edge to it; people we describe as gifted, as a population, report more mental-health problems and social issues than the general population. So while intelligent females may have good self-esteem, it isn't IQ that's producing it.

So many times we try to buck up a girl by telling her she is wonderful, smart, nice, worthy, or otherwise valued. It is usually a sign that the adult who is speaking recognizes that she has low self-esteem and is trying the old affective education method—*If I tell her all this stuff, she will believe me and she will start to believe it herself.* It never hurts a girl to hear genuine appreciation expressed, but compliments alone won't change the way she thinks about herself. Self-esteem is the ultimate hands-on, do-it-yourself project.

Emily: Into the Wilderness for Self-Discovery

Emily was thirteen, angry, and sad over the breakup of her parents' marriage and a move that separated her from her closest friends, when she was shipped off to a six-week summer wilderness extreme-challenge camp in Idaho. In the first weeks the campers learned basic backpacking and survival skills, and practiced teamwork and responsibility in a harsh and unforgiving geographic terrain. Day by day, as she grew physically stronger, she also began to feel a different kind of inner strength that previously she had not been aware she had. At one point during a long hike, she sprained an ankle on the trail, but still managed to haul her pack, plus part of another camper's things, so the team could keep up the pace needed to reach home camp before food and water ran out. Other moments along the way forced her to reach deep for energy, patience, and courage she didn't know she had. What she found within herself first surprised her, then thrilled her.

When she returned home six weeks later, nothing much had changed there, but she found that she had changed considerably, she said, recalling the experience in a conversation about a year later.

"At the point where I was at before, I was only looking for attention," she said, referring to outbursts of anger, and other beginnings of self-destructive behaviors she had been caught up in just prior to that summer trek. Her wilderness experience taught her a lot about surviving in a difficult environment, but even more about her own inner territory, she said.

"I learned that you don't have to get attention to be happy

with yourself. I can climb a mountain. I can carry a pack. I don't have to treat people like crap to get what I want. It doesn't matter how you look, or who you're dealing with—you need to look inside yourself to find your answer."

Her experience brought her closer to nature, and to the nature of the human experience: "It made me have more patience for things," she said. "When you're going up a mountain, you can't hurry it up . . . you have to move with the group. You have to think of other people and not only yourself.

"Being out in the woods changed the way I can look at things from a different perspective," Emily said. "Going through school, sometimes you think 'I can't get this test,' and think less of yourself, but now I can say I was twenty miles into this hike and couldn't even bend my legs anymore, but I kept going. I hiked ten miles with a sprained ankle. That's me. That's who I am!"

The Physiology of "3C" Self-Esteem

Why does *doing* work? Where does the magic come from? Groundbreaking research into the physiology and chemistry of the brain is beginning to shed a spotlight on the intricacies of the brain and how much of our thinking and feeling is related to neurology and body chemistry. The predisposition of females toward depression, anxiety, and fear was discussed in previous chapters. This is a real problem for females, as it relates to active doing in everyday life, and doing those things that create self-esteem. Fear and anxiety trigger flight and avoidance—not the risk-taking and determination needed to take on challenges that will help you grow. It is well-documented that depression is an action inhibitor. So with all three, the kind of doing that is positively active is inhibited by the limbic system that we are trying to enhance with feelings of confidence, competence, and connectedness.

That's why action therapy is so important and why I say to girls, I know you are afraid, sad, anxious, but you have to *do* it anyway.

The other chemistry and brain issue is related to endorphins. Physical activity, especially sustained physical activity, causes the body to produce endorphins, and endorphins cause the brain to produce more serotonin. Serotonin enhances neurotransmitter conduction and results in a feeling of well-being. So *doing* has a physiological, as well as a psychological, impact, causing a double-positive whammy for females. Conclusive research isn't in yet, but it makes logical sense that when a girl feels an overall sense of well-being, she is more apt to try and do the kinds of things that will build competence, confidence, and connectedness.

I Do, Therefore I Am—but Do What?

If doing results in feeling more confident, competent, and connected, and feeling confident, competent, and connected results in solid self-esteem, then doing what, is the next question. The not-so-simple but simple-sounding answer is: anything that causes a girl to feel confident, competent, and connected. And just like everything else related to human beings, that differs tremendously by individual. But as we look at the world and the world of girls, three key categories emerge.

Athletic Doing: Strong Bodies, Strong Minds

Access, success, and visibility has changed the world of girls and athletics. Now it is almost the opposite of what it was two decades ago: Girls who do not participate in sports are not in the groove. There is much correlational data that indicates that girls who participate in sports not only develop the useful skills of leadership, problem-solving, and physical coordination, but also often add to their reservoir of confidence, competence, and connectedness. In fact, probably more than any other category, sports can do it all. As a girl develops her skills as a basketball player, she feels more competent. As she scores baskets or blocks shots, she feels more confident; as the team huddles together before the game and after the game, the sense of connected-ness surges through her. Even girls who are not elite basketball talents can experience the three C's this way, especially if someone who understands girls coaches the team. However, being on a team that has a very critical or demeaning coach can have the opposite effect on sensitive girls.

I watched one ten-year-old girl struggle for several months with gymnastics. The big deal at her school was the gymnastics show before spring break. Each girl was to develop her own routine and perform it in front of a very large school audience. The year before, she had watched most of her friends add an aerial somersault to their routines. She was not able to do that, even after hours of practice, and it really bothered her. This year, she had put that into her routine, but each time she got to it in practice, she never made it. Her friends and family hoped she would just decide not to do the somersault when show time came. She had improved so much since the year before, and everyone was very proud of her; they didn't want this one snag to spoil her experience. But she didn't drop that piece from her routine.

On the day of the show, when her time came, the gym crowd of two hundred got uncharacteristically quiet when the music started for Kim's routine. As she stood in the corner of the mat, ready for the running start to the somersault, I could feel her determination and the audience's attempt to lift her up with telepathic levitation. Up she went, over she went, and down she came on two feet with her two arms shooting in the air in a mock Olympic stance. Ecstatic applause shook the gymnasium.

Not all athletic endeavors end this well, even the seemingly successful ones. Another older middle school girl was the tennis star in her school. Her coach and her team relied on her to win matches. As she moved into high school and onto the varsity team, there weren't just high hopes for a state championship; everyone was fairly convinced that she could win it all. The athletic director had even talked to all of the teachers about not having any classes the day before the state meets, so that the entire student body could go down to see them. Both of her parents told her that they would take the day off from work. Even her little brother had something nice to say to her.

She came to see me in the middle of the season to help her figure out how to get out of tennis. I thought that maybe she just needed some help in handling the pressure. It was true; the pressure was really tough. But the real issue was that tennis had become a grueling physical and emotional experience for her, and she felt that it was interfering with her learning, with her sleep, with her health and overall well-being. She was only a sophomore, and all she could see was two more years of this in high school, and then a big push to carry on in college, even to try for a scholarship. This was a girl not driven to compete, or win, or be better than everyone. She played tennis because she was naturally good at it, and had enjoyed the physicality and the camaraderie of the game. All of that had been lost in the all-encompassing drive to win.

Whatever sports you might consider encouraging your daughter to try, you'll need to take into account the matter of personal fit. Some girls do better with large team sports, like soccer and basketball. Some girls do better with small team sports, like track and field or tennis. And some girls do better with sports that are individual-based, like fencing or archery. Temperament, personality, and physical skills are all part of the analysis of which sport or sports are right for which girl. There are no magic answers or prescriptions, only thinking about these things and her own sampling and trying. It can be easier if girls begin playing sports recreationally, not highly competitively, early on in life. At this stage all girls are in the sampling and novice stage and there are (or should be!) no real pressures to succeed or to be a star. The exception to this is obviously the highly talented and skilled athletic girl. If she has Olympic swimming potential and the motivation, then the road is clear because *she* points it out.

It would be great if all girls could play some sport at some time in their lives, even if they are not gifted athletes. The enhancement of the three C's is a huge payoff, but there are other potential benefits. The production of the endorphins because of the physical exertion gives her attitude a very positive kick, and physical activity helps girls become fit and strong. Over time, both components enhance a feeling of well-being.

There is also something about the physical movement, the hard work, the sweating and being physical, without the focus on beauty, that has a much more hard-to-define overall positive effect on girls. So try hard to find something in the sports realm for a girl. Keep in mind that "sports" covers a wide range of options, from traditional school sports to horseback riding, jogging, or Ultimate Frisbee.

Creative Doing: Mind Over Matters

Writing, painting, dancing, singing, playing the tuba, inventing, and computer programming are all forms of creative doing that can and do build the reservoir of the three C's. I put this second on the doing list because although creative doing is a powerful venue for the benefits of doing, it also has some pitfalls. Girls often are very critical of their output. They look at what they have painted or written or how their voice sounds with an analytic eye. This happens with sports also, but there is something about playing a sport in which a girl understands that this is a process. Although creative endeavors are a process, too, they also have an immediately discernible product, and therein is the problem. There is something concrete to see and to be viewed by others. Many girls have a tendency to want it to be good and "right" from the get-go.

Andi had always enjoyed simple ceramics projects in elementary grades, and now, at thirteen, wanted to learn to do more. But when her mother tried to persuade her to take a summer class in pottery, she balked. She refused to sign up for an open class for twelve- and thirteen-year-olds, she said, because it would be embarrassing to be one of the oldest students there, with so little experience. When her mother found an open class for thirteen- to eighteen-year-olds, Andi refused it, too, saying that there she would be the youngest *and* the least experienced!

This is why I recommend to middle school art teachers that they switch from still-life painting to something such as using a digital camera for photography and then playing with ways of distorting the images on the computer. Then there is no definable product that is commonly recognizable as "good." This relieves the would-be perfectionist tendency of girls, and also keeps their creative doing a positive experience.

Carol Gilligan, in later collaboration with a theater professional, worked with girls and women on stage to strengthen their self-expression through speaking and acting. That is the power of this creative venue. If you don't want to tell the world about how you feel about high heels, or you don't have the chutzpah to tell your best friend you hate the way she makes fun of your red hair, you can get up on a stage and have a strong voice. It reminds me of Katharine Hepburn, when she was interviewed on TV, talking about how shy she was in public early on and how she would often throw up before she went on stage. Yet when she did step on the stage, she proved to be a powerhouse with an incredible voice and a powerful presence that eventually translated into a more confident voice offstage.

Connected Doing: Feeling the Power of Contribution and Partnership

This is probably the most natural fit for most females because of our predisposition to be a nurturer and caregiver of the species. Because of this, connected doing gives us a double shot of good feelings. Participating in Habitat for Humanity, tutoring younger children at your synagogue, walking animals at the local humane society, clearing trails in Ecuador with the Sierra Club, or simply reading to your father because his illness keeps him in bed for long periods of time are all forms of connected doing.

The key ingredients: The focus is not on the girl, and the activity is meaningful to the doer and to the receiver. A billionaire is not going to get a positive charge by giving a dollar to a street person, or by giving a million dollars if it's just to keep the fund-raisers away from the door.

Arthur Koestler, a brilliant philosopher and observer of humans, coined the term *holon*. It means something that is at once a whole and a part. Like a thumb is a whole entity, but it is part of a hand. A hand is a whole entity, but it is also a part of an arm. He and others have suggested that humans mistakenly believe that this holonic progression ends when we get to the whole individual. His point is that the progression continues: We are part of our families, our communities, our land, our world, our universe.

Some psychologists take this a step further and suggest that it is this next holonic connection, between the individual as a part and the many options as a whole with which to connect, that is most related to meaning in life and positive mental health. Remember the girl who was diagnosed with clinical depression, only to have it disappear when, at last, she felt connected to friends? That scenario plays out scores of times in a female's life. Why is a girl so devastated when a boyfriend breaks up with her, or when, many years later, her children have left the nest? Certainly there are many reasons, but this disconnect between self and others is a huge component. I love the old adage "Happiness is someone to love, something to do, and something to look forward to." The author is that very famous person named Ms. Anonymous.

This holonic connection of a girl to another person, group, or cause is the final component of a strong central core, of a thriving girl. It's the antidote for the extreme focus on self—how I look, how I feel, how many accoutrements of life I have—all of which move a girl to selfishness or dissatisfaction, the "not enough, never enough" syndrome. On the other hand, excessive or extreme connectedness or selflessness can be detrimental to that central core and diminish the sense of competence and confidence needed to be a thriving girl. So connected doing needs to be balanced, not only in terms of self and others, but also in terms of connectedness at the potential expense of competence and confidence. A girl who is too connected to others can be on the road to being an overpleaser and ultimately a very unhappy and ineffective person.

Other-Than-Self Experiences: Engaging in the World at Large

In a previous chapter, I talked about how important it is for tween and teen girls to find an anchor interest or passion, something in which they can invest themselves, and which helps them stay emotionally on course during typical turbulent stretches of growing-up years. In *Reviving Ophelia,* Mary Pipher called it a "North Star."

Mihaly Csikszentmihalyi, author, professor, and former head of the University of Chicago psychology department, coined the term *flow* as a state of mind in which we are fully engaged in optimal thinking.

Girls whose anchor or North Star is reading, for instance, may use it to disappear from the world, or escape into one, and it steadies them. A friend of mine was recently diagnosed with cancer; his daughter's reading habit has increased to a book a day. I know another girl who heads to the barn when she's had a bad day at school. Mucking out the stall, brushing the horse, and going for a ride envelops her in the flow.

I'd like to see girls have an anchor and experience flow, too. But I also believe girls benefit the most, especially in their teen years, when they put their anchor passion and their flow energy together, and focus their attention on what I call other-than-self experiences. Especially during the teen time of self-absorption and self-analysis, focusing on activities and others outside themselves provides the balance they need. Just as tutoring Joey was a breakthrough for Cecelia in the story that opened this chapter, outside-the-self experiences add an important dimension to every girl's experience of herself in relation to others.

Janine was just shy of her thirteenth birthday—her bat mitzvah—when she decided that, as her mitzvah (community service), she wanted to volunteer at the local humane society shelter. She had always loved animals, but mostly had been a dedicated reader about them and rescuer of orphaned animals in her neighborhood. She was underage for certain hands-on aspects of the shelter work, but the shelter supervisor agreed to let her walk dogs if her mother would do it with her. So the two began a weekly three-hour commitment at the shelter, where they helped clean and care for the dogs.

Within just a few months, Janine's mature approach to her work and her natural rapport with dogs became clear to everyone at the shelter, and her repeated requests to take on more duties finally met with success. Her work feels like an extension of herself, Janine says, and if she had a choice, she would do even more. "I like the responsibility. I have a job, I'm trustworthy, and I work with adults—and some of them think I'm eighteen!"

The magic of doing is available to every girl, and in enough variety to match any girl's interests. Activities that enhance competence, confidence, and connectedness, in varying degrees, include sports, any performance-based activity (theater, dance, gymnastics), speech or public speaking training, martial arts and wall rock-climbing, math or other content-based workshops for girls, training in learning styles, study skills courses and mentoring programs, Big/Little Sister programs, peer counseling, on-site volunteer programs (working at the hunger center instead of just bringing canned goods to school), and school government that has a meaningful role.

Girls on the Move: An Incredible Journey of Doing

I'd like to say I bicycled all the way across America with the extraordinary girls and women who participated in Outward Bound's Girls on the Move 2000 millennium project for ten weeks in the late summer and fall of that year. I didn't. However, as a member of the board of advisers, and a speaker at the rallies and programs across the country, I accompanied these women on various segments of the journey from Portland, Oregon, to New York City. I appreciated the opportunity to visit among these seventy-five or so bicyclists and support crew members, women aged seventeen to seventy-two, and their coast-to-coast admirers.

As fit as these women were, this challenge was not about physical fitness. The purpose of Girls on the Move was to celebrate the ability of girls to be active, to promote their courage to do important and difficult things, and to educate all of us that girls can do anything. So all along the ride route, festivals, speakers, and school visits were part of the event. The women wrote poems and songs and told stories to thousands of girls and women and men and boys at schools and public gatherings across the country. They pushed themselves physically to unbelievable levels. A few examples from this cast of impressive characters:

I (woman of the weak knee) often rode in the van with Nancy's guide dog. Nancy, who was blind, was the one out riding a tandem bike. She couldn't see to steer, but she could pedal like blue blazes, and was happy to keep a steady motivational chatter going with her riding partner.

Heidi was a mountain climber by profession. But at school stops, when she acted out the alphabet with music and dancing, the school audiences gave a standing ovation. She is a great communicator and artist—and she is deaf and mute.

The mother of one tween girl spent her time on the trip showing strength and stretching exercises to her peer riders. However, during the festivals in the major cities, she was the one who kept the audiences spellbound with her story of being a teenage single mother herself. Her stories of how she attended college with a baby and went on to become a successful professional left her audiences of young girls feeling like they could do anything if this petite little woman had that kind of inner and outer (her muscle definition was very apparent) strength.

And I will never forget the mother-daughter duo, B.J. and Robyn. Both had survived a devastating car crash in which B.J.'s other daughter—Robyn's sister—was killed. In that crash, B.J. had broken most of the bones in her body and was never expected to get out of bed again, let alone ride 3,600 miles across the country. I couldn't keep up with B.J. on the short spurts in which I participated. And Robyn talked about battling an eating disorder because she was so intent on having a perfect slim body during her high school and college years. Here was this gorgeous (inside and out) young woman who exuded personality, wit, charm, and intelligence. How could she have been so depleted in self-esteem?

These women and about fifty more pedaled their hearts out, waved to the people in towns all across the country, and stopped in many schools and cities to talk and perform and lead girls through climbing walls and challenge courses. They connected with each other and so many of the people they touched along the way.

Somewhere in the Midwest a boy in a wheelchair came to one of the festivals with his sister and their mother. He was stunned to see Candace, the rider I mentioned earlier, who used a hand-cycle because she was paralyzed from the waist down. She talked to the audience about how much she enjoyed participation in the para-Olympics each year. Afterward, this boy came up to talk to her. I still have the visual image of their wheelchairs pulled close together and the two of them talking animatedly. The next morning as I went out to help unload the bicycles from the trucks for the day's riding, I was surprised to see Candace's bicycle being pedaled around the parking lot, since Candace was sitting right in front of me in her wheelchair. Her young admirer was giving it a trial run; he had told his mother he was going to compete in the next para-Olympics.

A few weeks after the event ended and everyone was back in their home states getting back to the rest of their lives, I received an e-mail from one of the young riders. She had just gotten an e-mail from a young girl in Idaho. It simply said, "You probably don't remember me, but you came up and talked to me one day when you were visiting my school. You said that I reminded you of yourself when you were little, because you were shy, too, and didn't talk much in school. I just wanted you to know that I think you are great and I like the way you can talk in front of a group and everyone thought you were so interesting. So I've tried to talk more in class and everyone has noticed. Thanks!"

What a great event for the women participants and the observing girls: all three ways of doing rolled into one.

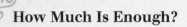

How Much Is Enough?

Whether it is sports, creative endeavors, or connected endeavors, participating in these activities enough over time develops the core self-esteem of girls. How much is enough? How long should a girl play sports? How many creative endeavors should she undertake? Is volunteering at the soup kitchen on Thanksgiving enough connectedness?

My grandmother, who never used a recipe in her life, probably came the closest to answering this question when I called her as I was trying to make Easter bread that tasted like hers. "How much vanilla should I put in, Grandma?" I could just see that little smile she would often get on her face.

"Well," she said, "just keep adding it until it feels right, looks right, and tastes like it is enough. You'll know."

So my answer to the enough question is that you have to just keep adding experiences until it feels right. Believe me—you'll know!

Pearls for Parents and Pearls for Girls:

- You can't give your daughter self-esteem, but if you are too critical or too demanding of her, you can take it away.

- You can make suggestions or support her choices (like paying for fencing lessons), but it will work better if she ultimately chooses her *doing* routes.

- Refrain from promoting the end product of the activity as her goal (e.g., winning awards, medals, or trophies, or earning credits).

- Model a doing life with a balance of physical activity, work and creativity, and connectedness.

- Make a contract with your daughter that she will do some activity each season of the year, and so will you!

- Put this sentence in your vocabulary: "It's okay to feel bad/sad/worried/scared for a while, but now it's time to *do* something . . ."

- Make it a family tradition to do some kind of volunteering or giving as a family at least once a year.

Epilogue: Girls in Progress

A man who paid millions to go into space with the astronauts came back and said the most valuable piece of the experience was the change of perspective. It would be great if there were a magic wand that could transport parents and significant adults in the lives of girls to a place where everyone could gain that feeling of perspective. We all get so involved in the daily stuff (and we need to) of living and making decisions, and yes, layering the strudel, that sometimes it is almost impossible to take the long view.

I'm so impressed by the sensitivity, resilience, and strength of young female beings—in the long run. Some very hard, traumatic, and trying things have occurred in the lives of so many girls (or they have provided those moments to their families and school!), yet most of them turn out to be fairly sturdy and healthy adults. So many mothers have asked whether they should be honest and divulge some of the mistakes they made and the terrible judgments they made as children or adolescents. When they begin to tell their stories, it's always amazing to compare this to the together woman sitting in front of me. I've now worked with girls for so long that I've also seen this metamorphosis among girls I've known as young students, and later as young women!

When I was an administrator interviewing a new teacher candidate, one of my former students came in to apply for the job. She confessed that she almost hadn't come in because she had been so wild as a student, she was sure that her history would be held against her in her bid for this teaching position. I had so many flashbacks of the years she kept us all on our toes in those few moments before responding. Her teaching references were glowing, the children loved her the day she spent in the class, and the other teachers felt she would be a great addition to their professional community. She ended up being one of the most talented and beloved of teachers. Ten years ago her parents and I would have been stunned at the thought!

Our hopes and dreams as adults in the lives of girls is that they will turn out to be healthy, happy, thriving human beings. We pray that all of our worries and work and caring and dreams translate into a young woman who adds to the world, and is content with who she is. We want to do a responsible and good job in parenting. The hard part is the journey, because I've never seen a totally smooth route for any girl or any parent.

If you've taken the time to read this book and think about your effect on a beloved girl, the chances are very high that you have done, and will continue to do, a good job. Just know that the obstacles in the road may make for some bumpy days; occasionally they'll even require that you take a detour, or take time out for a rest stop; but almost always they make all of us—girls, parents, and teachers—smarter, sturdier travelers for the journey of a lifetime.